The Winery
STEPHEN MATTHIAS

Washington State is the second-largest producer of wine in the country and home to more than 270 wineries, whose 30,000 acres of vineyards produce an amazing array of grapes. Distinctive for high quality, diversity, value and innovation, there is a wine for every palate and every meal. The amazing growth that has taken place in this industry over the past two decades is testament not only to consumers' increasing interest in wine, but also to the quality of Washington's products.

Throughout this book you will find a wine suggestion for many of the recipes. The wines selected highlight particular characteristics and qualities of what is grown in Washington. To round out the regional portfolio there are also lovely pinot noirs, pinot blancs and pinot gris from Oregon. Experiment and learn what you like.

Tasty Tomato Tapenade Bruschetta

This is a no-fuss crowd-pleaser. While tapenade typically refers to a spread based on chopped olives, this tomato-only version is equally tasty. The bruschetta will be best served right away after assembling, so the toasted bread doesn't become soggy with sitting. The topping and toasts can be made up to a day ahead, though, and quickly assembled just before serving.

Preheat the oven to 400°F. Cut the baguette on the diagonal into twenty-four ⅓-inch-thick slices. Brush 1 side of each slice with some of the olive oil and set them on 2 baking sheets. Bake until lightly toasted, about 4 minutes, then set aside to cool on a wire rack.

Gently stir together the plum tomatoes, olive oil, sun-dried tomatoes, basil, parsley, vinegar, oregano, and garlic. Spread the mixture on the non-oiled side of the bread slices, sprinkle with the feta, and serve.

MAKES 6 TO 8 SERVINGS

◆ Sangiovese (the grape behind Italy's chianti wines), with it's high acid, will partner well with ripe tomatoes and creamy feta.

1	baguette (about 12 ounces)
1/4	cup extra virgin olive oil, plus more for brushing
1 1/2	cups seeded and diced plum (Roma) tomatoes
3	tablespoons minced sun-dried tomatoes (dry, not oil-packed)
3	tablespoons minced fresh basil
1	tablespoon minced fresh parsley
2	teaspoons balsamic vinegar
1	teaspoon dried oregano
1	clove garlic, minced
1/2	cup crumbled feta cheese

Recipe pictured on page 25

SOME LIKE IT HOT BRUSCHETTA

1   baguette (about 12 ounces)

1/3   cup extra virgin olive oil, plus more for brushing

8   ounces cream cheese, at room temperature

3/4   cup freshly grated Parmesan cheese, plus more for sprinkling

1   jalapeño chile, cored and cut into pieces

3   cloves garlic, minced

2   teaspoons dried basil

1/2   teaspoon dried oregano

Recipe pictured on page 25

This is a great spread to make ahead and have on hand for a last-minute appetizer when friends drop in, or for an impromptu dinner party. An extra dose of heat comes from the jalapeño seeds; leave them out if you'd prefer to tone down the heat level.

Preheat the oven to 400°F. Cut the baguette on the diagonal into twenty-four ⅓-inch-thick slices. Brush 1 side of each slice with olive oil and arrange them on 2 baking sheets. Bake until lightly toasted, about 4 minutes, then set aside to cool on a wire rack. Leave the oven set at 400°F.

Combine cream cheese, Parmesan cheese, olive oil, jalapeño, garlic, basil, and oregano in the bowl of a food processor and purée until smooth.

Spread 1 tablespoon of the cheese mixture on the non-oiled side of each bread slice and sprinkle with a pinch of Parmesan. Bake until golden, about 5 minutes. Serve warm.

MAKES 6 TO 8 SERVINGS

Any baguette left over after cutting the 24 slices needed here can be diced, tossed lightly with olive oil, salt, and pepper, and toasted in a 350°F oven until crisp—perfect salad croutons!

CLASSIC COSMOPOLITAN

1/3   cup Finlandia vodka

Splash Triple Sec

Splash cranberry juice

Lime twist, for garnish

Fill a cocktail shaker with ice. Add all the ingredients, cover, and shake vigorously. Strain into a martini glass and garnish with a lime twist.

MAKES 1 SERVING

WILD MUSHROOM GALETTES

An outing to Seattle's Pike Place Market will open your eyes to the bountiful wild mushroom varieties in the Northwest. If you can't find fresh wild mushrooms, use cultivated types such as shiitake and cremini.

Put the dried mushrooms in a small bowl and add enough hot water to cover; let stand 1 hour to soften. Lift the mushrooms from the liquid and drain briefly on paper towels, then finely chop them.

Melt 2 tablespoons of the butter in a medium skillet over medium-high heat, add the leeks, and cook until tender and aromatic, about 2 minutes. Add the remaining 2 tablespoons of the butter, the reconstituted dried mushrooms, and the fresh mushrooms and sauté until tender, about 5 minutes. Add the wine and simmer to reduce the liquid by half, 3 to 5 minutes. Add 2 tablespoons of the goat cheese and take the skillet from the heat. Stir in the green onions and season to taste with salt and pepper.

Preheat the oven to 400°F. Line a baking sheet with parchment paper or a silicone sheet. Cut out four 4-inch rounds from the puff pastry sheet and set them on the prepared baking sheet. Cut out decorative designs from the remaining pastry scraps, either free-hand or using small cookie cutters, and set them alongside the rounds on the baking sheet. Spread or crumble 1 tablespoon of the remaining goat cheese on each pastry round. Drain away any accumulated liquid from the mushroom mixture and spoon the mushrooms onto the pastry, turning the pastry edges up slightly to hold the filling.

Bake until the pastry is puffed and golden, 10 to 15 minutes. The decorative pieces may be ready before the galettes. If so, remove them from the baking sheet, and allow the galettes to continue baking. Serve warm, sprinkled with parsley and topped with the pastry cut-outs.

MAKES 4 SERVINGS

◆ A classic chardonnay, with little or no oak, will make the mushrooms' earthy flavors shine. As a spirited alternative, a Classic Cosmopolitan (page 28) would match the Galette's sophisticated presentation.

1	ounce dried chanterelle, morel, or porcini mushrooms
4	tablespoons unsalted butter, divided
1/2	cup chopped leeks (white part only)
6	ounces mixed wild mushrooms such as chanterelles, morels, and porcini, brushed clean, trimmed, and coarsely chopped
1/2	cup dry white wine
3	ounces goat cheese, crumbled or grated, at room temperature, divided (preferably a crottin or other full-bodied goat cheese)
1/4	cup chopped green onions
	Salt and freshly ground black pepper
1	sheet frozen puff pastry, thawed
3	tablespoons minced fresh parsley

Celebrate the Rain

Cooking with the
Fresh & Abundant Flavors
of the Pacific Northwest

The Junior League of Seattle

in association with

FOOD WRITER *Cynthia Nims* ◆ WINE WRITER *Anne Nisbet*
PHOTOGRAPHER *Angie Norwood Browne* ◆ FOOD STYLIST *Patty Wittmann*

The Junior League of Seattle is an organization of women committed to promoting voluntarism, developing the potential of women, and to improving the community through the effective action and leadership of trained volunteers. Its purpose is exclusively educational and charitable.

Each year the Junior League of Seattle members contribute over 100,000 volunteer hours to community projects in the areas of education, the arts, human services, and to issues involving women, children and families.

Profits from the sale of this cookbook are used to support the community projects of the Junior League of Seattle.

NORDSTROM *Celebrate the Rain* is proudly sponsored by Nordstrom. The Junior League of Seattle recognizes and thanks Nordstrom for their generous donation and support toward the publication of this book.

Celebrate the Rain: Cooking with the Fresh & Abundant Flavors of the Pacific Northwest

© 2004 by the Junior League of Seattle, Inc. All rights reserved. No part of this book may be reproduced in any form, except for brief reviews, without the written permission of the publisher.

First Edition   April 2004   35,000 copies

This cookbook is a collection of favorite recipes, which are not necessarily original recipes.

Library of Congress Number: 2003115071
ISBN: 0-9636088-5-1

Manufactured by Favorite Recipes® Press
An Imprint of

FRP

PO Box 305142
Nashville, Tennessee 37230
1-800-358-0560

Art Director *Steve Newman*

The Junior League of Seattle

Editor *Beth Gaskill Douglass*
Design Editor *Barbara Goodwin McClure*
Text Editor and Art Writer *Mary Chapman Mascarella*
Project Chair *Elizabeth Benson Arganian*

Credits

Food Writer and Recipe Editor *Cynthia Nims*
Wine Writer *Anne Nisbet*
Photographer *Angie Norwood Browne*
Food Stylist *Patty Wittmann*
Graphic Designer *Mary Cunningham*

Cover Art *Summer Picking by Pierce Milholland*

Table of Contents

Chapter Sponsors

We wish to thank the following individuals and businesses for their generous support:

JoAnne and Clayton Jones ✦ Lesa Sroufe ✦ Evelyn Zabo and Rick Schroder ✦ Marcia Zech
Brown - Forman ✦ Microsoft Corporation
Nordstrom

THE JUNIOR LEAGUE OF SEATTLE & NORTHWEST ART

*N*orthwest Art is the Junior League of Seattle's oldest ongoing community project. Since its inception in 1960, this unique traveling collection of contemporary fine art has been viewed by thousands of school children and is recognized by the community for its excellence in teaching children about creativity and imagination through art. This project was created because the Junior League of Seattle felt that it was important for all Seattle area children to become familiar with the unusually rich artistic environment of the Northwest.

The Junior League of Seattle members receive specialized training in multi-sensory approaches to teaching children about art. Children are encouraged to see beyond what a piece of art looks like and to imagine how it might feel, smell, taste or sound. As a result, the children develop a more receptive and exploratory point of view toward art. This interactive experience with original artworks reinforces their own ability to be active participants in the world of art.

Two People Waiting
JOE MAX EMMINGER

Today the JLS Collection contains over sixty prints, paintings, sculptures, mixed media pieces and art glass by more than forty Northwest artists. Some well-known artists in this Collection include Guy Anderson, Dale Chihuly, Mark Tobey and Jacob Lawrence.

Introduction

The rain for which Seattle is so well known, that some prefer to call "liquid sunshine," is a major reason for the wondrous bounty of foods we celebrate in this book. The culinary riches of the Northwest include a rainbow of crops that make menu planning in the Emerald City a treat: asparagus and pears, lentils and sweet onions, cherries and Asian greens. The list includes exceptional wine grapes: Washington is the second largest producer of wine in the country and home to more than 270 wineries. When autumn rain begins, the lush green forests produce exquisite wild mushrooms. In summer, families flock to U-Pick berry farms just outside the city to pluck their share. This city on the Puget Sound harbors oysters, clams, mussels, Dungeness crab and plenty of fish for our dining pleasure. Dozens of neighborhood P-Patch gardens and farmers' markets turn out amazing fresh-as-it-gets food. Longtime locals, and newcomers, too, secretly relish the blustery storms of Seattle, which draw us to the home fires and perhaps a relaxing Saturday afternoon baking treats with our children or cooking a fancy dinner for friends. There is, indeed, plenty of reason to celebrate the rain and the array of foods it provides us in the Northwest.

Cynthia Nims

All of the original paintings included within *Celebrate the Rain* were created by talented local artists. Each piece reflects the beauty and lifestyle of our region. Of special note are three paintings which also belong to the Junior League of Seattle's Northwest Art Collection:

Summer Picking by Pierce Milholland (cover art)
Two People Waiting by Joe Max Emminger
Our Father by Sherry Markovitz

Pike Market Fish
BETTY OLSON VACCA

$\mathcal{F}$armers' markets dot the landscape all over Washington State, and the historic Pike Place Market in Seattle is one of the most notable. Located in the bustling center of downtown, where tourists, residents, and business people mingle throughout the day, it is a favorite place to find the freshest produce and seafood. Locals and tourists are entertained daily by the fish merchants who theatrically toss every purchase overhead before packaging.

Appetizers

Seattle Szechwan Salmon Cakes
with Ginger Garlic Dipping Sauce 8

Broiled Westcott Bay Oysters
with Pepper Cheese 9

Crabmeat, Apple, and Mango Salad
on Cumin Apple Crisps 11

Spicy Shrimp and Scallop Dip 12

Dijon Marinated Shrimp 13

Knock Your Socks Off Shrimp 15

Apple-Filled Potato Puffs 16

Toasted Coconut Chicken Bites
with Cilantro Dipping Sauce 17

Pesto and Peppercorn Rotolo 18

Warm and Smoky Bacon
Gorgonzola Dip 20

Roast Beef and Couscous Wraps 21

Szechwan Eggplant Salsa
with Pita Crisps 22

Warm Harvest Goat Cheese Spread 23

Pear Bruschetta
with Tarragon Pesto 24

Tasty Tomato Tapenade Bruschetta 27

Some Like It Hot Bruschetta 28

Wild Mushroom Galettes 29

Tomato, Feta, and Pancetta Tart 31

Vegetable Pita Rounds 33

SEATTLE SZECHWAN SALMON CAKES WITH GINGER GARLIC DIPPING SAUCE

I	pound salmon fillet, skin and pin bones removed, cut into 1-inch pieces
8	ounces sea scallops, cut into 1-inch pieces, or bay scallops
1/4	cup finely chopped fresh cilantro
2	green onions, thinly sliced
I	egg, lightly beaten
2	tablespoons minced pickled ginger with its juice
I	tablespoon grated lemon zest
I	tablespoon minced garlic
2	teaspoons chili garlic paste
2	teaspoons soy sauce
1/2	teaspoon salt
1/4	teaspoon freshly ground black pepper
I	cup fresh bread crumbs
	Vegetable oil, for frying

GINGER GARLIC DIPPING SAUCE

1/4	cup rice vinegar
2	tablespoons soy sauce
2	tablespoons minced fresh cilantro
I	teaspoon minced or grated ginger
I	teaspoon sugar
I	teaspoon minced garlic
I	teaspoon hot pepper sauce

Seattle has always been in the forefront of fusion cooking, combining Northwestern ingredients with elements of traditional Asian cuisines. The Cilantro Dipping Sauce (page 17) is a great alternative to the Ginger Garlic Dipping Sauce.

Pulse the salmon and scallops together in a food processor until the pieces are the size of peas. Avoid overmixing, as you don't want to make a purée.

In a medium bowl, combine the cilantro, green onions, egg, pickled ginger, lemon zest, garlic, chili garlic paste, soy sauce, salt, and pepper. Add the salmon mixture and bread crumbs and stir to thoroughly blend. Form the mixture (it will be rather loose, but the cakes firm up when cooked) into 12 cakes about 2½ inches across and ¾ inch thick or form smaller bite-sized cakes of about 1½ inches across for cocktail fare. Set the cakes on a waxed paper-lined baking sheet, cover, and refrigerate at least 1 hour or up to 4 hours.

For the dipping sauce, whisk together the vinegar, soy sauce, cilantro, ginger, sugar, garlic, and hot sauce. Set aside.

When ready to cook the cakes, preheat the oven to 250°F. Heat about 3 tablespoons of oil in a large nonstick skillet over medium heat. When the oil is hot, add half of the salmon cakes and cook until nicely browned and cooked through, 2 to 3 minutes per side. Transfer the cakes to a baking sheet and keep warm in the oven while cooking the remaining cakes, adding more oil to the skillet as needed. Serve hot, with the dipping sauce alongside.

MAKES 6 SERVINGS

◆ The sweetness of a riesling will tame the heat and spice in these salmon cakes.

BROILED WESTCOTT BAY OYSTERS WITH PEPPER CHEESE

The Puget Sound region is known for its great quality and quantity of oysters. Found in the San Juan Islands, in the far northwest corner of Washington State, Westcott Bay produces an oyster with a creamy texture accompanied by a nice briny flavor.

12	medium oysters
4	ounces Viking or Monterey Jack hot pepper cheese, grated
	Tabasco or other hot pepper sauce
	Chopped fresh parsley and lemon wedges, for serving

Shuck the oysters, discarding the top flatter shell and leaving the oyster in the bottom cupped shell.

Preheat the broiler and set a rack about 6 inches from the top element. Cover a rimmed baking sheet with rock salt or a large piece of crumpled foil and set the oysters on top so they sit evenly. Sprinkle the cheese over the oysters and add 1 to 2 dashes of Tabasco to taste. Broil the oysters until the cheese bubbles and browns and the oysters are firm to the touch, but not rubbery, 3 to 5 minutes.

Remove the oysters from the oven and carefully transfer them to a serving platter, sprinkle with chopped parsley, and serve right away with lemon wedges alongside for squeezing.

MAKES 6 SERVINGS

◆ A dark, porter style beer from the Northwest would be a good companion to this spicy cheese and oyster combination.

SAN JUAN OYSTER WASH

A great and easy sauce for barbecued oysters or as a zesty topper for raw halfshell oysters.

Combine all the ingredients in a small bowl and let sit for 1 hour to let the flavors meld. Strain and serve drizzled over freshly barbecued oysters or raw oysters on the halfshell.

MAKES ABOUT 1/4 CUP

2	tablespoons rice vinegar
1	tablespoon freshly squeezed lime juice
1	tablespoon chopped fresh cilantro
1	tablespoon minced shallot
1/4	teaspoon minced serrano chile

CRABMEAT, APPLE, AND MANGO SALAD ON CUMIN APPLE CRISPS

Sweet-spiced apples serve as the base for a flavorful crab-enhanced salad. A mandoline slicer is the ideal tool for making even, thin apple slices.

Preheat the oven to 225°F. Line 2 large baking sheets with a silicone nonstick sheet or with parchment paper.

Trim the top and bottom from the apples and cut them horizontally into 1/16-inch slices, popping out the seeds as you slice. Combine the cumin and sugar in a small bowl, spoon into a small sieve, and lightly dust the apple slices on both sides as evenly as possible. Lay the slices on the prepared baking sheets and bake until they begin to crisp, about 2 hours. Some slices may brown more quickly than others; remove them as they are ready, returning the pan to the oven until all the slices are crisp. Peel the slices from the baking sheet and let cool on a wire rack.

For the salad, whisk together the olive oil, vinegar, green onion, garlic, cumin, and mustard in a small bowl until blended. Pick over the crabmeat to remove any bits of shell or cartilage, and squeeze gently to remove excess liquid. Put the crabmeat in a separate bowl with the mango and apple. Add the dressing, tossing gently to mix.

Top each apple slice with 1 tablespoon of the crabmeat salad, and sprinkle with some of the cilantro. Arrange on a platter and serve right away.

MAKES 8 TO 12 SERVINGS

You could omit the apple crisps and simply serve the salad on crackers or tortilla crisps made by brushing wedges of flour tortilla with oil, sprinkling with cumin, and toasting in the oven until crisp.

◆ The Lemon Cassis Martini (page 12) would be elegant alongside this sophisticated appetizer.

2	medium Granny Smith apples
3	tablespoons powdered sugar
1	teaspoon ground cumin

SALAD

1/3	cup extra virgin olive oil
1	tablespoon apple cider vinegar
1	tablespoon finely chopped green onion
1	clove garlic, minced
1/8	teaspoon ground cumin
1/8	teaspoon Dijon mustard
8	ounces Dungeness crabmeat
1/2	cup diced mango
1/2	cup diced Granny Smith apple
2	tablespoons chopped fresh cilantro

SPICY SHRIMP AND SCALLOP DIP

8	ounces bay scallops, halved if large
8	ounces bay shrimp, cooked
2	plum (Roma) tomatoes, seeded and diced
1/2	cup cooked black beans
1/4	cups diced avocado
1/3	cup chopped fresh cilantro
1/4	cup diced red onion
1/2	serrano chile, cored, seeded, and minced
1	tablespoon chopped fresh parsley
1/2	teaspoon cumin
1/4	cup olive oil
	Juice of 1 lime
	Salt and freshly ground black pepper
	Tortilla chips, for serving

This dip is a breeze to make and transports well for sharing with friends while watching a big game or just catching up. Be sure there's ice cold beer alongside, the ideal accompaniment!

Bring a medium pot of water to a rolling boil. Add the scallops and poach until barely cooked through, about 1 minute. Drain the scallops well and cool to room temperature before proceeding.

Combine the scallops, shrimp, tomatoes, black beans, avocado, cilantro, onion, chile, parsley, and cumin in a medium bowl and stir to mix. Add the oil and lime juice and toss to mix thoroughly. Season to taste with salt and pepper. Cover and refrigerate until chilled. Serve, with tortilla chips alongside for dipping.

MAKES 4 SERVINGS

LEMON CASSIS MARTINI

1/2	lemon
1/4	cup Finlandia vodka
1	teaspoon sugar
1	teaspoon crème de cassis
1	blackberry, for garnish

Recipe pictured on page 10

Squeeze 1 teaspoon of juice from the lemon and use a vegetable peeler to peel away a 2-inch strip of the zest. Reserve the remaining lemon rind.

Fill a cocktail shaker with ice. Add the vodka, lemon juice, sugar, crème de cassis, and lemon zest, cover, and shake until very cold. Rub the reserved lemon rind around the lip of a large martini glass and strain the martini into it. Add the blackberry and serve.

MAKES 1 SERVING

Dijon Marinated Shrimp

Mustard and dill are a classic combination with shrimp that reflects the Scandinavian heritage that is part of Seattle's ethnic mix. The lettuce cups help contain the marinade while also serving as an edible package for this tasty appetizer. You could instead serve the shrimp with toothpicks.

Heat the 2 tablespoons of oil in a large skillet over medium-high heat. Add the shrimp and sauté until just opaque, about 3 minutes. Take the shrimp from the skillet and set aside to cool at room temperature.

For the marinade, whisk together the olive oil, lemon zest, lemon juice, mustard, and dill in a large bowl. Add the shrimp with any accumulated liquid, the capers, green onions, and garlic. Cover and refrigerate for at least 3 hours or overnight. Bring to room temperature before serving, as the dressing will solidify slightly in the refrigerator.

Arrange the lettuce leaves on a serving platter or individual plates. Spoon the shrimp onto the lettuce leaves with some of the sauce, garnishing with lemon slices and fresh dill.

MAKES 8 SERVINGS

For a shortcut, buy pre-cooked large shrimp, or smaller bay shrimp, and toss with the marinade, rather than starting with raw shrimp.

◆ Try a crisp sauvignon blanc to complement both the sweetness of the shrimp and the herbal flavor of dill.

2	tablespoons olive oil
1 1/2	pounds large shrimp, peeled and deveined

DIJON MARINADE

1/2	cup olive oil
1	tablespoon grated lemon zest
3	tablespoons freshly squeezed lemon juice
2	tablespoons Dijon mustard
2	tablespoons chopped fresh dill, plus more for garnish
1/3	cup drained capers
2	green onions, thinly sliced
1	clove garlic, minced
8	leaves butter lettuce, for serving
	Lemon slices, for garnish

Path to Grandma's Cove
NANCY SPAULDING

*H*iking, biking and walking outdoors are pastimes that can be enjoyed year-round in the Northwest and its large expanse of National Parks. Washington in particular is called the "Evergreen State" for its thick forests of pine, cedar and Douglas fir.

KNOCK YOUR SOCKS OFF SHRIMP

This simple shrimp dish is perfect for casual entertaining. The spicy sauce is spooned over lightly toasted baguette slices and topped with baked shrimp. They'd make a flavorful start to a Mardi Gras or Cinco de Mayo party.

Preheat the oven to 400°F. Lightly grease a 9- or 10-inch shallow oven-to-table baking dish, and arrange the shrimp in it in a single layer.

Combine the butter, wine, Worcestershire, garlic, black pepper, chili powder, salt, and cayenne pepper in a small saucepan. Bring the mixture just to a boil over medium-high heat and pour evenly over the shrimp. Bake until the shrimp are pink and just cooked through, 8 to 10 minutes. Sprinkle with the parsley and serve with the baguette slices alongside.

MAKES 8 SERVINGS

1	pound medium shrimp, peeled and deveined
3	tablespoons unsalted butter
2	tablespoons dry red wine
1	tablespoon Worcestershire sauce
2	cloves garlic, minced
1	teaspoon freshly ground black pepper
1	teaspoon chili powder
1/4	teaspoon salt
1/8	teaspoon cayenne pepper
2	tablespoons chopped fresh parsley
36	slices baguette, for serving

CIDER WITH A PUNCH

	Block of ice
10	cups clear apple cider
5	cups club soda
2 1/2	cups high quality bourbon, such as Woodford Reserve
1	cup Grand Marnier or other orange liqueur
1/4	cup Jack Daniel's Tennessee whiskey
	Small orange slices, for garnish
	Cinnamon sticks, for a swizzle (optional)

Put the ice block in a large punch bowl. Slowly pour the cider, club soda, bourbon, Grand Marnier, and Jack Daniel's over and stir to mix. (Alternatively, ladle over ice in individual glasses.) Garnish with orange slices. If you like, put cinnamon sticks in individual glasses for serving. Best if served very cold.

MAKES 18 SERVINGS

APPLE-FILLED POTATO PUFFS

2   eggs

1/4   cup vegetable oil

1/3   cup chopped green onions

1/4   cup dry bread crumbs

1   teaspoon salt

1/2   teaspoon baking powder

1 1/4   pounds yellow-fleshed potatoes, such as Yukon Gold

    Chopped fresh parsley, for garnish

CHUNKY APPLESAUCE

4   tart apples, peeled, cored, and cut into chunks

1   cup water

1/2   cup sugar

1   tablespoon freshly squeezed lemon juice

1/2   teaspoon cinnamon

This sweet-and-savory appetizer is delicious as an accompaniment to sliced ham on a buffet or simply as a nibble to have with cocktails or a glass of champagne.

For the applesauce, combine the apples, water, sugar, lemon juice, and cinnamon in a medium saucepan and cook over medium heat until the apples are tender and the mixture is thickened, 15 to 20 minutes. Press the apple pieces against the side of the pan as they begin to soften during cooking to help make a coarse purée. Set the applesauce aside to cool.

Preheat the oven to 400°F. Thoroughly grease 36 mini-muffin cups (1¾- by 1-inch).

In a large bowl, whisk together the eggs and oil to blend, then whisk in the green onions, bread crumbs, salt, and baking powder. Working quickly, in 2 batches, peel and quarter the potatoes and pulse them in a food processor to finely chop them (avoid over-processing to a purée). Add the potatoes to the egg mixture and stir to evenly mix.

Fill each muffin cup halfway with the potato mixture. Spoon ½ teaspoon of the applesauce mixture into each cup, followed by enough potato mixture to fill the cups completely. Bake until golden brown and the potatoes are tender when pierced with the tip of a knife, about 30 minutes (or if using a nonstick, dark muffin tin, 20 to 25 minutes). Let stand 5 minutes in pan (important to make unmolding easier) before turning them out. Serve warm, sprinkled with chopped parsley.

MAKES 8 TO 12 SERVINGS

◆ Hot Scandinavian Glogg (page 32) would be a delicious warm beverage to complement this appetizer on a cold, wintery day.

TOASTED COCONUT CHICKEN BITES WITH CILANTRO DIPPING SAUCE

Easy to make, the chicken and sauce can be prepared the night before and the chicken baked just before your guests arrive.

For the Cilantro Dipping Sauce, combine the cilantro, green onions, jalapeño, lemon juice, salt, pepper, cumin, and turmeric in a food processor and blend until finely chopped. With the blades running, slowly add the oil and process until smooth. Refrigerate until ready to serve.

Preheat the oven to 325°F. Spread the coconut on a baking sheet and bake until golden brown, about 5 minutes, stirring frequently. Watch carefully, as it can burn easily. Take the coconut from the oven and let cool, then coarsely chop it in a food processor and put it aside in a medium bowl.

Combine the cumin, coriander, cayenne, salt, and pepper in a large bowl and stir to mix. Add the chicken pieces and toss to coat. Add the eggs and toss to coat again. Dredge the chicken pieces in the coconut one by one, coating them well. Transfer the chicken to 2 greased baking sheets, allowing space between the pieces for even cooking. Cover and refrigerate 1 hour. (Can be prepared to this point 1 day ahead.)

Shortly before ready to cook the chicken, preheat the oven to 400°F. Bake the chicken until crisp and golden, about 12 minutes. Arrange the chicken on a platter and serve warm or at room temperature with the sauce alongside for dipping.

MAKES 8 TO 12 SERVINGS

In place of the Cilantro Dipping Sauce, you could instead serve the chicken bites with a simple "sauce" of Dijon mustard.

3	cups sweetened shredded coconut
2	teaspoons ground cumin
3/4	teaspoon ground coriander
1/2	teaspoon cayenne pepper
1/4	teaspoon salt
	Pinch freshly ground black pepper
2	pounds boneless, skinless chicken breasts, cut into 1-inch pieces
2	eggs, lightly beaten

CILANTRO DIPPING SAUCE

1	cup lightly packed cilantro leaves
3/4	cup chopped green onions
1	jalapeño chile, stemmed, cored, and seeded
2	tablespoons freshly squeezed lemon juice
1/2	teaspoon salt
1/2	teaspoon freshly ground black pepper
1/4	teaspoon ground cumin
1/4	teaspoon ground turmeric
1/3	cup extra virgin olive oil

PESTO AND PEPPERCORN ROTOLO

8   ounces cream cheese or Neufchâtel cheese, at room temperature

1   cup ricotta cheese

3   tablespoons mixed peppercorns (black, white, pink, and/or green)

Arugula leaves, olives, fresh or sun-dried tomato slices, and/or red bell pepper strips, for garnish

Sliced dark bread and/or crackers, for serving

PESTO

2   cups lightly packed fresh basil leaves

1/4   cup olive oil

2 – 3   cloves garlic

2   tablespoons freshly grated Parmesan cheese

Salt

Colorful and fragrant crushed peppercorns decorate the outside of this striking spiraled cheese log. You'll need cheesecloth to help form this log.

Beat the cream cheese and ricotta with a mixer at medium speed until thoroughly combined and smooth.

Prepare a 2-layer rectangle of cheesecloth, about 11 by 14 inches, and set on a tray or baking sheet. Spread the cheese mixture onto the cheesecloth, making a rectangle about 9 by 12 inches. Tidy the edges by pressing in from the sides with the flat edge of a table knife. Refrigerate, lightly covered with a piece of plastic wrap, for at least 3 hours before filling.

For the pesto, combine the basil, olive oil, garlic, and Parmesan in a food processor or blender. Purée until smooth, then season to taste with salt. Remove the cheese rectangle from the refrigerator and spread the pesto on top to within ½ inch of the edges.

Lifting the cheesecloth from one of the longer ends, roll it up as you would a jelly roll, lifting away the cheesecloth as you go and using it to help form an even, compact cylinder. Lay out a fresh piece of double-layered 9- by 12-inch cheesecloth, then take the rotolo from its cheesecloth and set it on the fresh cheesecloth. Put the peppercorns in a resealable plastic bag, seal it (with most of the air extracted), and then use a mallet or the bottom of a small saucepan to coarsely crush the peppercorns. Sprinkle the cracked peppercorns over the rotolo, covering the surface as evenly as possible, using the cheesecloth to help roll the cylinder of cheese slightly to cover the sides and bottom. Roll the rotolo up in the cheesecloth, and set it seam-side down on a tray or baking sheet. Cover it tightly with plastic wrap and refrigerate for 12 to 24 hours before serving.

To serve, unwrap the plastic and cheesecloth from the rotolo and place it on a serving plate. Frame it lavishly with the arugula, olives, tomato, and/or bell pepper, and serve it with dark bread and/or crackers.

MAKES 8 SERVINGS

Store-bought pesto or olive tapenade can be used in place of the homemade pesto.

WARM AND SMOKY BACON GORGONZOLA DIP

7   slices bacon, diced

2   cloves garlic, minced

8   ounces cream cheese,
     at room temperature

1/4 cup half-and-half

4   ounces Gorgonzola or other blue
     cheese, crumbled

2   tablespoons minced fresh chives,
     plus more for garnish

4   tablespoons finely chopped smoked
     almonds, divided

     Grapes, for serving

     Sliced baguette, crackers,
     crostini, celery, and/or carrot
     sticks, for dipping

This hearty, rich-and-cheesy dip is perfect for a party on a chilly evening.

Preheat the oven to 350°F. Cook the bacon in a large skillet over medium heat until almost crisp, 4 to 5 minutes. Scoop out the bacon with a slotted spoon onto a small plate, drain the grease from the skillet, and return the bacon to the pan. Add the garlic and continue to cook until the bacon is crisp, 2 to 3 minutes longer.

Blend the cream cheese and half-and-half in a food processor until smooth. Put the mixture in a medium bowl and stir in the bacon and garlic, Gorgonzola, and chives. Spoon the mixture into a 2-cup oven-to-table baking dish. Cover with foil and bake until heated through, about 30 minutes.

Stir 3 tablespoons of the almonds into the hot dip, then sprinkle the remaining almonds and some minced chives evenly over the top. Serve with grapes, bread, crackers, and/or vegetables alongside for dipping.

MAKES 6 TO 8 SERVINGS

◆ The sweet smokiness of bacon shows off the rich and ripe fruit flavors of syrah. If you prefer a cocktail, try a Classic Manhattan to complement the richness of this dip.

CLASSIC MANHATTAN

1/3 cup Woodford Reserve bourbon

1   tablespoon sweet vermouth

1   dash bitters

1   dash grenadine

1   maraschino cherry

Fill a cocktail shaker with ice. Add all ingredients, except cherry, and shake well. Strain into a chilled martini glass, add the cherry, and serve.

MAKES 1 SERVING

ROAST BEEF AND COUSCOUS WRAPS

There is a subtle sweet-and-savory combination in these impressive appetizers of roast beef wrapped around a couscous filling.

Combine the broth, 1 tablespoon of the olive oil, and the herbes de Provence in a small saucepan and bring to a boil over high heat. Stir in the couscous, take the pan from the heat, cover, and let sit for 5 minutes. Fluff the couscous with a fork and stir in the remaining 2 tablespoons of oil with the marmalade, Parmesan, sliced green onion, parsley, red wine and balsamic vinegars, and salt and pepper to taste. Set aside to cool.

Once the couscous has cooled, lay out a few slices of roast beef on the counter. Spoon about 2 tablespoons of the couscous mixture along a short side of each slice of roast beef and use your fingers to press the couscous together to help make a tidy mound. Set a strip of bell pepper alongside and roll the roast beef tightly to enclose. Each cylinder should be about 1 inch in diameter. Tie the rolls at 1-inch intervals with the green parts of the green onions. Repeat with the remaining slices of beef and couscous filling. (The rolls can be prepared the night before up to this point, wrapped well in plastic and refrigerated.)

When ready to serve, cut the rolls on the diagonal into 1-inch lengths (you should have about 50 pieces in all), and arrange them cut side up on a lettuce-lined serving platter.

MAKES 12 TO 16 SERVINGS

You can use toothpicks to secure the rolls rather than tying them with the green onions tops before cutting.

◆ Rich and robust, zinfandel can handle both the savory and sweet flavors of these do-ahead wraps.

1	cup chicken broth
3	tablespoons olive oil, divided
1/2	teaspoon herbes de Provence
3/4	cup couscous
1/2	cup orange marmalade
1/3	cup freshly grated Parmesan cheese
1/4	cup thinly sliced green onion, white part only, green tops reserved and cut into 1/4" wide strips
3	tablespoons minced parsley
2	tablespoons red wine vinegar
1	tablespoon balsamic vinegar
	Salt and freshly ground black pepper
1	pound thinly sliced (about 1/8-inch) deli roast beef, regular or Italian style
1	red bell pepper, cored, seeded, and cut lengthwise into 1/4-inch strips
	Lettuce, for garnish

SZECHWAN EGGPLANT SALSA WITH PITA CRISPS

1/4	cup vegetable oil
1	large eggplant (about 1 1/4 pounds), cut into 1/2-inch cubes
1/4	cup chicken broth
1	tablespoon rice vinegar
1	tablespoon dry sherry
1	teaspoon minced garlic
1	tablespoon minced or grated ginger
1	teaspoon Szechwan chili paste
1	teaspoon hoisin sauce
1	red bell pepper, cored, seeded, and cut into 1/4-inch dice
2	tablespoons soy sauce
1	tablespoon packed light brown sugar
3	green onions, thinly sliced
1/2	teaspoon toasted sesame oil
	Baked pita crisps

There is a touch of sweetness in this aromatic, Asian-inspired sauce, deftly absorbed by the eggplant. It makes a great do-ahead snack. Allow the salsa to come back to room temperature after refrigerating, so that the flavors will be more pronounced. You can use triangles of flour tortilla lightly fried in olive oil in place of the pita chips. Other hot pepper sauces can be used instead of the Szechwan chili paste.

Heat the oil in large heavy skillet over medium-high heat. Add the eggplant and stir-fry until tender and lightly browned, 3 to 5 minutes. Transfer to paper towels to drain.

Add the broth, vinegar, sherry, garlic, ginger, chili paste, and hoisin sauce to the skillet and cook for 30 seconds. Add the bell pepper, soy sauce, brown sugar, and eggplant and cook until the eggplant has absorbed most of the liquid, about 1 minute. Take the skillet from the heat, add the green onions and sesame oil, and stir well. Set aside to cool.

Serve the salsa at room temperature, with baked pita crisps alongside for dipping.

MAKES 8 SERVINGS

Pita crisps are easily made by first halving pocket-style pitas horizontally, then cutting each half into wedges. Bake the wedges in a 350°F oven until lightly browned and crisp, about 10 minutes.

◆ The exotic flavors of gewürztraminer echo this appetizer's savory seasonings.

WARM HARVEST GOAT CHEESE SPREAD

Tangy goat cheese is dotted with a red, orange, and green bell pepper topping, then gently warmed in the oven for a quick and easy appetizer that is full of the colors and flavors of harvest time.

Preheat the oven to 300°F. Lightly oil an ovenproof serving dish just large enough to hold the cheese slices in an even layer.

Heat 1 tablespoon of the oil in a large skillet over medium heat and sauté the bell peppers and garlic until tender and aromatic, about 5 minutes. Add the remaining 3 tablespoons of olive oil with the rosemary, coriander, fennel, pepper, thyme, and bay leaf. Take the skillet from the heat, season to taste with salt, and stir in the balsamic vinegar.

Arrange the goat cheese slices in the prepared dish and press down gently so that the cheese forms an even layer. Spoon the bell pepper topping over and sprinkle with the pine nuts. (This can be made ahead to this point and refrigerated for up to 4 hours.) Bake until warm, about 10 minutes. Discard the bay leaf and serve the warm cheese spread with toasted baguette slices or crackers.

MAKES 4 TO 6 SERVINGS

This recipe can easily be transformed into bruschetta: Set the cheese slices atop toasted baguette slices and top with the bell pepper mixture and pine nuts. Bake at 350°F until warmed.

◆ Cabernet franc will offer a unique contrast to this spread's seasonings.

4	tablespoons extra virgin olive oil, divided
1/4	cup diced green bell pepper
1/4	cup diced red bell pepper
1/4	cup diced orange bell pepper
4	cloves garlic, minced
2	teaspoons minced fresh rosemary
1/2	teaspoon coriander seeds, crushed
1/4	teaspoon fennel seeds, crushed
1/4	teaspoon freshly ground black pepper
1/4	teaspoon dried thyme
1	bay leaf
	Salt
1	teaspoon balsamic vinegar
8	ounces fresh goat cheese, such as Montrachet, cut into 8 slices
2	tablespoons toasted pine nuts
	Toasted baguette slices or crackers, for serving

PEAR BRUSCHETTA WITH TARRAGON PESTO

1   baguette (about 12 ounces)

     Olive oil, for brushing

1   medium pear, peeled, cored, and quartered, tossed with 2 tablespoons lemon juice

1 1/2   cups grated Gruyère cheese

     Freshly ground black pepper

TARRAGON PESTO

1 1/2   cups lightly packed fresh parsley leaves

1/2   cup freshly grated Parmesan cheese

1/4   cup olive oil

3   tablespoons coarsely chopped fresh tarragon

2   cloves garlic, minced

Pears are abundant in the Pacific Northwest through the fall and winter, with many colorful and juicy varieties to choose from, any of which will be good for this twist on bruschetta. You will be pleasantly surprised by the subtle sweetness that complements the aromatic tarragon and nutty Gruyère.

Preheat the oven to 400°F. Put 1 oven rack about 4 inches from the top element and another in the center of the oven.

For the tarragon pesto, combine the parsley, Parmesan, olive oil, tarragon, and garlic in a food processor and process until smooth. Set aside.

Cut the baguette on the diagonal into twenty-four 1/3-inch slices. Brush 1 side of each slice with olive oil, set them on a baking sheet, and bake in the center of the oven until lightly toasted, about 4 minutes. Set aside and turn on the broiler.

Spread the non-oiled side of each baguette slice with the pesto. Cut each pear quarter into 6 slices and top the pesto with a pear slice. Sprinkle with grated cheese and a small pinch of pepper. Broil the bruschetta until the cheese melts, watching carefully to avoid burning, 1 to 2 minutes. Serve warm.

MAKES 6 TO 8 SERVINGS

ARTISAN CHEESE

While Cheddar used to suffice on the subject of cheese, today there are dozens of quality cheeses available in stores, many supplied by small regional producers who often work with milk from their own farms. It's a change that has forever broadened our options in the kitchen, whether a question of cheese to sprinkle over a green salad or one with which to make a delectable sauce for a steak. Many of these European-influenced artisan cheeses are made locally, including goat cheeses that range from soft, fresh logs to nutty aged *crottin* and robust sheep's milk cheeses. Consider sampling a number of artisan cheeses side-by-side, with some delicious Washington wines as well, for a distinctly "Seattle" wine and cheese party. With sliced crusty bread alongside, perhaps some dried fruits and toasted nuts, you'll be set for a fun evening of exploration.

TOMATO, FETA, AND PANCETTA TART

Whether you gather them from your own sun-drenched garden or from the neighborhood farmers' market, summer's plump ripe tomatoes are a big treat and well showcased in this delicious tart.

For the tart dough, combine the flour, thyme, and salt in a large bowl. Using a pastry blender, cut in the butter until the mixture resembles coarse meal. (Alternatively, pulse the ingredients together in a food processor, then transfer to a large bowl.) Stir in the ice water and olive oil just until blended and the dough holds together. Form the dough into a disc, wrap in plastic, and refrigerate for at least 1 hour.

Preheat the oven to 425°F. Roll out the dough on a lightly floured surface to an 11-inch round. Gently fit the dough into a 9-inch tart pan with a removable base. Prick the bottom of the tart shell several times with a fork. Line the crust with foil and fill with pie weights or dried beans. Bake the tart shell until the edges begin to brown, 10 to 12 minutes. Remove the foil and beans and continue baking until the crust is golden, about 10 minutes longer. Remove the tart shell from the oven and let cool on a wire rack; reduce the oven temperature to 375°F.

Cook the pancetta or bacon in a nonstick skillet over medium-high heat until it is crisp and the fat has rendered, about 5 minutes. Add 1 tablespoon of the oregano and cook another 30 seconds. Drain the bacon on paper towels and remove all but 1 tablespoon of the drippings from the skillet.

recipe continued on next page

1/2	cup chopped pancetta or bacon (about 2 ounces)
2	tablespoons chopped fresh oregano, divided
1	small red onion, halved and thinly sliced
3	cloves garlic, very thinly sliced
2	tablespoons dried bread crumbs
6 – 8	plum (Roma) tomatoes or other small tomatoes, preferably heirloom, cut into 1/4- to 1/2-inch-thick slices)
1/4	cup crumbled feta cheese
1/4	cup finely chopped fresh basil
1/2	teaspoon salt
1/4	teaspoon freshly ground black pepper

THYME TART DOUGH

1 1/4	cups all-purpose flour
1	tablespoon minced fresh thyme or 1 teaspoon dried thyme
1/2	teaspoon salt
6	tablespoons unsalted butter, cut into pieces and refrigerated
3	tablespoons ice water
2	tablespoons olive oil

Return the skillet to the heat, add the onion and garlic and cook until the onion is golden and aromatic, 8 to 10 minutes. Sprinkle the bread crumbs evenly into the tart shell. Spread the onion mixture over the bread crumbs, then arrange the tomato slices over the onions in an overlapping circle. Sprinkle with the bacon, feta, remaining oregano, basil, and salt and pepper to taste. Bake until the filling is heated through, 10 to 12 minutes. Let the tart cool slightly on a wire rack, then remove the edges from the tart pan, cut into wedges, and serve warm or at room temperature.

MAKES 8 SERVINGS

◆ Fruit forward sauvignon blancs have enough weight to handle both the tang of tomatoes and the sharpness of feta.

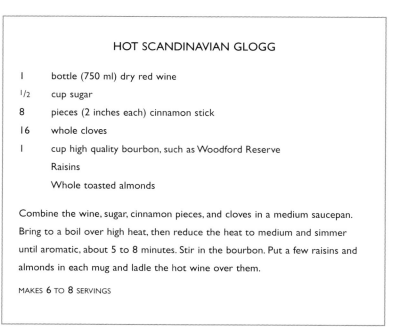

HOT SCANDINAVIAN GLOGG

1	bottle (750 ml) dry red wine
1/2	cup sugar
8	pieces (2 inches each) cinnamon stick
16	whole cloves
1	cup high quality bourbon, such as Woodford Reserve
	Raisins
	Whole toasted almonds

Combine the wine, sugar, cinnamon pieces, and cloves in a medium saucepan. Bring to a boil over high heat, then reduce the heat to medium and simmer until aromatic, about 5 to 8 minutes. Stir in the bourbon. Put a few raisins and almonds in each mug and ladle the hot wine over them.

MAKES 6 TO 8 SERVINGS

VEGETABLE PITA ROUNDS

This is great finger food for a party buffet or cocktail snacks. It's important to choose the pocket-style pita bread for this recipe, as the pita is halved to make thinner rounds that serve as a base for the vegetable mixture.

Preheat the oven to 350°F. Heat the olive oil in a large skillet over medium heat, add the onion and garlic and cook until tender and aromatic, 3 to 5 minutes. Add the red and green bell peppers and cook until just softened, about 5 minutes. Add the zucchini, mushrooms, and oregano, with salt and pepper to taste, and cook until the zucchini is just tender, 2 to 3 minutes longer. Stir in half the mozzarella and take the skillet from the heat.

Halve the pita rounds horizontally to form 4 rounds and arrange them cut side up on a baking sheet. Brush the pita rounds lightly with oil and sprinkle with salt. Bake until lightly browned, about 5 minutes. Sprinkle the pita rounds with half of the remaining mozzarella and return to the oven until the cheese is melted, about 1 minute. Take the pan from the oven and turn on the broiler.

Divide the vegetable topping among the pita rounds, top with the remaining mozzarella, the tomato, Parmesan, and basil, and broil until bubbly, about 3 minutes. Cut each pita into 6 pieces and serve warm.

MAKES 6 TO 8 SERVINGS

◆ The delicate flavor of fresh vegetables and herbs would be best showcased by a high acid sauvignon blanc.

3	tablespoons olive oil, plus more for brushing
1	small red onion, thinly sliced
2	cloves garlic, minced
1	small red bell pepper, cored, seeded, and thinly sliced
1	small green bell pepper, cored, seeded, and thinly sliced
3/4	cup thinly sliced zucchini
4	button mushrooms, brushed clean, trimmed, and sliced
1	teaspoon crumbled dried oregano
	Salt and freshly ground black pepper
1 1/3	cups grated mozzarella cheese, divided
2	whole-wheat pita rounds (about 6 inches across)
2/3	cup seeded, chopped tomato
3	tablespoons freshly grated Parmesan cheese
3	tablespoons shredded fresh basil

Delphinium by the Sea
NANCY SPAULDING

The San Juan Islands, close to the Canadian border, are a well-loved weekend getaway. There are dozens of cozy bed & breakfasts and port-side restaurants that seem magically far from daily life. Visitors can enjoy excellent seafood, pickings from island orchards, unique shopping, and local artwork in the midst of a relaxed, natural environment.

Brunch

Wine Crab Soufflé 36

Rolled Omelet with Smoked Salmon,
Spinach and Crème Fraîche 37

The Best Bacon 38

Roasted Red Pepper, Mushroom,
and Spinach Frittata 39

Goat Cheese and Asparagus Strata 40

Tomato Cobbler with Gruyère Crust 41

Herbed Prosciutto and
Gruyère Croque Monsieurs 42

Roasted Potatoes 44

Apricot Hazelnut Scones 45

Crispy Pecan Waffles 47

Ricotta Cheese Pancakes
with Orange Butter Sauce 48

Baked Blueberry Pecan French Toast
with Blueberry Syrup 49

Minted Melon Salad 51

Almond Pastry Puff 52

Pumpkin Apple Bread 53

Cranberry Orange Sweet Rolls 55

Espresso Chocolate Chip Muffins 57

WINE CRAB SOUFFLÉ

1/2	loaf French bread, crust removed and torn into bite-sized pieces
3	tablespoons unsalted butter, melted
8	ounces grated Swiss cheese
4	ounces grated Monterey Jack cheese
1 1/2	cups Dungeness crabmeat
2	green onions, minced
8	eggs
1/2	cup milk
1/4	cup dry white wine
1 1/2	teaspoons Dijon mustard
1/8	teaspoon freshly ground black or white pepper
3/4	cup sour cream
1/2	cup freshly grated Parmesan cheese

Elegant and make-ahead—what could be better! This recipe could also be served as an appetizer, cut into small squares. Note that the recipe needs to be started the night before to allow the bread to fully soak up the flavorful egg custard before baking.

Butter a 9- by 13-inch baking dish. Scatter the bread evenly in the dish and drizzle the butter over the bread, then layer the cheeses on top. Pick over the crabmeat to remove any bits of shell or cartilage and sprinkle the crab over the cheese, followed by the green onions.

Whisk together the eggs, milk, wine, mustard, and pepper in a medium bowl. Pour the egg mixture into the baking dish, cover with foil, and refrigerate overnight.

Remove the baking dish from the refrigerator 30 minutes before baking. Preheat the oven to 325°F. Bake, covered, until set and a knife inserted in the center comes out clean, about 1 hour. Meanwhile, stir together the sour cream and Parmesan. Remove the soufflé from the oven, uncover, and spread the sour cream mixture over the top. Return the baking dish to the oven and continue to bake, uncovered, until golden brown, about 10 minutes. Let stand 5 minutes before cutting. Serve warm or at room temperature.

MAKES 10 SERVINGS

Small cooked shrimp can be used in place of the Dungeness crabmeat, or consider using a combination of both. If the shrimp are on the large size, coarsely chop them before sprinkling over the cheese.

◆ The high acids in a sparkling wine will refresh the palate while enjoying this rich dish.

Rolled Omelet with Smoked Salmon, Spinach, and Crème Fraîche

This is a very showy, elegant way to serve eggs at your next brunch! The vivid colors of deep orange smoked salmon and green spinach play off the light eggs beautifully.

Preheat the oven to 350°F. Line a 15- by 10-inch jelly roll pan or other rimmed baking sheet with foil, making sure the foil goes all the way up all four sides of the pan. Generously coat the foil with nonstick cooking spray or vegetable oil. (Do not use butter as it will cause the egg to stick.)

Combine the crème fraîche and 2 tablespoons of the milk in a small bowl and stir together until smooth and liquid enough to be drizzled, adding a bit more milk if needed. Set aside.

Combine the remaining 1 cup of milk, eggs, flour, melted butter, salt, and pepper in a blender and blend until smooth. Pour the egg mixture into the prepared pan. Lay the smoked salmon slices over the egg, then sprinkle with the onion and minced chives. Bake until the eggs are set, 15 to 18 minutes. Take the pan from the oven and sprinkle with the spinach. Beginning at one of the shorter ends of the omelet, roll it up into a cylinder, using the foil to lift and help roll the omelet. Cut the omelet into 8 slices and set them on individual plates. Drizzle with the crème fraîche, garnish with the caviar and chives (if using), and serve.

MAKES 4 SERVINGS

◆ A chilled pinot gris, with its balance of fruitiness and acidity, offers a nice contrast to this creamy omelet.

1/3	cup crème fraîche
1	cup plus 2 tablespoons milk, divided, more if needed
4	eggs
1/2	cup all-purpose flour
2	tablespoons unsalted butter, melted
1/2	teaspoon salt
	Pinch freshly ground white or black pepper
4	ounces thinly sliced cold-smoked salmon (lox style)
1/4	cup finely chopped red onion
3	tablespoons minced fresh chives
1	cup chopped, packed spinach leaves
	Caviar, for garnish (optional)
	Whole chives, for garnish (optional)

THE BEST BACON

2   tablespoons packed light
    brown sugar

1/4 teaspoon cayenne pepper

1/4 teaspoon freshly ground
    black pepper

1   pound thick-sliced bacon

For those days when everyday bacon just won't do, this easy but dressed-up variation is sure to get raves. Your friends will be surprised how well the salty flavor of the bacon melds with the sweetness of brown sugar.

Preheat the oven to 425°F. Line a rimmed baking sheet with foil. Set a wire cooling rack or other slotted rack on top of the foil-lined pan.

Stir together the brown sugar, cayenne, and black pepper in a small bowl until well blended. Lay the bacon strips in a single layer on the rack. (Use 2 pans if all the bacon will not fit in a single layer.) Sprinkle the bacon with the brown sugar mixture. Bake until the bacon is browned, 15 to 20 minutes. Transfer the bacon immediately to individual plates and serve warm.

MAKES 6 SERVINGS

ROASTED RED PEPPER, MUSHROOM, AND SPINACH FRITTATA

The frittata is one of the most versatile brunch dishes, a great easy-to-make egg dish that doesn't require precision cooking or fancy folding. You can combine any number of ingredients in this recipe, tailoring it to seasonal offerings and your family's favorite ingredients.

Heat the oil in a large nonstick ovenproof skillet over medium heat. Add the onion and sauté until tender and aromatic, about 8 minutes. Add the mushrooms and continue to cook until the mushrooms release their liquid and begin to brown, about 5 to 7 minutes. Stir in the chopped red pepper, followed by the vinegar, stirring to scrape up any browned bits stuck to the bottom of the pan. Cook until the vinegar has evaporated, about 2 minutes. Add the spinach and stir until fully wilted, about 2 to 3 minutes. Stir in ¼ cup of the basil with salt and pepper to taste.

In a medium bowl, whisk together the eggs, Parmesan, ½ teaspoon salt, and ¼ teaspoon pepper until well blended. Pour the eggs over the hot vegetables in the skillet and gently stir for a few seconds to combine. Reduce the heat to medium-low and cook without further stirring until the eggs are set on the bottom, 5 to 8 minutes. Preheat the broiler.

Sprinkle the feta cheese over the frittata and broil until the cheese melts and begins to brown, about 2 to 4 minutes. Take the skillet from the oven, sprinkle with the tomatoes and remaining 2 tablespoons of basil, cut into wedges, and serve.

MAKES 4 SERVINGS

2	teaspoons olive oil
1/2	cup chopped red onion
1 1/2	cups assorted sliced mushrooms
1	red bell pepper, roasted (see sidebar below) and chopped
2	tablespoons balsamic vinegar
1/2	small bunch spinach, rinsed, dried, and tough stems removed
1/4	cup plus 2 tablespoons chopped fresh basil, divided
	Salt and freshly ground black pepper
6	eggs
1/2	cup freshly grated Parmesan cheese
1	cup crumbled feta cheese
3/4	cup chopped tomatoes, drained

HOW TO ROAST BELL PEPPERS

Roast the bell pepper(s) whole over a gas flame or under the broiler until the skin blackens, turning occasionally to roast evenly, about 10 minutes total. Put the pepper(s) in a plastic bag, securely seal it, and set aside to cool. When cool enough to handle, peel away and discard the skin. Remove the core and seeds and proceed as directed in the recipe.

GOAT CHEESE AND ASPARAGUS STRATA

8	cups 1-inch bread cubes, crusts removed
2	cups milk
1/4	cup olive oil
1 1/2	cups whipping cream
5	eggs
1	tablespoon minced garlic
1/2	teaspoon freshly grated or ground nutmeg
	Salt and freshly ground black pepper
12	ounces goat cheese, crumbled
2	tablespoons finely chopped fresh sage
1 1/2	teaspoons herbes de Provence
12	ounces ham, cut into 1/2-inch cubes
1	pound asparagus, trimmed, cut into 2-inch pieces, and blanched
1	cup grated fontina cheese
1 1/2	cups freshly grated Parmesan cheese

This elegant strata combines spring's fresh asparagus with creamy goat cheese and cubes of ham (which can be omitted for a vegetarian version). When asparagus is out of season, you can substitute it with 2 1/2 cups of artichoke hearts.

Preheat the oven to 350°F. Butter a 9- by 13-inch baking dish.

Put the bread in a large bowl. Whisk together the milk and oil, pour this over the bread, and let stand until absorbed, 10 to 15 minutes, stirring occasionally. Whisk together the cream, eggs, garlic, nutmeg, and a good pinch each of salt and pepper. Stir in the goat cheese, sage, and herbes de Provence.

Spoon half of the bread mixture into the prepared dish and sprinkle the top with half of the ham, half of the asparagus, and half the fontina and Parmesan cheeses. Pour half of the cream mixture evenly over the layers. Repeat the layering with the remaining ingredients. Bake, uncovered, until the eggs are fully cooked (the tip of a knife inserted in the center should come out clean) and the top is nicely browned, about 1 hour. Let the strata sit for about 5 minutes before cutting into pieces to serve.

MAKES 12 SERVINGS

The strata can be assembled the night before, refrigerated, and baked in the morning just before serving. Take the strata from the refrigerator about 30 minutes before baking to take off some of the chill before it goes into the hot oven.

Tomato Cobbler with Gruyère Crust

Resist temptation and allow the cobbler to cool to room temperature before serving so the tomato juices collect. For brunch, this will be delicious served with scrambled eggs and The Best Bacon (page 38), or it will make a good dinnertime accompaniment to roasted meat or chicken. The Gruyère crust dough can be made a day in advance.

For the Gruyère crust, combine the flour, cheese, thyme (if using), salt, and sugar in the bowl of a food processor and pulse to mix. Add the butter and pulse until the mixture resembles coarse meal, 8 to 10 seconds. Still pulsing the machine, drizzle the ice water in little by little through the chute until the dough begins to hold together without becoming wet or sticky. Do not process more than 30 seconds or the dough will be tough rather than tender. To test, press a small amount of the dough together; if it is crumbly add more water 1 teaspoon at a time. Form the dough into a disk about 1 inch thick, wrap in plastic, and refrigerate for at least 1 hour.

Preheat the oven to 375°F. Lightly grease a 9½- or 10-inch deep-dish pie pan.

Melt the butter in a large skillet over medium heat. Add the onion and garlic and cook, stirring occasionally, until the onion is tender and aromatic, about 5 to 7 minutes. Set aside to cool slightly.

Put the tomatoes in a large bowl, add the basil, flour, salt, sugar, and pepper, and toss gently to mix. Stir in the cooled onion mixture, then spoon into the prepared pie pan.

Roll the dough out on a floured surface to a circle that is 1 inch larger in diameter than the pie pan. Transfer the dough to the top of the dish, tuck the edges in around the tomato filling, and crimp the edge. Make 3 or 4 small slits in the crust to allow steam to escape. Whisk the egg and water together in a small bowl. Brush the crust with the egg wash and sprinkle with the Gruyère cheese.

Set the pie pan on a baking sheet to catch any drips. Bake until the crust is golden and the filling is bubbly, about 45 to 50 minutes. Cover the cobbler loosely with foil if the crust is browned before the filling is hot. Let it cool to room temperature before serving.

MAKES 6 TO 8 SERVINGS

1	tablespoon unsalted butter
1	large onion, diced
3	cloves garlic, minced
2	pounds cherry tomatoes, preferably assorted varieties, stemmed
1/2	cup chopped fresh basil
1/4	cup plus 2 tablespoons all-purpose flour
1 1/2	teaspoons salt
1 1/2	teaspoons sugar
	Pinch freshly ground black pepper
1	egg
1	teaspoon water
1/4	cup grated Gruyère cheese

GRUYÈRE CRUST

1 1/4	cups all-purpose flour
1/2	cup grated Gruyère cheese
1	tablespoon fresh thyme leaves or 1 teaspoon dried (optional)
1/2	teaspoon salt
1/2	teaspoon sugar
1/2	cup unsalted butter, cut into 1/2-inch pieces and refrigerated
2 – 3	tablespoons ice water

Herbed Prosciutto and Gruyère Croque Monsieurs

2   eggs

1   tablespoon milk

12   slices (1/2 inch thick) dense, white, artisan bread

1   tablespoon finely chopped fresh parsley

2   teaspoons finely chopped fresh thyme

12   ounces thinly sliced prosciutto

12   ounces grated Gruyère cheese

4   tablespoons unsalted butter, divided, more if needed

   Whole-grain mustard, for serving

This is a unique take on a traditional Parisian café dish, adding a dip in an eggy batter to form an even more golden and rich exterior.

Preheat oven to 200°F. Put a large ovenproof serving platter in the oven to warm while preparing sandwiches.

In a shallow bowl or pie pan, whisk together the eggs and milk until well blended. Dip one side of 6 of the bread slices briefly into the egg mixture. Sprinkle the eggy sides of the bread with half of the parsley and half of the thyme and set the slices egg-side down on a piece of parchment paper or foil. Top the dry side of the bread with the prosciutto and cheese. Dip 1 side of the remaining 6 slices of bread in the egg mixture and set on top of the sandwiches, egg-side up. Sprinkle with the remaining parsley and thyme.

Melt 2 tablespoons of the butter in a large skillet over medium-low heat. Cook 2 or 3 sandwiches until golden brown on the bottom and the cheese begins to melt, about 3 to 4 minutes. Turn the sandwiches and cook until the second side is golden brown, the cheese is melted, and the sandwiches are warmed through, another 3 to 4 minutes, adding a bit more butter to the skillet if needed. Transfer the sandwiches to a baking sheet and keep warm in the oven while cooking the remaining sandwiches. Cut the sandwiches in half and serve, passing the whole-grain mustard separately.

MAKES 6 SERVINGS

♦ Weightier than most whites and as flavorful as many reds, a rose wine can handle the distinct flavors of Gruyère and prosciutto.

ROASTED POTATOES

2   pounds small potatoes, scrubbed and quartered (or cut into large chunks for big potatoes)

2   tablespoons olive oil

1 – 2   teaspoons herbes de Provence (optional)

     Salt and freshly ground black pepper

1/4   cup chopped fresh parsley

No brunch is complete without some crispy, delicious potatoes. This simple herb-enhanced roasted potato is a glorious accompaniment to any brunch spread. You can use any kind of potato for this recipe.

Preheat the oven to 450°F. Put the potatoes in a shallow baking dish, drizzle the olive oil over, and sprinkle with the herbes de Provence, if using, and salt and pepper to taste, tossing gently to mix and evenly coat the potatoes with the oil. Roast the potatoes in the lower third of the oven, without stirring or turning, until the undersides are golden brown, about 20 minutes. Turn the potatoes and roast until tender, 10 to 15 minutes longer. Transfer to a serving bowl and toss with the parsley. Serve warm.

MAKES 4 TO 6 SERVINGS

MOJITO

1/2   cup freshly squeezed lime juice, rinds reserved

     Leaves from 8 mint sprigs

1/4   cup sugar

3/4   cup light rum

     Club soda

Put the lime juice in a small bowl, add the mint and sugar, and crush the mint with the back of a spoon until the sugar is dissolved. Stir in the rum. Cut the lime rind into quarters. Fill 4 tall glasses with ice and add 1 piece of lime rind. Pour the mojito into the glasses, top with a splash of club soda, and serve.

MAKES 4 SERVINGS

APRICOT HAZELNUT SCONES

Scones are a wonderfully versatile pastry treat, great for breakfast, as a snack with an afternoon cup of tea, or as a base for a quick dessert, topped with fresh fruit and a dollop of whipped cream.

Preheat the oven to 400°F. Lightly grease a baking sheet.

Stir together the flour, brown sugar, baking powder, baking soda, and salt in a large bowl. Using a pastry cutter or your fingers, work in the cold butter until the mixture resembles coarse meal. Stir in the sour cream, hazelnuts, apricots, and vanilla until a cohesive dough forms. Turn the dough out onto a lightly floured surface and gently knead until smooth, about 10 turns. Flatten the dough into an 8-inch round and cut into 8 wedges. Set the wedges on the baking sheet and sprinkle lightly with brown sugar. Bake the scones until nicely puffed and golden, about 20 minutes. Serve warm with jam and butter.

MAKES 8 SCONES

2	cups all-purpose flour
1/4	cup packed light brown sugar, plus more for sprinkling
2	teaspoons baking powder
1/2	teaspoon baking soda
1/2	teaspoon salt
5	tablespoons unsalted butter, cut into 1/2-inch pieces and refrigerated
1	cup sour cream
1/2	cup toasted, coarsely chopped hazelnuts
1/2	cup chopped dried apricots
1	teaspoon vanilla extract
	Jam and unsalted butter, for serving

VERY BERRY MARGARITAS

Combine 2/3 cup of the sugar and the lime juice in a small bowl and set aside until the sugar is dissolved, stirring occasionally. Purée the blackberries, raspberries, and lime juice mixture in a blender until smooth. Strain through a fine sieve into a large measuring cup. Refrigerate for at least 1 hour and up to 1 day.

Stir the tequila and Grand Marnier into the berry purée. Transfer half of the purée to the blender; add half the frozen strawberries and half the ice (work in smaller batches if your blender is not large enough). Blend until smooth and transfer to a pitcher. Repeat with the remaining berry purée, frozen strawberries, and ice.

Combine the salt and remaining 3 tablespoons sugar in a shallow dish and stir well to evenly mix. Run a lime rind along the rim of each margarita glass to moisten, then dip into the salt-sugar mixture. Pour the margarita mixture into the glasses and garnish with strawberries and/or lime wedges.

MAKES 8 TO 10 SERVINGS

2/3	cup plus 3 tablespoons sugar, divided
1/2	cup freshly squeezed lime juice, rinds reserved
1 1/2	pints blackberries
1/2	pint raspberries
1 1/2	cups tequila
2/3	cup Grand Marnier or other orange liqueur
2	pints strawberries, sliced, frozen 1 hour
5	cups ice
3	tablespoons kosher salt
	Strawberries and lime wedges, for garnish

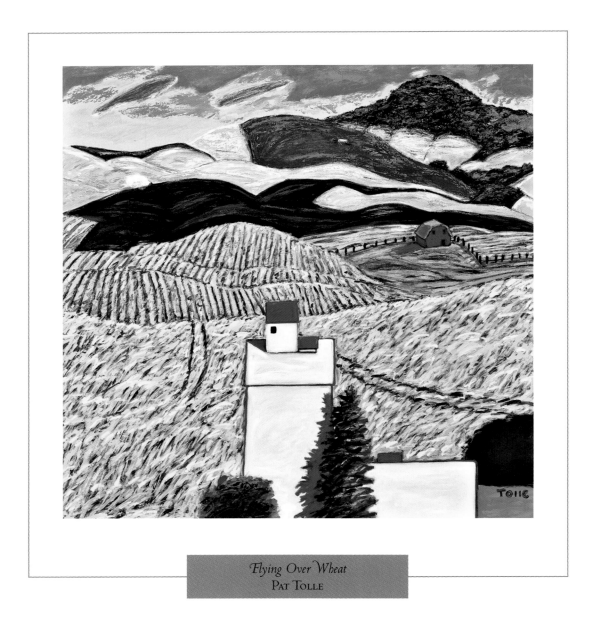

Flying Over Wheat
PAT TOLLE

*B*runch is a great time for enjoying Washington specialties such as scones, pancakes or freshly baked bread. Washington is home to many a wheat farm in the eastern part of the state, where long, hot summers prevail. Some may be surprised to know that our state produces the second largest wheat crop in the nation.

CRISPY PECAN WAFFLES

What makes these tasty, pecan-enhanced waffles extra crispy is keeping them warm directly on the oven rack so that excess moisture is drawn away from the surface, leaving the waffles crispy outside and still tender inside.

Preheat the oven to 200°F and preheat a waffle iron. Combine the flour, pecans, cornstarch, salt, baking powder, and baking soda in a large bowl and stir to mix. In a separate bowl, whisk together the buttermilk, oil, milk, and egg yolk. Whip the egg white in a medium bowl until it forms soft peaks. Add the sugar and continue beating until stiff peaks form, then beat in the vanilla. Pour the buttermilk mixture into the dry ingredients and whisk together just until incorporated. Gently fold in the egg white.

Pour a generous ½ cup of the batter (more or less depending on the size of your iron) onto the waffle iron. Close the waffle iron and cook until well browned and cooked through, 5 to 7 minutes. As each waffle is cooked, set it directly on the oven rack to keep warm while cooking the rest of the waffles. Do not stack the waffles or they'll be soft rather than crispy. Once all the waffles are cooked, serve right away.

MAKES 4 SERVINGS

Serve these waffles with butter, if you like, and your favorite syrup, lightly warmed. They are also tasty topped with sliced bananas.

3/4	cup all-purpose flour
1/2	cup toasted, chopped pecans
1/4	cup cornstarch
1/2	teaspoon salt
1/2	teaspoon baking powder
1/4	teaspoon baking soda
3/4	cup buttermilk
6	tablespoons vegetable oil
1/4	cup milk
1	egg, separated
1	tablespoon sugar
1/2	teaspoon vanilla extract

RICOTTA CHEESE PANCAKES WITH ORANGE BUTTER SAUCE

1 cup all-purpose flour

1 tablespoon sugar

1 teaspoon baking powder

1/2 teaspoon salt

4 eggs

2 cups ricotta cheese

3/4 cup milk

1 teaspoon vanilla extract

1/2 teaspoon grated orange zest

1 – 2 tablespoons unsalted butter, more if needed

Fresh raspberries and powdered sugar, for serving

ORANGE BUTTER SAUCE

1/2 cup freshly squeezed orange juice

1/3 cup sugar

4 tablespoons unsalted butter

1 teaspoon freshly squeezed lemon juice

1 teaspoon grated orange zest

2 tablespoons Grand Marnier or other orange liqueur

These are rich, delicate, and moist—a striking variation on traditional pancakes. For a shortcut, you can omit the orange butter sauce and simply serve the pancakes with your favorite fruit preserves.

For the orange butter sauce, combine the orange juice, sugar, butter, lemon juice, and orange zest in a small saucepan. Bring to a boil over medium-high heat, stirring to help dissolve the sugar. Continue to boil just until slightly thickened, 2 to 3 minutes. Stir in Grand Marnier. Return the sauce to a boil and cook for another 30 seconds. Keep warm over very low heat while making the pancakes. Preheat the oven to 250°F.

Whisk together the flour, sugar, baking powder, and salt in a medium bowl. In another bowl, lightly beat the eggs, then stir in the ricotta cheese, milk, vanilla, and orange zest until the mixture is very smooth. Gradually add the egg mixture to the flour mixture, whisking just until combined and smooth. Don't overmix; a few small lumps are okay.

Heat a large heavy skillet over medium heat and lightly coat with butter. Form pancakes of about 3 tablespoons each in the skillet. When the pancakes begin to bubble, flip to brown the other side. Transfer the pancakes to a lightly buttered baking sheet and keep warm in the oven while cooking the remaining pancakes, adding more butter to the skillet as needed.

To serve, drizzle individual plates with orange sauce and top with pancakes. Top with raspberries and dust lightly with powdered sugar.

MAKES 6 SERVINGS

For more informal family-style service, you could arrange the pancakes on a warmed platter and pass them at the table, also passing the orange butter sauce separately for guests to spoon onto their own plates.

BAKED BLUEBERRY PECAN FRENCH TOAST WITH BLUEBERRY SYRUP

The French toast can be assembled and the blueberry syrup made the day before serving. The next morning, simply bake the French toast and reheat the syrup before serving.

Preheat the oven to 350°F. Spread the pecan halves evenly on a baking sheet. Toast them until fragrant, about 8 minutes. Sprinkle the salt over the pecans and toss to evenly coat; set aside.

Butter a 9- by 13-inch baking dish. Cut the baguette into 1½-inch-thick slices and arrange them in an even layer in the baking dish (if some of the bread slices won't fit, save them for another use). Whisk together the eggs, milk, ½ cup of the brown sugar, vanilla, and nutmeg in a large bowl, and pour the mixture evenly over the bread. Turn the bread slices to coat them evenly. Chill the mixture, covered with plastic wrap, until all the liquid is absorbed by the bread, at least 8 hours or overnight.

Preheat the oven to 400°F. Take the baking dish from the refrigerator and let sit for about 30 minutes to take some of the chill off. Just before baking, sprinkle the pecans and blueberries evenly over the soaked bread. Combine the butter with the remaining ¼ cup brown sugar in a small saucepan and warm over medium heat, stirring, until the butter is melted. Drizzle the butter mixture over the bread and bake until blueberry juices are bubbling around the edge of the pan and the bread is heated through, 20 to 25 minutes.

While the French toast is baking, make the syrup. Cook the blueberries and maple syrup in a small saucepan over medium heat until most of the blueberries burst, 3 to 5 minutes, stirring occasionally. Pour the syrup through a sieve into a heatproof pitcher, pressing on the solids to extract as much blueberry flavor as possible. Stir in the lemon juice; set the pitcher in a pan of warm water to keep warm until ready to serve.

MAKES 6 SERVINGS

◆ The Very Berry Margaritas (page 45) will take advantage of other fresh summer berries that ripen during our warm Northwest summers.

1	cup pecan halves
1/4	teaspoon salt
1	baguette (about 12 ounces), preferably day-old
5	eggs
1 1/2	cups milk
3/4	cup packed light brown sugar, divided
1	teaspoon vanilla extract
1/2	teaspoon freshly grated or ground nutmeg
4	tablespoons unsalted butter, cut into pieces
2	cups blueberries, fresh or frozen (about 12 ounces)

BLUEBERRY SYRUP

1	cup blueberries, fresh or frozen (about 6 ounces)
1/2	cup pure maple syrup
1	tablespoon freshly squeezed lemon juice

Minted Melon Salad

Serve this refreshingly light, summer fruit salad for brunch or an afternoon luncheon. It's a bit less sweet than many melon salads and the crème de cassis draws out the juices from the fruit while giving the salad a subtle purple hue. Dense fruit nectar is an excellent, non-alcoholic substitute for the crème de cassis. Look for it at your local natural foods market or well-stocked grocery shelves near other juices.

Stir together the crème de cassis, lemon juice, and honey in a small bowl until the honey has dissolved. Adjust the sweetness to taste by adding either more lemon juice or more honey. Gently toss together the melons with the mint in a large bowl, then stir in the cassis dressing. Serve either chilled or at room temperature.

Makes 6 servings

◆ Celebrate the fruits of summer by pairing this melon salad with Sunset Sangria.

1/4	cup crème de cassis, berry liqueur, or currant nectar
1/4	cup freshly squeezed lemon juice, more to taste
2	tablespoons honey, more to taste
4	cups cubed, seeded watermelon
1/2	cantaloupe, cut into melon balls
1/2	honeydew, cut into melon balls
2/3	cup chopped fresh mint, more or less to taste, plus additional sprigs for garnish

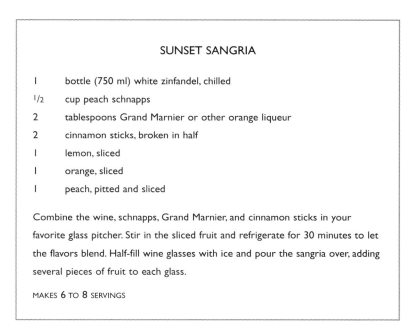

SUNSET SANGRIA

1	bottle (750 ml) white zinfandel, chilled
1/2	cup peach schnapps
2	tablespoons Grand Marnier or other orange liqueur
2	cinnamon sticks, broken in half
1	lemon, sliced
1	orange, sliced
1	peach, pitted and sliced

Combine the wine, schnapps, Grand Marnier, and cinnamon sticks in your favorite glass pitcher. Stir in the sliced fruit and refrigerate for 30 minutes to let the flavors blend. Half-fill wine glasses with ice and pour the sangria over, adding several pieces of fruit to each glass.

MAKES 6 TO 8 SERVINGS

ALMOND PASTRY PUFF

This elegant pastry is surprisingly quick and easy to prepare since both doughs—a pastry crust and the rich pastry puff filling—are made in the food processor.

PASTRY CRUST

1 1/2	cups all-purpose flour
3/4	cup unsalted butter, cut into pieces
3 – 4	tablespoons ice water
1/2	teaspoon salt

PASTRY FILLING

1	cup water
1/2	cup unsalted butter
	Pinch salt
1	cup all-purpose flour
4	eggs
1 1/2	teaspoons almond extract

FROSTING

1 1/2	cups powdered sugar
2	tablespoons milk
1	tablespoon unsalted butter or 2 tablespoons cream cheese, at room temperature
1	teaspoon freshly squeezed lemon juice
1/2	teaspoon vanilla extract
1/4	cup toasted slivered almonds

Preheat the oven to 400°F. Lightly grease a baking sheet.

For the crust, combine the flour, butter, 3 tablespoons of the ice water, and salt in a food processor and pulse just until evenly blended, but avoid overworking the dough. Add the extra water ½ tablespoon at a time if needed to form a smooth dough. On the prepared baking sheet, pat the dough into an 11- by 13-inch rectangle, pinching up the sides ½ inch all the way around. Rinse out the food processor for the next step.

For the pastry filling, combine the water, butter, and salt in a medium saucepan and bring to a boil over high heat. Take the pan from the heat and whisk in the flour all at once. Pour the mixture into the food processor and allow to cool slightly. With the motor running, add the eggs one at a time through the chute, then add the almond extract. Use a spatula to spread the filling onto the crust. Bake until golden brown, about 35 minutes. Allow to cool slightly.

For the frosting, stir together the sugar, milk, butter, lemon juice, and vanilla until smooth. Spread the frosting on the warm pastry, then sprinkle with the slivered almonds. Let cool completely, then cut into pieces to serve.

MAKES 8 SERVINGS

To avoid any accidental addition of egg shell to the pastry puff filling, first crack each egg into a small dish, then tip the egg from the dish into the chute of the food processor.

PUMPKIN APPLE BREAD

The flavorful, aromatic qualities of holiday pumpkin pie show up here in a delicious quick bread, with crisp, tart apples embellishing the rich pumpkin and warm spices.

For the topping, combine the sugar, flour, butter, and cinnamon and blend with your fingers to an even, crumbly texture. Set aside.

Preheat the oven to 350°F. Butter and flour two 9- by 5-inch loaf pans. Sift together the flour, baking soda, cinnamon, nutmeg, cloves, salt, and allspice into a large bowl. In another large bowl, whisk together the pumpkin, sugar, eggs, and oil. Add the flour mixture to the pumpkin, stirring to evenly mix, then fold in the apples. Divide the batter between the pans, smoothing the tops. Sprinkle each loaf with the cinnamon-sugar topping. Bake until a toothpick inserted in the center comes out clean, about 1 hour.

MAKES 2 LOAVES

These loaves hold up well and can be baked a day or two before being served. They also freeze well for up to 1 month, securely wrapped in plastic, then wrapped one more time in foil.

3	cups all-purpose flour
2	teaspoons baking soda
1 1/2	teaspoons ground cinnamon
1	teaspoon freshly grated or ground nutmeg
1	teaspoon ground cloves
3/4	teaspoon salt
1/4	teaspoon ground allspice
1	can (16 ounces) pure pumpkin purée
2 1/4	cups sugar
4	eggs, lightly beaten
3/4	cup vegetable oil
1	large Granny Smith apple, peeled, cored, and cut into 1/4-inch dices

CINNAMON-SUGAR TOPPING

5	tablespoons sugar
1	tablespoon all-purpose flour
1	tablespoon unsalted butter, at room temperature
1	teaspoon cinnamon

CRANBERRY ORANGE SWEET ROLLS

This dough is buttery and rich and oh-so-tasty. It's a fun twist on the cinnamon roll theme, with tangy cranberries, aromatic orange zest, and toasty walnuts embellishing the filling.

For the dough, stir together the warm water, yeast, and a pinch of the sugar in a small bowl. Let stand until frothy, 5 to 10 minutes. Combine the flour, salt, and remaining sugar in the bowl of an electric mixer fitted with the dough hook. Blend at low speed until combined. Whisk together the milk and eggs in a small bowl, then add to the flour mixture along with the yeast mixture and continue blending until the flour is incorporated. Increase the speed and beat until a soft dough forms, about 2 minutes. Add the butter and continue beating until the dough is smooth, soft, and elastic, about 4 minutes (it will still be quite sticky). Rinse a large bowl with hot water and pour out the water. Add the dough to the damp bowl and cover it tightly with plastic wrap. Let it rise in a warm place until doubled in bulk, 45 minutes to 1 hour.

For the filling, combine 1 cup of the granulated sugar and the water in a medium saucepan and bring to a boil over medium-high heat, stirring until the sugar has dissolved. Add the cranberries and simmer just until they begin to burst, about 2 minutes. Strain the berries and set aside to cool, discarding the cooking liquid. Combine the butter and orange zest in a small bowl and stir to evenly mix. In another small bowl, stir together the remaining ⅓ cup granulated sugar, brown sugar, and cinnamon.

Turn the dough out onto a well-floured surface, dust the top with flour, and roll out into a 16-inch square. Brush off any excess flour from the surface and spread with the orange butter. Sprinkle with the brown sugar mixture, scatter the cranberries evenly over the dough, and sprinkle with the walnuts.

Beginning with the side nearest to you, roll up the dough firmly but not too tightly into a log, pinching the seam gently to seal. Trim 1 inch off each end and discard. Slice the log into 12 pieces.

recipe continued on next page

DOUGH

½	cup warm water (110°F to 115°F)
2	packages (5 teaspoons) active dry yeast
½	cup granulated sugar
5½	cups all-purpose flour
1½	teaspoons salt
1	cup warm milk
2	eggs
½	cup unsalted butter, at room temperature

FILLING

1⅓	cups granulated sugar, divided
¼	cup water
2	cups fresh or frozen cranberries
½	cup unsalted butter, at room temperature
	Finely grated zest of 1 orange
¼	cup packed light brown sugar
1	teaspoon ground cinnamon
1	cup toasted, chopped walnuts

FROSTING

4	ounces cream cheese, at room temperature
2	tablespoons unsalted butter, at room temperature
½	teaspoon vanilla extract
	Pinch salt
2	cups powdered sugar

Generously butter two 9-inch cake pans or a 9- by 13-inch baking dish and arrange the roll slices cut side up in the pan(s). Cover with a clean dish towel and let rise in a warm place until doubled in bulk, about 1 hour. While the rolls are rising, preheat the oven to 350°F. Bake the rolls until puffed and nicely browned, 30 to 35 minutes. Let cool in the pan(s) on a wire rack for 10 minutes, then turn them out onto a platter or serving plates and let them cool slightly.

For the frosting, beat together the cream cheese and butter in a medium bowl until smooth. Add the vanilla and salt, then gradually stir in the powdered sugar and beat until smooth. Spread the frosting over the warm rolls before serving.

MAKES 12 SERVINGS

◆ The cinnamon and spice flavors of the Spiced Coffee with Whipped Cream will be a delicious accompaniment to these sweet rolls.

SPICED COFFEE WITH WHIPPED CREAM

3/4	cup whipping cream, well-chilled
1 1/2	tablespoons powdered sugar
1	tablespoon high quality bourbon, such as Woodford Reserve
3/4	cup plus 2 tablespoons freshly ground mild-roast coffee
4	teaspoons ground cardamom
1	tablespoon sugar
2	teaspoons ground cinnamon
1	teaspoon freshly grated or ground nutmeg
6	cups water

Whip the cream with an electric mixer at medium-high speed until soft peaks form. Add the powdered sugar and bourbon and beat to medium-stiff peaks.

Combine the coffee, cardamom, sugar, cinnamon, and nutmeg in the coffee filter of your coffee machine and stir gently with a small spoon. Add water to the coffee maker and brew according to manufacturer's instructions. Pour the coffee into individual cups or mugs, top with a dollop of whipped cream, and serve.

MAKES 8 SERVINGS

ESPRESSO CHOCOLATE CHIP MUFFINS

This sweet muffin would be as welcome as a dessert-time treat as for an element on your brunch spread.

Preheat the oven to 375°F. Prepare a 12-cup muffin tin by either lining the cups with paper liners or greasing them well.

For the topping, stir together the brown sugar and flour in a small bowl. Using your fingers or the back of a fork, work in the butter until the mixture has a crumbly texture. Set aside.

In the bowl of an electric mixer, beat the butter until light and fluffy. Gradually add the sugar and beat until well blended. Sift together the flour, baking powder, baking soda, and salt into a large bowl. In a separate bowl, whisk together the sour cream, eggs, espresso, and vanilla. Add the dry ingredients to the butter, alternating with the liquid in 3 batches, ending with the liquid ingredients. Use a wooden spoon to stir in the chocolate chips.

Fill the muffin cups ¾ full with batter and sprinkle with the topping. Bake until a toothpick inserted in the center of a muffin comes out clean, 15 to 18 minutes. Turn the muffins out onto a wire rack to cool slightly, then serve warm.

MAKES 12 MUFFINS

3/4	cup unsalted butter, at room temperature
1	cup granulated sugar
3 1/2	cups all-purpose flour
2	teaspoons baking powder
1	teaspoon baking soda
1	teaspoon salt
1/2	cup sour cream
2	eggs
3	tablespoons fresh espresso or 2 tablespoons instant espresso dissolved in 2 tablespoons hot water
2	teaspoons vanilla extract
1 1/2	cups chocolate chips

TOPPING

5	tablespoons packed light brown sugar
1	tablespoon all-purpose flour
1	tablespoon unsalted butter, at room temperature

West Side
KRISTY GJESME

The rocky, dramatic coastline of Washington State is shaped by the winds and waters of the Pacific Ocean. On the Olympic Peninsula, the westernmost tip of the United States, there is a microclimate of dense rainforests, ideal for hiking and camping. The Makah and Quileute peoples still live on their ancestral homelands in this area and a fascinating native cultural center welcomes visitors in Neah Bay.

Soup & Salad

Saffron Mussel Bisque 60

Salmon Corn Chowder 61

Thai Shrimp Bisque 63

Shrimp Stock 64

Zesty Chicken Soup 65

Cheese Tortellini Soup with
White Beans, Kielbasa, and Spinach 66

Wild Rice and Sausage Soup 67

Seattle Style Chili 68

Chunky Five-Bean Chili 70

Walla Walla Onion Soup 71

Curried Carrot Soup with
Nutty Fall Garnish 73

Lentil and Roasted Tomato Soup 74

Wild Mushroom Soup 75

Chilled Cherry Soup 76

Serrano Ham and
Manchego Cheese Toasts 78

Beer Bread 79

Sunflower Loaf 80

Herbed Cheese Bread 81

Rosemary Bread 82

Hearts of Romaine with
Hazelnut Roquefort Dressing 84

Mixed Greens with
Hazelnut Crusted Goat Cheese 85

Mixed Greens with Yakima Nectarines and
Honey Poppy Seed Dressing 87

Ruby Green Salad with
Creamy Mustard Balsamic Vinaigrette 88

Spinach and Apricot Salad 90

Wilted Spinach and Apple Salad 91

Toasted Couscous Salad with
Grilled Summer Vegetables 92

Summer Tomato Salad 94

Roasted Corn and Avocado Salad 95

Orecchiette and Spring Pea Salad 96

Smoked Salmon Pasta Salad 97

Wheat Berry Salad with Autumn Dried Fruits 98

Middle Eastern Lentil and Orzo Salad 100

Curried Couscous Salad 101

Lemon Garlic Shrimp with Greens 103

Elliott Bay Ceviche 104

Mediterranean Potato Salad 105

Spicy Greens with
Miniature Wasabi Crab Cakes 106

Gingered Chicken Salad with
Hoisin Vinaigrette 109

Tri-Color Coleslaw with Miso Dressing 111

SAFFRON MUSSEL BISQUE

2	tablespoons unsalted butter
1	cup chopped onion
1/2	cup chopped leek, white and pale green parts
1	sprig savory or thyme
4	cups clam juice or fish stock
1	teaspoon saffron threads, crushed
3	pounds Penn Cove mussels, scrubbed and debearded
1	pound russet potatoes, peeled and cut into 1/4-inch dice
1 1/2	cups dry white wine
1	cup whipping cream
1	cup half-and-half
	Salt and freshly ground black pepper
2	tablespoons chopped chives, for garnish

Saffron and mussels were just made for each other. The briny and slightly sweet flavor of the mussels beautifully complements the uniquely earthy, aromatic flavor of saffron. Saffron is celebrated as being one of the world's most expensive foods—but rest assured that a little goes a long way.

Melt the butter in a large pot over medium heat. Add the onion, leek, and savory or thyme and sauté until the onion is tender and aromatic, about 5 minutes. Add the clam juice and saffron and bring to a low simmer over medium-high heat. Add the mussels, cover, and cook until most of the mussels have opened, 3 to 5 minutes, gently shaking the pan once or twice during cooking. Scoop out the mussels with a slotted spoon and set aside in a large bowl, discarding any mussels that did not open.

Add the potatoes and wine to the pot and simmer over medium heat until the potatoes are tender when pierced with a fork, about 15 minutes. Meanwhile, remove the mussels from their shells. Remove the savory sprig, then stir in the cream and half-and-half and season the soup to taste with salt and pepper.

To serve, distribute the mussels evenly among individual bowls and ladle the hot bisque over the mussels. Garnish with chopped chives and serve.

MAKES 6 SERVINGS

Salmon Corn Chowder

Sweet corn and rich salmon make a wonderful duo in this tasty soup, nearly a meal in itself. This is a great way to use leftover salmon.

Set the salmon pieces on a plate, season lightly with salt and pepper, wrap in plastic, and refrigerate while preparing the chowder base.

Cut the kernels off 4 of the ears of corn: hold a cob upright on the chopping board with the broader end down. Slide the knife blade vertically down the length of the cob, cutting away a strip of kernels. Turn the cob slightly and repeat around the ear to remove all the kernels. Turn the knife and rub the back of the blade down the cob, all the way around, to remove the milky tender flesh that remains. Grate the corn from the fifth ear on the large holes of a hand grater. Set the corn aside.

Melt the butter in a large saucepan over medium heat. Add the onion and cook, stirring occasionally, until tender and aromatic, about 5 to 7 minutes. Add the wine and boil over medium-high heat until reduced by half, about 3 minutes. Add the fish stock, savory, and cayenne and bring to a simmer. Add the potatoes, reduce the heat to medium, and simmer until the potatoes are nearly tender when pierced with a fork, about 8 to 10 minutes. Add the corn and cream and cook until the corn is almost tender but still slightly crunchy, about 3 to 5 minutes longer.

Add the salmon and simmer until the fish is opaque throughout, about 5 to 7 minutes. Stir in the milk with 2 tablespoons of the chives. Heat until warmed through, but do not boil. Season the chowder to taste with salt and pepper, ladle into individual bowls, and serve right away, with the remaining chives sprinkled on top.

MAKES 6 SERVINGS

◆ Sweet corn and creamy chowder suit a lightly toasted, buttery chardonnay.

1 1/4	pounds salmon fillet, skin and pin bones removed, cut into 1-inch pieces
	Salt and freshly ground black pepper
5	ears tender sweet corn, husks and silk removed
2	tablespoons unsalted butter
1	cup diced onion
3/4	cup dry white wine
2	cups fish stock or canned or bottled clam juice
2	teaspoons minced fresh savory or thyme or 1/2 teaspoon dried savory or thyme
1/8	teaspoon cayenne pepper
5	medium red potatoes, peeled and cut into 3/4-inch dice
1	cup whipping cream
2	cups milk
1/4	cup minced fresh chives, divided

THAI SHRIMP BISQUE

Lighter than many classic bisques, this soup relies on Asian flavor accents such as coconut milk, fresh ginger, and cilantro to liven up the flavors. It's easy enough for any night of the week, but elegant enough for company.

For the marinade, combine the lime zest, lime juice, soy sauce, cilantro, garlic, ginger, coriander, cumin, curry, and garlic chili sauce in a resealable plastic bag. Add the shrimp and toss to evenly coat in the marinade, seal the bag well, and marinate in the refrigerator for 30 minutes.

Heat the oil in a large saucepan over medium heat. Add the onion, celery, and carrot, and sauté until the vegetables begin to soften and lightly brown, about 5 to 7 minutes. Add the flour and cook for 2 minutes, stirring constantly to evenly mix. Add the coconut milk, clam broth, bell pepper, milk, and tomato paste, scraping the pan to loosen any browned bits. Bring the mixture to a boil over high heat, then reduce the heat to medium-low and simmer until thick, about 3 minutes, stirring often. Add the shrimp and marinade to the pan and cook until the shrimp turn pink and are cooked through, about 5 minutes. Stir in the lime zest and cilantro and season to taste with salt. Spoon into bowls and garnish with more chopped cilantro.

MAKES 4 SERVINGS

1 1/2	pounds medium shrimp, peeled and deveined (shells reserved for stock, if desired)
2	tablespoons olive oil
1/2	cup chopped onion
1	stalk celery, chopped
1	medium carrot, chopped
1/4	cup all-purpose flour
1	can (14 ounces) coconut milk
1	cup clam broth or shrimp stock (see recipe on page 64)
1	medium red bell pepper, cored, seeded, and chopped
1	cup milk
1	tablespoon tomato paste
1	tablespoon grated lime zest
1	tablespoon minced cilantro, plus more for garnish
	Salt

MARINADE

1	tablespoon grated lime zest
1/3	cup freshly squeezed lime juice
2	tablespoons soy sauce
2	tablespoons chopped cilantro
2	cloves garlic, minced
1	tablespoon plus 2 teaspoons finely minced ginger
1	teaspoon ground coriander
1	teaspoon ground cumin
1	teaspoon curry powder
1/2	teaspoon Asian garlic chili sauce or 1/4 teaspoon cayenne pepper

SHRIMP STOCK

Shells from 1 1/2 pounds shrimp

2 cups water

1/4 cup dry white wine

1 tablespoon tomato paste

Shrimp stock is incredibly easy to make. This flavorful liquid is a great addition to seafood soups, chowders, or to use in sauces to serve with shrimp. You can omit the tomato paste for use in recipes in which the red hue would not be desirable.

Combine the shells, water, wine, and tomato paste in a medium saucepan. Bring to a boil over medium-high heat, then reduce the heat to low and simmer until the liquid is aromatic and reduced to about 1 cup, about 10 minutes, stirring occasionally. Strain the stock through a sieve and discard the solids. Use right away or freeze for up to 1 month.

MAKES ABOUT 1 CUP

WALLA WALLA ONIONS

Walla Walla onions are among the most celebrated sweet onions in the country—right up there with Vidalia and Maui onions, which can be used in place of the Walla Wallas, though we're partial to this Northwest product! Walla Walla onions grow in the eastern part of Washington state (and in a bit of northeastern Oregon, too) and are harvested primarily during the late spring and summer months. The onions have a higher water content than regular yellow onions, so tend to spoil more quickly than other onions. Plan to use sweet onions within a week or so of purchase and store them in a cool, dark place. Walla Walla sweets are a great Northwest treat to savor while in season.

ZESTY CHICKEN SOUP

There's a touch of Indian flair in this chicken soup with the addition of curry powder, ginger, currants, and some heat from red pepper flakes.

Heat the oil in a large stockpot over medium-high heat. Add the onion and sauté until tender and aromatic, about 3 to 5 minutes, then add the garlic and sauté 1 minute longer. Stir in the curry and sauté for 1 minute, then add the chicken, red pepper, ginger, and red pepper flakes and stir for 2 minutes. Add the broth, tomatoes, and apple and bring to a boil. Reduce the heat to low and simmer for 20 minutes. (The soup can be made a day ahead to this point; cover and refrigerate, then bring to a simmer before continuing.)

Add the orzo and currants to the soup and simmer until the orzo is tender, about 10 minutes. Season the soup to taste with salt and pepper and ladle it into bowls. Garnish with cilantro and a dollop of yogurt or sour cream.

MAKES 6 SERVINGS

Dried cranberries or raisins can be used in place of the currants in this recipe, or consider using a combination if you have more than one on hand.

1	tablespoon olive oil
3/4	cup chopped onion
4	cloves garlic, chopped
1	tablespoon curry powder
4	boneless, skinless chicken breasts or 6 boneless, skinless chicken thighs, cut into 1/2-inch pieces
1/2	cup chopped red bell pepper
1	teaspoon grated or minced ginger
1/4	teaspoon dried red pepper flakes
2	cans (14 ounces each) chicken broth
1	can (14 ounces) diced tomatoes, with their liquid
1	large Granny Smith apple, cored, peeled, and coarsely chopped
1/2	cup orzo
3	tablespoons dried currants
	Salt and freshly ground black pepper
	Chopped cilantro, for garnish
	Plain yogurt or sour cream, for garnish

Cheese Tortellini Soup with White Beans, Kielbasa, and Spinach

2   tablespoons olive oil

12   ounces thinly sliced, fully cooked, smoked kielbasa sausage

1/2   cup diced onion

4   cloves garlic, minced

1 1/2   teaspoons chopped fresh thyme or 1/2 teaspoon dried thyme

   Scant 1/2 teaspoon red pepper flakes, or to taste

5   cans (14 ounces each) chicken broth

1   can (14 1/2 ounces) diced tomatoes, with liquid

1   can (15 ounces) white cannellini beans, rinsed and drained

1   package (9 ounces) fresh cheese tortellini

1/2   bunch fresh spinach, rinsed, dried, and tough stems removed

   Grated Parmesan cheese, for serving

An ideal quick supper for those busy weeknights, just add a crisp green salad and crusty rolls.

Heat the olive oil in a Dutch oven or other large pot over medium-high heat. Add the kielbasa, onion, garlic, thyme, and red pepper flakes and sauté until browned, about 12 minutes (if the garlic seems to be getting too brown, reduce the heat to medium to avoid burning it).

Add the broth and tomatoes and bring to a boil. Reduce the heat to low, and simmer for 15 minutes. Add the beans and tortellini to the soup. Simmer until the pasta is just tender to the bite, about 10 minutes. Stir the spinach into the soup and turn off the heat; let stand for about 2 minutes. Ladle the soup into bowls and sprinkle with Parmesan cheese before serving.

Makes 6 servings

WILD RICE AND SAUSAGE SOUP

Hearty, soul-satisfying flavors to help warm things up on a brisk, cold day. For a great shortcut, use pre-washed spinach. And if you have some leftover rice on hand—whether wild or long-grain white rice—it will make this recipe even quicker!

Bring 1½ cups of the water to a boil in a small saucepan over high heat. Add the wild rice, cover, reduce the heat to low, and simmer until the rice is tender, about 50 to 60 minutes. Drain away any excess water and set the rice aside.

Cook the sausage links in a Dutch oven or other large pan over medium-high heat until browned and cooked through, about 5 to 7 minutes. Drain the sausage on paper towels and let cool, then halve the links lengthwise and cut across into ¼-inch half moons; set aside.

Add the oil to the Dutch oven and heat over medium-high heat. Add the onion and sauté until tender and aromatic, about 3 minutes. Add the garlic and cook for 1 minute longer. Add the sausage, broth, remaining 2 cups water, tomatoes, tomato paste, oregano, and basil. Bring to a boil, then reduce heat to medium and simmer for 20 minutes. Stir in the wild rice and spinach and season to taste with salt and pepper. Ladle the soup into bowls and sprinkle each with some Parmesan cheese.

MAKES 8 SERVINGS

You can use any type of sausage here to suit your taste: hot or mild, pork or chicken, plain or seasoned.

3½	cups water, divided
½	cup wild rice
1	pound Italian sausage links or any type of link sausage
1	teaspoon olive oil
1	cup chopped onion
3	cloves garlic, minced
4	cans (14 ounces each) chicken broth
1	can (14½ ounces) diced tomatoes, with liquid
3	tablespoons tomato paste
1	teaspoon dried oregano
1	teaspoon dried basil
3	cups packed torn spinach leaves
	Salt and freshly ground black pepper
	Grated Parmesan cheese, for garnish

SEATTLE STYLE CHILI

2 | tablespoons olive oil, divided

1 | large onion, chopped

5 | cloves garlic, minced

3 | pounds sirloin steak, cut into 1/2-inch cubes

1 | cup strong coffee

3 | tablespoons chili powder

2 | teaspoons dried oregano

2 | teaspoons dried thyme

2 | teaspoons ground cumin

2 | teaspoons freshly ground black pepper

2 | cans (14 1/2 ounces each) crushed peeled tomatoes

1 | can (14 ounces) beef broth

2 | cans (15 ounces each) small red or kidney beans, rinsed and drained

Salt

Sour cream, grated Monterey Jack cheese, diced avocado, chopped cilantro, and/or chopped green onion, for garnish

The addition of strong coffee may be unexpected in chili, but the dark brew adds another level of flavor to this meat-and-beans chili recipe. It's a great dish to take to a wintertime potluck or to warm things up on a cold, rainy day.

Heat 1 tablespoon of the olive oil in a large saucepan over medium heat, add the onion and garlic, and sauté until tender and golden, about 8 to 10 minutes. Scoop out the onion mixture into a small bowl and set aside.

Heat the remaining tablespoon of oil in the pan, add the beef, and cook to brown it on all sides, about 5 minutes. (It's important to not crowd the pan when browning the beef; brown in batches if needed.) Add the coffee, chili powder, oregano, thyme, cumin, and black pepper to the beef and stir to evenly coat the meat in the spices, then add the tomatoes and the onion mixture. Bring just to a boil, stirring occasionally, then reduce the heat to medium and simmer for 10 minutes. Add the beef broth and the beans, return to a low boil once again, then reduce the heat to low and simmer until the meat is tender, about 1 hour. Season the chili to taste with salt.

To serve, ladle the chili into bowls and top with the chosen garnishes.

MAKES 6 TO 8 SERVINGS

Among the chili-toppers suggested to garnish this aromatic, hearty recipe, choose as many as you like—or even just one—to suit your taste. Instead of garnishing each bowl, you could instead pass the garnishes separately and let guests customize their toppings.

◆ Beer Bread (page 79) would be ideal alongside as well as a glass of Northwest porter-style beer with a dark malt flavor.

Northwest Passage
ROSS BUCKLAND

Long before airports were built in convenient locations, floatplanes were busy shuttling people up and down the coastal and inland waters of Washington. Fresh seafood was also frequently part of the cargo, which helped spread the popularity of each delectable variety of salmon and shellfish. Floatplanes are still a common sight today, popular for their quick service between Seattle, British Columbia and points in between.

CHUNKY FIVE-BEAN CHILI

2	tablespoons olive oil
1 1/2	cups chopped onion
1	green bell pepper, cored, seeded, and chopped
1	red or yellow bell pepper, cored, seeded, and chopped
3	cloves garlic, minced
2	tablespoons chili powder
2	teaspoons ground cumin
1	teaspoon salt
1/2	teaspoon freshly ground black pepper
1/2	teaspoon dried oregano
1/2	teaspoon dried basil
	Dash cayenne pepper
2	cans (14 ounces each) chicken or vegetable broth
1	can (28 ounces) stewed tomatoes
2	tablespoons Dijon mustard
1	tablespoon Worcestershire sauce
1	can (15 ounces) pinto beans, rinsed and drained
1	can (15 ounces) black beans, rinsed and drained
1	can (15 ounces) butter beans, rinsed and drained
1	can (15 ounces) kidney beans, rinsed and drained
1	can (15 ounces) white cannellini beans, rinsed and drained
1/2	cup chopped fresh parsley
	Chopped red onion, sour cream, and grated cheddar cheese, for garnish

Don't be daunted by the list of ingredients; this is a quick-and-easy chili recipe that will make for a hearty cold-weather dinner any day of the week. Add some crusty bread alongside, a crisp green salad, and call it a meal!

Heat the olive oil in a Dutch oven or other large pot over medium heat. Add the onion, bell peppers, and garlic, and sauté until slightly softened, about 5 minutes. Add the chili powder, cumin, salt, pepper, oregano, basil, and cayenne and cook 2 minutes longer, stirring constantly to evenly coat the vegetables with the spices. Stir in the broth, tomatoes, mustard, and Worcestershire and bring to a boil. Cover, reduce the heat to low, and simmer 20 minutes. Add the beans and parsley, and cook until the beans are heated through, about 10 minutes longer.

Spoon the chili into individual bowls and top with red onion, sour cream, and cheddar cheese, or pass the garnishes separately for guests to add to taste.

MAKES 6 SERVINGS

The chili can be made up to 2 days in advance and gently reheated before serving, making it a great option for casual weekend entertaining. In fact, the flavors will be more developed if the chili is made at least a few hours before serving.

◆ Zinfandel can take the heat, and its ripe fruit is a good match for any tomato-based dish.

WALLA WALLA ONION SOUP

The sweet onions that come from Eastern Washington are one of the highlights of summertime cooking in the Northwest. This is a time-consuming recipe—primarily because it requires patience to slowly cook the onions to their caramelized goodness—but the results are well worth it.

Combine the beef broth, apple cider, bay leaves, thyme, pepper, and a good pinch of salt in a large stockpot. Bring to a boil over high heat, reduce the heat to medium-low, and simmer, covered, for 1 hour.

While the broth is simmering, melt the butter in a large skillet over medium heat. Add the onions and sauté until beginning to soften, about 8 minutes. Add the sugar and cook, covered, but stirring occasionally, until the onions are very tender and nicely browned, about 40 to 45 minutes. You may have to add 1 to 2 tablespoons of water if the pan gets dry. When the onions are soft and brown, stir the sherry into the pan, scraping up any cooked bits from the bottom.

Add the onions and sherry to the broth. Cover and simmer for 1 hour. Remove the bay leaves and thyme sprigs and taste the soup for seasoning, adding more salt to taste.

Preheat the broiler. Ladle the soup into ovenproof bowls, top with a slice of baguette, sprinkle with Parmesan and top with 1 or 2 slices of Gruyère. Broil until the cheese is melted and bubbly, about 1 to 2 minutes. Top with the diced apple and serve.

MAKES 8 SERVINGS

Onions may be caramelized in advance using a slow cooker (page 129), and stored in freezer for later use.

◆ The sweetness of the slow-cooked onions suits a mellow merlot.

5	cans (14 ounces each) beef broth
3	cups apple cider or apple juice
2	bay leaves
6	sprigs fresh thyme or 1 teaspoon dried thyme
2	teaspoons freshly ground black pepper
	Salt
4	tablespoons unsalted butter
3	pounds Walla Walla sweet onions, thinly sliced
1	teaspoon sugar
2/3	cup dry sherry
8	baguette slices (1 inch thick)
1	cup freshly grated Parmesan cheese
	Sliced Gruyère cheese
2/3	cup finely diced red apple, such as Red Delicious, chilled

CURRIED CARROT SOUP WITH NUTTY FALL GARNISH

The aromatic, spicy nature of curry powder is a wonderful foil for the earthy sweetness of carrots, a match made in soup heaven! In place of the Nutty Fall Garnish, you could simply top the deep orange soup with a sprinkle of toasted coconut.

For the garnish, toss the diced apple with the lemon juice and set aside. Combine the water, wild rice, and wheat berries in a small saucepan and bring just to a boil. Reduce the heat to low, cover the pan, and cook until the rice and wheat berries are tender, about 45 minutes; drain away any excess liquid and set aside.

Heat the oil and butter in a medium skillet over medium heat. Add the shallots and cook until tender and aromatic, about 3 to 5 minutes. Add the rice and wheat berries and warm through. Take the skillet from the heat, stir in the nuts and herbs, and season to taste with salt and pepper. Stir in the diced apple just before serving.

For the soup, melt the butter in a large saucepan over medium heat. Add the green onions and garlic and sauté until tender and aromatic, about 2 to 3 minutes. Sprinkle the flour and curry powder over the mixture and cook, stirring to evenly coat the onions, about 1 minute. Gradually stir in the broth, then add the carrots. Bring to a boil over medium-high heat, then reduce the heat to low, cover, and simmer until the carrots are very tender, about 20 minutes. Take the pan from the heat and let cool slightly. Purée the soup in batches in a blender or food processor until smooth and return the soup to the saucepan (or use an immersion blender to purée the mixture). Add the milk with salt and pepper to taste. Reheat but do not allow it to boil. Spoon some of the Nutty Fall Garnish into the center of each soup bowl and serve hot, passing extra garnish separately.

MAKES 4 TO 6 SERVINGS

3	tablespoons unsalted butter
1	cup chopped green onions, white and light green parts only, about 3 large bunches
3	cloves garlic, minced
3	tablespoons all-purpose flour
2	teaspoons curry powder
2	cans (14 ounces each) chicken broth
4	cups carrots, cut into 1/4-inch slices
2	cups milk
	Salt
	Dash of white or black pepper

NUTTY FALL GARNISH

1	cup water
1/4	cup wild rice
1/4	cup hard red wheat berries (pearl barley can be substituted)
2/3	cup diced apple
2	tablespoons lemon juice
1	teaspoon vegetable oil
1	teaspoon unsalted butter
1/4	cup diced shallots
2/3	cup toasted and chopped pistachios, almonds, or skinned hazelnuts
1	tablespoon minced fresh herbs (thyme, parsley, sage, and/or mint)
	Salt and freshly ground black pepper

LENTIL AND ROASTED TOMATO SOUP

4 – 5 large, ripe tomatoes (about 2 pounds), stemmed and halved crosswise

3 tablespoons olive oil, divided

3 ounces pancetta or prosciutto, chopped

1 1/2 cups chopped onion

1 1/2 cups finely diced carrots

1 1/2 cups finely diced celery

1 1/2 tablespoons minced garlic

1/4 cup balsamic vinegar

1/2 teaspoon dried thyme

1/2 teaspoon dried marjoram

5 cans (14 ounces each) vegetable or chicken broth

2 cups French green lentils

Salt and freshly ground black pepper

Earthy and delicious flavors converge in this wonderful soup. The Serrano Ham and Manchego Cheese Toasts (page 78) make a soulful accompaniment.

Preheat the broiler and set the oven rack about 6 inches from the top element. Lightly oil a rimmed baking sheet and arrange the tomatoes in a single layer, cut side down. Use 1 tablespoon of the olive oil to lightly brush each tomato. Broil them until they darken, soften, and begin to blister, 4 to 6 minutes. Take the baking sheet from the oven, cover the tomatoes with a towel, and set aside on a wire rack to cool. When cool, gently peel away as much of the skin as you can with a small sharp knife. Cut the tomato halves into 1/2-inch dices.

Cook the pancetta in a large saucepan over medium-high heat until crisp, about 3 to 5 minutes, stirring occasionally. Scoop out the pancetta onto paper towels to drain and pour off the grease. Heat the remaining 2 tablespoons of olive oil in the same pan, add the onion, carrots, celery, and garlic and sauté until tender, aromatic, and richly browned, about 7 to 8 minutes (take care to not scorch the vegetables; reduce the heat a bit if needed). Stir in the balsamic vinegar, scraping up any browned bits from the bottom of the pan. Stir in the thyme, marjoram, and pancetta and cook for 1 minute longer. Add 7 cups of the broth with the tomatoes and lentils and bring to a low boil. Reduce the heat to medium-low, cover, and simmer until the lentils are tender, about 40 minutes. If the soup is quite thick, add a bit more broth. Season to taste with salt and pepper.

MAKES 6 SERVINGS

◆ For a classic combination, try a hefeweizen unfiltered wheat beer with hints of barley and hops.

WILD MUSHROOM SOUP

This rich and delicious soup gets a boost of flavor and aroma from a splash of dry sherry. Paired with the Ruby Green Salad with Creamy Mustard Balsamic Vinaigrette (page 88), it makes a lovely early spring luncheon.

Melt 6 tablespoons of the butter in large pot over medium-high heat. Add the celery, shallots, onion, and garlic and sauté until tender and aromatic, about 8 minutes. Add the shiitake, cremini, and oyster mushrooms, and sauté until they begin to soften, about 4 to 5 minutes. Add the white wine and sherry and simmer until the liquid is reduced to a glaze, about 6 to 8 minutes.

In a small bowl, combine the remaining 2 tablespoons of butter and the flour and mix to a smooth paste. Add the paste to the mushroom mixture in the pot, stirring until the mixture melts and coats the vegetables. Gradually add the broth and bring to a boil, stirring often. Reduce the heat to medium-low and simmer until slightly thickened, stirring often, about 10 minutes. Stir in the cream, dill, and parsley, and season to taste with salt and pepper. Ladle the soup into individual bowls, garnish with dill sprigs, and serve.

MAKES 8 TO 10 SERVINGS

◆ Echo the forest origins of mushrooms with an earthy pinot noir.

1/2	cup unsalted butter, at room temperature, divided
2	cups sliced celery
1	cup sliced shallots
3/4	cup chopped onion
3	cloves garlic, minced
6	ounces shiitake mushrooms, brushed clean, stemmed, and thinly sliced
6	ounces cremini mushrooms, brushed clean, trimmed, and sliced
4 1/2	ounces oyster mushrooms, brushed clean, trimmed, and thinly sliced
1/2	cup dry white wine
1/2	cup dry sherry
1/4	cup all-purpose flour
5	cans (14 ounces each) chicken broth
1/2	cup whipping cream
1	tablespoon chopped fresh dill, plus dill sprigs for garnish
1	tablespoon chopped fresh parsley
	Salt and freshly ground black pepper

WILD MUSHROOMS

So few of the foods we enjoy are truly "wild" any longer, but forest mushrooms are hold-outs that draw foragers into the wilderness in search of these distinctive treats. Most types of wild mushrooms flourish in the fall, when the abundant Northwest rain brings forth countless pounds of chanterelles, porcini, hedgehogs, and even the prized matsutake mushrooms that are among the most celebrated foods of Japan. Another premier mushroom holds court in spring, the morel with its hollow cap that has an interesting network of deep ridges on the surface. Wild mushrooms are sometimes available in grocery stores, though a trip to a farmers' market—particularly Seattle's Pike Place Market—will provide an array of delicious options when the season is in full gear. Dried wild mushrooms are a good off-season alternative.

CHILLED CHERRY SOUP

3 cups cold water

1/3 cup sugar

1 cinnamon stick

4 cups pitted fresh or frozen Bing or other dark sweet cherries (about 2 pounds)

4 teaspoons cornstarch

1/2 cup whipping cream

1/2 cup dry red wine

Crème fraîche, for serving

Milk, for serving

This is a very versatile recipe, an interesting first course on a hot summer day (perhaps with the Mixed Greens with Hazelnut Crusted Goat Cheese on page 85), served in small cups as a palate cleanser for a fancy dinner party, or even a great dessert to serve with the Hazelnut Butter Cookies (page 223). For dessert, you could sweeten the soup a little more if you like.

Combine the water, sugar, and cinnamon stick in a large saucepan and bring to a boil. Add the cherries and simmer over low heat, partially covered, until the cherries are very tender, about 30 minutes. Remove and discard the cinnamon stick. Stir together the cornstarch with 2 tablespoons of the cherry cooking liquids in a small bowl to make a paste. Add this to the soup, stirring constantly. Bring to a boil, then reduce the heat to low and simmer until the soup thickens slightly, about 3 minutes. Take the pan from the heat and let the soup cool slightly, then purée in batches in a blender or food processor. Refrigerate the soup until thoroughly chilled.

Just before serving, whisk in the cream and wine and ladle the soup into bowls. Thin the crème fraîche with 1 to 2 teaspoons of milk until it is the consistency of whipping cream, then put into a squirt bottle and garnish each bowl with a swirl, or simply use a spoon to lightly drizzle the cream over the soup.

MAKES 8 TO 10 SERVINGS

◆ Avoid big, oaky red wines for this soup, or the oaky flavor will overwhelm the balance of flavors. A beaujolais (not nouveau) or light style of pinot noir would be an ideal choice.

Serrano Ham and Manchego Cheese Toasts

2 – 3 ounces thinly sliced Serrano ham
or prosciutto

2 ounces manchego or
Parmesan cheese

4 slices (about 3/4 inch thick) ciabatta
bread or other dense, crusty loaf

Extra virgin olive oil

2 cloves garlic, halved

Coarsely ground black pepper

2 – 3 tablespoons chopped fresh parsley

These will quickly become a family favorite, as the cheesy toasts are an ideal side dish for a hearty soup or salad.

Trim any excess fat from the edges of the Serrano ham. Shave the manchego cheese into thin strips (a vegetable peeler works well for this).

Preheat the oven to 350°F. Cut each bread slice in half and lightly brush or spray one side with extra virgin olive oil. Put the bread on a wire rack set on a baking sheet and toast just until golden brown around the edges, but still soft in the center. Lightly rub the oiled side of the bread with the cut garlic and sprinkle with pepper. Top with Serrano ham and manchego cheese and sprinkle with parsley. Serve right away while the toast is still warm.

Makes 4 servings

Serrano ham is a cured ham from Spain similar to prosciutto (which can be substituted), but with a smoother, richer flavor. Also from Spain, manchego is a firm cheese that, when aged, is comparable to Parmesan, which can be used in its place.

BEER BREAD

This savory loaf is just the right thing for a weeknight soup dinner. A pilsner or ale works well. Allow the bread to cool at least a bit before serving, or the loaf will be too soft to slice. Because this is not a yeast bread, it doesn't require rising time.

Preheat the oven to 350°F. Butter a 9- by 5-inch loaf pan.

Combine the flour, sugar, baking powder, fennel seeds (if using), and salt in a large bowl and stir to evenly mix. Add the beer and stir until just combined. Spoon the batter into the prepared pan and smooth the top with a spatula. Drizzle the melted butter evenly over the top and bake until golden and a toothpick inserted in the center comes out clean, about 50 minutes. Turn the bread out onto a wire rack to cool at least 15 minutes before slicing to serve.

MAKES 1 LOAF

Minced fresh herbs—such as rosemary, thyme, or oregano—can be used in place of the fennel seed in this recipe.

3	cups all-purpose flour
1/4	cup sugar
4 1/2	teaspoons baking powder
2	tablespoons whole fennel seeds (optional)
1 1/2	teaspoons salt
1	bottle (12 ounces) beer, such as a Northwest pilsner or ale
1/4	cup unsalted butter, melted

SUNFLOWER LOAF

1 package (about 2 1/2 teaspoons) active dry yeast

1 teaspoon sugar

1 1/4 cups warm water (110°F to 115°F)

1/2 cup buttermilk

1/4 cup honey

1 1/2 teaspoons salt

3 cups whole-wheat flour

1 cup all-purpose flour, more if needed

1/2 cup toasted shelled sunflower seeds

1 egg yolk

1 tablespoon milk

3 tablespoons raw shelled sunflower seeds

The nutty crunch of sunflower seeds—both in the dough and scattered over the loaf—give distinctive character to this hearty whole-wheat bread.

Dissolve the yeast and sugar in the warm water in a large bowl. Let stand until the yeast is frothy, about 10 minutes. Add the buttermilk, honey, and salt, stirring to dissolve the honey. Add the whole-wheat and all-purpose flours and toasted sunflower seeds, mixing with a large wooden spoon to thoroughly blend. (The dough will be slightly sticky until after it rises.) Turn the dough out onto a lightly floured board and knead until smooth and satiny, for about 10 minutes, incorporating up to 1/2 cup more all-purpose flour if needed. Shape the dough into a ball and put it in a lightly oiled bowl, turning the dough so the surface is lightly, evenly coated in oil. Cover the bowl with plastic wrap and let rise in a warm place for 20 minutes. Gently punch down the dough, kneading gently once or twice, and form it into a ball. Return the dough to the bowl, cover, and let rise for 40 minutes. Shape the dough into a cylinder about 8 inches long and set it in a greased 9- by 5-inch loaf pan.

Combine the egg yolk and milk in a small dish and blend with a fork. Brush the top of the bread loaf with this glaze and sprinkle the raw sunflower seeds evenly over, pressing very gently to help them adhere, without deflating the dough. Cover the pan lightly with plastic wrap and let rise until the dough has risen about 1 inch above the top edge of the pan, about 45 minutes.

Preheat the oven to 375°F. Bake the bread until it is nicely browned and the loaf sounds hollow when tapped on the bottom, about 40 minutes (if the seeds on top are nicely browned before the bread is cooked, lightly cover the pan with foil to avoid burning). Turn the bread out onto a wire rack to cool before slicing to serve.

MAKES 1 LOAF

HERBED CHEESE BREAD

**This is a creative variation on everyone's favorite garlic bread,
perfect to serve with soups, salads or on a casual buffet.**

Preheat the oven to 350°F. Use a large bread knife to cut 1½-inch
slices into the loaf of bread, but not through the bottom crust so that
the loaf remains intact. Make more slices perpendicular to the others,
forming squares, or at a slight angle to form diamonds.

In a small saucepan over low heat, melt the butter with the parsley,
poppy seeds, onion, and mustard, stirring to evenly mix. Drizzle the
butter mixture into the slits in the bread, then insert the cheese slices
into the slits. Wrap the bread well in foil so that butter won't drip out
as it heats (you may want to double-wrap it; the bread can be made
up to a day in advance to this point).

Set the wrapped loaf on a baking sheet and bake for 15 minutes.
Loosen the foil to expose the top and bake until lightly brown, about
15 minutes longer. Discard the foil and serve hot, guests tearing off
individual portions of the bread.

MAKES 6 TO 8 SERVINGS

*The bread can be prepared up to 3 days in advance, wrapped in foil, and
refrigerated until ready to bake.*

1	round loaf sourdough or French bread
½	cup unsalted butter
2	tablespoons chopped parsley
2	tablespoons poppy seeds
1	tablespoon grated onion
1	tablespoon Dijon mustard
8	ounces Monterey Jack cheese, sliced

ROSEMARY BREAD

3¾ teaspoons active dry yeast

1 cup warm water (110°F to 115°F)

1 cup milk, at room temperature

¼ cup olive oil

About 5 cups unbleached all-purpose flour, divided

¼ cup minced fresh rosemary or 1½ tablespoons crushed dried rosemary

4 teaspoons fine salt

1–1½ teaspoons coarse salt, preferably kosher

Cornmeal, for baking

These beautiful, crusty loaves will have your friends wondering where you bought them! The savory rosemary flavor is delicious, particularly if using fresh rosemary, making the bread a great accompaniment for stews or hearty soups.

In the bowl of an electric mixer, stir the yeast into the warm water; let stand until frothy, about 10 minutes. Stir in the milk and oil. Combine 4½ cups of the flour in another bowl with the rosemary and fine salt, and stir to mix. Add the flour mixture to the yeast mixture and blend with the paddle attachment at low speed until the flour is absorbed, about 1 to 2 minutes. Using the dough hook, knead the dough on medium speed until velvety, elastic, smooth, and somewhat moist, about 5 minutes. Gradually add enough of the remaining flour until the dough does not stick to the bottom and sides of the bowl. Finish kneading the dough by hand on a lightly floured surface for a few minutes. Put the dough in an oiled bowl, turning the dough so the surface is lightly and evenly coated in oil all over, cover with plastic wrap, and let rise in a warm place until doubled in bulk, about 1½ hours.

Gently punch the dough down on a lightly floured surface but do not knead it. Cut the dough in half and shape each into a round ball. Put the loaves on a lightly floured bread board, cover loosely with plastic wrap, and let rise until almost doubled, about 45 to 55 minutes.

Preheat the oven to 450°F. Put a baking stone in the cold oven and preheat in the oven 30 minutes before baking. Just before you put the loaves in the oven, make an asterisk of shallow slashes in the top of each loaf with a razor blade or sharp knife, and sprinkle the coarse salt into the slits. Carefully sprinkle the heated baking stone with cornmeal, then slide the loaves onto it or simply form the loaves on a lightly oiled baking sheet and bake directly on the sheet, omitting the cornmeal. Bake for 10 minutes, during which time use a small spray bottle of water (the kind you keep by your ironing board or outdoor grill) to spray the inside of the oven 3 times; this helps develop a chewy crust. Reduce the oven to 400°F and bake until the bread is nicely browned and the loaves sound hollow when tapped on the bottom, about 30 to 35 minutes longer. Let cool on wire racks before cutting into slices to serve.

MAKES 2 LOAVES

HEARTS OF ROMAINE WITH HAZELNUT ROQUEFORT DRESSING

2   heads romaine lettuce, center hearts only, rinsed, dried, and torn into pieces

2   small heads radicchio, rinsed, dried, and torn into pieces

1/2   cup dried cranberries

1/2   cup hazelnuts, toasted, skinned, and chopped

    Salt and freshly ground black pepper

HAZELNUT ROQUEFORT DRESSING

1   tablespoon Dijon mustard

1/4   teaspoon coarsely ground black pepper, more to taste

1/3   cup hazelnut oil

2   tablespoons red wine vinegar

2   tablespoons cranberry juice

1   tablespoon olive oil

1   tablespoon minced shallot

1   teaspoon minced garlic

3 – 4   ounces Roquefort or other blue cheese, crumbled, more to taste

This is not your basic blue cheese dressing, thanks to the addition of hazelnut oil and a bit of tang from cranberry juice. Next time you need a simple salad to begin a meal, look no further. Hazelnut oil is available in gourmet shops, as well as in many supermarkets. If necessary, you could substitute extra virgin olive oil, though the dressing will lack that touch of nutty flavor.

For the dressing, put the Dijon mustard and pepper in a small bowl and slowly drizzle in the hazelnut oil, whisking constantly, until the mixture is emulsified (slightly thickened and creamy). Whisk in the vinegar and cranberry juice. Heat the oil in a small skillet over medium heat, add the shallot and garlic, and sauté until tender and aromatic, 2 to 3 minutes. Add the vinaigrette and cheese and immediately take the pan from the heat. Stir just until warmed through, then let cool to room temperature.

Put the romaine and radicchio in a large bowl. Taste the dressing for seasoning, adding salt or pepper to taste, then toss the lettuce with the dressing so that it evenly coats the leaves. Arrange the salad on individual plates, sprinkle with cranberries and hazelnuts, and serve immediately.

MAKES 4 SERVINGS

The "heart" of a head of romaine lettuce simply refers to the inner leaves, which are lighter in color and more tender than the big outer leaves. The outer leaves could be used in another salad or wrapped around fish for steaming.

◆ Typically, a red wine would seem too bold to pair with salad, but powerful blue cheese meets its match with tannic cabernet.

Mixed Greens with Hazelnut Crusted Goat Cheese

A treat for those who love cheese, this green salad is topped with a warm round of goat cheese crusted with hazelnuts and bread crumbs. The vinaigrette sports delicious herbal flavor from fresh sage, though you could use another favorite herb in its place, such as chives, chervil, or parsley. This is quite a dressed-up salad!

Stir together the hazelnuts and bread crumbs in a shallow bowl and spread them out in an even layer. Lightly beat the egg whites in a separate shallow bowl. Dip each goat cheese round in egg white, allowing excess to drip off, then dip each side into the hazelnut mixture, lightly pressing the nuts into the cheese. Refrigerate for at least 30 minutes.

For the dressing, whisk together vinegar, shallot, mustard, sage, and garlic with a good pinch each of salt and pepper. Let stand for at least 15 minutes to allow the shallot to "pickle" slightly. Slowly drizzle in the oil, whisking constantly, until emulsified (slightly thickened). Taste the dressing for seasoning, adding more salt, pepper, or vinegar to taste. Put the salad greens in a large bowl and set aside.

Melt the butter in a medium nonstick skillet over medium-high heat. Fry the goat cheese rounds until golden brown and warmed through, 1 to 2 minutes on each side. (Take care when turning them.)

As soon as the cheese is done, drizzle the dressing over the greens and toss well. Arrange the greens on individual plates, top each salad with a warm goat cheese round, and garnish with more chopped toasted hazelnuts. Serve right away.

MAKES 4 SERVINGS

◆ The soft cherry and strawberry fruit of pinot noir are complemented by the creamy goat cheese and toasted nuts.

2/3	cup hazelnuts, toasted, skinned, and finely chopped, plus more for garnish
1/4	cup dried bread crumbs
2	egg whites
4	slices (1/2 inch thick) Montrachet goat cheese, well chilled
6	cups lightly packed mixed wild and baby greens, rinsed and dried
2 – 3	tablespoons unsalted butter

SAGE DRESSING

2	tablespoons Champagne vinegar or white wine vinegar
1	tablespoon minced shallot
2	teaspoons Dijon mustard
2	teaspoons minced fresh sage
1/2	teaspoon minced garlic
	Salt and freshly ground black pepper
1/4	cup hazelnut oil or extra virgin olive oil, or a blend of both

MIXED GREENS WITH YAKIMA NECTARINES AND HONEY POPPY SEED DRESSING

Yakima Valley nectarines capture the essence of Eastern Washington's summers. Beyond simply eating them out of hand as a delicious, juicy snack, nectarines are most appreciated in simple preparations that let the fruit shine. This quick-to-make summer salad is an ideal example and versatile enough to complement any summer meal.

For the dressing, whisk together the honey, vinegar, olive oil, mustard, shallot, lemon juice, and poppy seeds in a small bowl and season to taste with salt and pepper. Whisk well to thoroughly blend and dissolve the honey. Taste the dressing for seasoning, adding more salt, pepper, or lemon juice to taste.

Combine the greens, nectarine slices, almonds, and green onions in a salad bowl or other large bowl. Drizzle the dressing over, toss to mix, and serve.

MAKES 4 SERVINGS

◆ The berry hue and flavor of Blackberry Lemonade contrast nicely with the nectarines and greens in this salad.

6	ounces mixed greens, rinsed and dried, leaves torn if large
1	large ripe nectarine, pitted and thinly sliced
1/2	cup toasted slivered almonds
1/2	cup thinly sliced green onions

HONEY POPPY SEED DRESSING

2	tablespoons honey
1	tablespoon plus 2 teaspoons cider vinegar
1	tablespoon olive oil
1	tablespoon Dijon mustard
1	tablespoon minced shallot
1	teaspoon freshly squeezed lemon juice, more to taste
1/2	teaspoon poppy seeds
	Salt and freshly ground black pepper

BLACKBERRY LEMONADE

Peel the zest from 4 of the lemons with a vegetable peeler and squeeze enough juice from all the lemons to measure 1 cup. Combine 2 cups of the water and the sugar in a medium saucepan and bring to a boil over high heat, stirring, until the sugar is dissolved. Stir in the zest pieces, cover, and steep for 30 minutes. Add the lemon juice and remaining 2 cups water. Let cool.

Purée the blackberries with 1/2 cup of the lemonade mixture and stir into the remaining lemonade. Strain into a pitcher and refrigerate until fully chilled, up to 2 days. Serve over ice in tall glasses garnished with lemon slices.

MAKES 6 SERVINGS

6	large lemons
4	cups water
1	cup sugar
1/2	cup fresh blackberries
6	lemon slices, for garnish

RUBY GREEN SALAD WITH CREAMY MUSTARD BALSAMIC VINAIGRETTE

10–12 ounces fresh, trimmed baby red beets, scrubbed, or small beets, scrubbed and quartered

1 small head spinach (about 8 ounces), rinsed, dried, and tough stems removed

1 small head frisée, rinsed, dried, and tough outer leaves discarded

1 small head radicchio, rinsed, dried, and leaves torn

MUSTARD BALSAMIC VINAIGRETTE

2 tablespoons balsamic vinegar, more to taste

3 tablespoons minced shallot

1 tablespoon Dijon mustard

2 teaspoons minced garlic

2 tablespoons crème fraîche or sour cream

1/4 cup plus 2 tablespoons walnut oil or olive oil

TOASTED SPICED PUMPKIN SEEDS

1 tablespoon unsalted butter, melted

1 tablespoon packed light brown sugar

1/4 teaspoon ground cinnamon

1/8 teaspoon ground cardamom

1/8 teaspoon ground allspice

Salt and freshly ground black pepper

1 vanilla bean or 1/2 teaspoon vanilla extract

1 cup green pumpkin seeds (*pepitas*) or slivered almonds

The striking presentation, complex flavors, and textures make this a salad to remember.

Set a collapsible steamer basket in the bottom of a large saucepan, add a couple inches of water, and bring to a boil. Add the beets to the basket, cover the pan, and steam them until tender, 12 to 15 minutes. Allow the beets to cool, then peel and quarter the baby beets or cut the larger beets into ½-inch slices. (To keep the beets from coloring your hands, wear rubber gloves.)

For the dressing, whisk together the balsamic vinegar, shallot, mustard, and garlic with salt and pepper to taste. Let rest for 15 to 20 minutes to allow the shallot to "pickle" slightly. Whisk in the crème fraîche and then slowly whisk in the walnut oil. Taste the dressing for seasoning, adding more balsamic vinegar, salt, or pepper to taste.

For the Toasted Spiced Pumpkin Seeds, preheat the oven to 350°F. Combine the butter, brown sugar, cinnamon, cardamom, allspice, and ⅛ teaspoon salt in a medium bowl. Split the vanilla bean lengthwise (if using) and scrape out the tiny black seeds with the tip of the knife. Add the vanilla seeds (or extract) to the bowl with the pumpkin seeds and stir to coat the pumpkin seeds evenly with the spices.

Spread the pumpkin seeds in a single layer on a rimmed baking sheet. Bake until golden and aromatic, about 15 minutes. Shake the pan twice during the baking time to ensure they toast evenly; the seeds will crackle and puff as they cook. Transfer the spiced seeds to a bowl and set aside to cool.

Combine the beets, spinach, frisée, and radicchio in a large bowl and drizzle the dressing over. Toss the salad to evenly mix, then divide it among individual plates, being careful to distribute the beets evenly. Scatter the pumpkin seeds over and serve.

MAKES 4 SERVINGS

Into The Cedars
Nancy Spaulding

With so much water surrounding the cities in Western Washington, it is no wonder people here enjoy many types of water sports. From power boating to kayaking, there are many rivers, bays and inlets to enjoy while afloat. The mild climate is conducive to spending the entire day outdoors and a picnic lunch or a hearty salad is just the right thing to take along.

SPINACH AND APRICOT SALAD

6 ounces dried apricots, coarsely chopped

1 cup boiling water, more if needed

3 tablespoons cider vinegar

3 tablespoons apricot preserves

1/2 teaspoon powdered mustard

1/4 cup olive oil

1 large bunch spinach (about 10 ounces), rinsed, dried, tough stems removed, and large leaves torn

3/4 cup toasted walnuts, chopped, or toasted pine nuts

4 ounces Gorgonzola or feta cheese, crumbled

Salt

This salad couldn't be simpler. Serve it with roasted chicken, on a lunch buffet, or as part of a summer barbecue.

Put the apricots in a small bowl and add enough boiling water to cover. Let sit until softened, about 10 minutes. Drain, set aside, and let cool completely. Combine the vinegar, apricot preserves, powdered mustard, and a pinch of salt in a blender or food processor and pulse to mix. With the motor running, slowly drizzle in the oil. Taste the dressing for seasoning, adding more salt to taste.

Combine the spinach, apricots, nuts, and cheese in a large salad bowl, drizzle the dressing over, and toss to evenly mix. Serve right away.

MAKES 4 TO 6 SERVINGS

When chopping dried apricots or other dried fruits, first spray the knife blade with nonstick spray (or lightly and carefully rub it with vegetable oil) to help prevent the fruits from sticking to the blade while you chop.

WILTED SPINACH AND APPLE SALAD

Enjoy this new take on classic wilted spinach salad for your next luncheon or as an ideal complement to the Wild Mushroom Soup (page 75). For a time-saver, use bagged, pre-cleaned spinach in place of the bunch spinach.

Cook the bacon in a large skillet over medium heat, stirring frequently, until crisp and browned, 5 to 7 minutes. Spoon the bacon onto paper towels to drain; discard all but 1 tablespoon of the drippings from the skillet.

Add the apple and shallot to the skillet and sauté over medium heat, stirring, for 1 minute. Add the cider, cider vinegar, and apple juice concentrate. Bring to a boil over medium-high heat and boil, stirring occasionally, until the liquid is reduced to about ½ cup, 8 to 10 minutes. Take the skillet from the heat and whisk in the mustard and oil with salt and pepper to taste.

Put the spinach in a large bowl, drizzle the warm dressing over, and toss until the spinach is just lightly wilted. Divide the salad among individual plates and top with the bacon, egg slices, and walnuts. Serve right away, while still warm.

MAKES 4 SERVINGS

To hard-boil eggs, put them in a small pan of cold water and set on medium-high heat. When the water comes to a boil, set the timer for 10 minutes and reduce the heat to medium so the water simmers but doesn't boil vigorously. Drain the eggs and rinse with cold water to help cool quickly.

5	slices lean bacon, finely chopped
3/4	cup finely chopped apple, such as Fuji, Gala, or Braeburn
3	tablespoons minced shallot
1 1/4	cups apple cider
1/4	cup cider vinegar
1/4	cup apple juice concentrate
1	tablespoon Dijon mustard
3	tablespoons olive oil
	Salt and freshly ground black pepper
1	bunch spinach (about 10 ounces), rinsed, dried, tough stems removed, and large leaves torn
2	hard-boiled eggs, sliced
1/2	cup toasted walnuts, chopped

Toasted Couscous Salad with Grilled Summer Vegetables

2	zucchini, quartered lengthwise
2	yellow summer squash, quartered lengthwise
4	plum (roma) tomatoes
12	spears asparagus, trimmed
1	red bell pepper, cored, seeded, and quartered
1	yellow or orange bell pepper, cored, seeded, and quartered
1	medium red onion, quartered and layers separated (optional)
1/4	cup finely shredded fresh basil (chiffonade)
2	tablespoons fresh thyme leaves
1/4	cup chopped fresh parsley
2	cans (14 ounces each) vegetable or chicken broth
2	tablespoons olive oil
3	cups Israeli couscous*

VINAIGRETTE

1/2	cup balsamic vinegar
2	teaspoons finely minced garlic
1	teaspoon Dijon mustard
	Salt and freshly ground black pepper
1	cup extra virgin olive oil

Refer to couscous information on page 101

This hearty salad could be served as a vegetarian main course or a satisfying, make-ahead side dish for your favorite lunch or dinner.

For the vinaigrette, whisk together the vinegar, garlic, and mustard with a good pinch each of salt and pepper in a small bowl. Slowly drizzle in the olive oil, whisking constantly, until emulsified (slightly thickened). Taste the dressing for seasoning, adding more salt or pepper to taste.

Combine the zucchini, yellow squash, tomatoes, asparagus, red and yellow peppers, and onion in a large shallow dish. Pour half of the vinaigrette over the vegetables, toss to evenly coat, and let marinate at room temperature for at least 45 minutes or up to 2 hours.

Preheat an outdoor grill (to high if using a gas grill). Take the vegetables from the marinade and grill them, preferably on a grill screen, just until cooked through and lightly browned, about 10 minutes. They should be tender to the bite, but not soft. (Note that the vegetables will cook at different rates, so remove the softer, quicker-cooked vegetables as they are done.) All the vegetables, except the tomatoes, can be spread in a single layer on a baking sheet and roasted in a 425°F oven for 40 minutes. Add the tomatoes during the last 15 minutes of roasting.

Let the vegetables cool to room temperature. Cut the zucchini and yellow squash into ½-inch pieces. Quarter the tomatoes, discarding the skin if it slips off, and cut the asparagus into 2-inch pieces. Cut the peppers and onion into 1-inch pieces.

Put the broth in a small saucepan and bring just to a low boil over medium heat; reduce the heat to low to keep the broth warm.

Heat the olive oil in a sauté pan or deep skillet over medium-high heat. Add the couscous and cook, stirring often, until toasted to golden brown. Add enough stock to the couscous to cover it by about 1 inch (add extra water if needed to cover) and bring to a boil. Cook until *al dente*, about 10 minutes. Drain well and let cool to room temperature in a large bowl.

Add the vegetables, basil, thyme, and parsley to the cooled couscous, drizzle the remaining vinaigrette over, and toss to evenly mix. Taste the salad for seasoning, adding more salt or pepper to taste.

MAKES 8 TO 10 SERVINGS

SUMMER TOMATO SALAD

1 1/2   pints (about 12 ounces) teardrop, cherry, currant, and/or grape tomatoes (mixed colors), stemmed and halved

2   large, firm, ripe tomatoes (preferably 1 yellow or orange and 1 red)

   Basil leaves, for garnish

FETA VINAIGRETTE

2   tablespoons red wine vinegar

1   tablespoon minced shallot

1   teaspoon minced garlic

   Salt and freshly ground black pepper

1/4   cup extra virgin olive oil

1   cup crumbled feta cheese

1   tablespoon chopped fresh oregano

2   teaspoons chopped fresh basil

Recipe pictured on page 93

Perfectly ripe, fresh summer tomatoes need little else, but this simple vinaigrette is a snap to make and it's a fabulous accent for the tomatoes. Try to find an interesting mix of tomato types, including heirloom varieties that tend to be particularly flavorful. If you are unable to find the varieties listed here, substitute any mix of the best tomatoes you can find, cut into bite-sized pieces.

For the vinaigrette, whisk together the vinegar, shallot, and garlic with a good pinch each of salt and pepper in a small bowl and set aside for 30 minutes to allow the shallot to "pickle" slightly. Slowly drizzle in the olive oil, whisking constantly, until the mixture is emulsified (slightly thickened). Stir in the feta cheese, oregano, and basil and taste for seasoning, adding more salt or pepper if needed. Toss two-thirds of the dressing with the halved tomatoes in a medium bowl.

Slice the remaining tomatoes into 1/4-inch-thick slices and arrange the slices, overlapping, on individual plates. Drizzle with the remaining dressing and top with the halved tomatoes. Garnish with basil leaves and serve.

MAKES 4 SERVINGS

This recipe can be altered to make a version of the traditional caprese salad (tomatoes and fresh mozzarella). Replace the red wine vinegar, garlic, and feta cheese with balsamic vinegar, garlic, and 1 cup of diced fresh mozzarella. Also, reverse the quantities of herbs, using instead 1 tablespoon basil and 2 teaspoons oregano.

ROASTED CORN AND AVOCADO SALAD

The sweetness of summer corn and the creamy richness of avocados are a wonderful pairing in this salad. Serve it with Cajun Pacific Snapper Tacos (page 149) and a cold beer.

Preheat the oven to 400°F. Lightly oil a rimmed baking sheet.

Cut the kernels from the corn cobs: hold a cob upright on the chopping board with the broader end down. Slide the knife blade vertically down the length of the cob, cutting away a strip of kernels. Turn the cob slightly and repeat around the ear to remove all the kernels. Put the kernels on the baking sheet and roast in the oven until slightly shriveled, golden brown, and aromatic, about 15 minutes, turning with a spatula once or twice.

For the dressing, whisk together the lime juice, olive oil, vinegar, garlic, cumin, chili powder, and salt in a small bowl. Add cayenne and pepper sauce to taste. Toss the corn with the black beans in a large bowl, then toss in the red pepper, onion, oregano, and jalapeño. Gently stir the dressing into the corn mixture and taste the salad for seasoning, adding more salt, cayenne, or pepper sauce to taste. Let sit for at least 30 minutes before serving.

Just before serving, peel and pit the avocados and cut them into ½-inch pieces. Gently stir the avocados and tomatoes into the salad. Set the lettuce leaves on individual plates, spoon the salad into the center of the leaves, and garnish with lime wedges or oregano sprigs.

MAKES 6 TO 8 SERVINGS

You could also make this recipe as a green salad. Simply toss the finished corn-avocado mixture with 4 cups of rinsed, dried, and torn leaf lettuce. Add additional lime juice or other seasonings if desired.

4	large ears sweet corn, husks and silk removed
1	cup canned small black beans, drained and rinsed
3/4	cup diced red bell pepper
3/4	cup minced red onion
1/4	cup minced fresh oregano
1	tablespoon minced jalapeño chile
3	ripe avocados
1 1/2	cups seeded, diced tomatoes
6 – 8	leaves red leaf lettuce
	Lime wedges or oregano sprigs, for garnish

LIME CUMIN DRESSING

1/2	cup freshly squeezed lime juice
1/3	cup extra virgin olive oil
1/4	cup red wine vinegar
1	tablespoon minced garlic
1	tablespoon ground cumin
2	teaspoons chili powder
3/4	teaspoon salt
	Pinch cayenne pepper, more to taste
8 – 10	drops hot pepper sauce

ORECCHIETTE AND SPRING PEA SALAD

8	ounces orecchiette pasta
1 1/2	cups fresh peas or frozen petit peas, blanched
3/4	cup diced, seeded tomatoes
1/2	cup grated asiago cheese
2	tablespoons chopped fresh parsley

LEMON THYME DRESSING

2	teaspoons finely grated lemon zest
2	tablespoons freshly squeezed lemon juice, more to taste
1	teaspoon minced garlic
	Salt and freshly ground black pepper
5	tablespoons extra virgin olive oil
1/3	cup minced red onion
2	tablespoons chopped fresh lemon thyme or regular thyme

What better way to celebrate the flavors of spring than with this deliciously simple salad? Spring's fresh, plump, sweet peas will be tastiest in this pasta salad, though good frozen peas are a decent substitute; don't be tempted to use canned peas.

Bring a large saucepan of salted water to a boil over high heat. Add the pasta, reduce the heat to medium, and simmer until the pasta is *al dente*, about 12 minutes. Drain well and let the pasta cool in the colander in the sink, tossing occasionally to keep the orecchiette from sticking together.

For the dressing, combine the lemon zest, lemon juice, and garlic in a small bowl and add salt and pepper to taste. Slowly drizzle in the olive oil, whisking constantly, until emulsified (slightly thickened). Stir in the onion and thyme. Let rest at least 30 minutes to allow the onion to "pickle" slightly.

Combine the pasta, peas, and tomatoes in a large bowl. Drizzle the dressing over and add the asiago and parsley, tossing to evenly mix. Taste the salad for seasoning, adding more lemon juice, salt, or pepper if needed. Serve at room temperature.

MAKES 6 SERVINGS

Orecchiette are a small, concave, disk-shaped pasta; the name translates to mean "little ears" in Italian. If you are unable to find orecchiette, you could use farfalle (bowties) or fusilli (corkscrews) instead.

SMOKED SALMON PASTA SALAD

This light, refreshing salad is an ideal way to highlight the rich flavors of a traditional Northwest favorite—smoked salmon. Serve it for lunch with a grilled sandwich for a great mid-day treat. Be certain to use a firm hot-smoked salmon, as opposed to softer cold-smoked salmon such as lox.

For the dressing, whisk together the olive oil, lemon juice, shallot, vinegar, mustard, and brown sugar, then season to taste with salt and a liberal dose of pepper. Set aside for at least 30 minutes.

Bring a large pot of salted water to a boil. When the water is at a rolling boil, add the pasta and cook until *al dente*, about 10 to 12 minutes. Drain the pasta well, put it in a large bowl, and drizzle with the olive oil. Toss to evenly coat the pasta in the oil, then set aside and let cool to room temperature.

Add the smoked salmon, artichoke hearts, green onions, parsley, onion, capers, and lemon zest to the pasta. Rewhisk the dressing and pour about ⅔ of it over the salad, tossing gently to mix. Let sit for at least 1 hour so the flavors can blend (refrigerate if preparing more than an hour in advance). Season the salad to taste with salt and pepper. Serve at room temperature with lemon wedges garnishing the plates, passing extra dressing separately to be added to taste.

MAKES 4 SERVINGS

12	ounces dry pasta, such as farfalle or fusilli
12	ounces hot-smoked salmon, flaked, skin and bones discarded
3/4	cup coarsely chopped artichoke hearts (in simple brine rather than marinated)
1/2	cup thinly sliced green onions
1/2	cup chopped fresh parsley
1/4	cup minced red onion
3	tablespoons coarsely chopped capers
1	teaspoon grated lemon zest
	Salt and freshly ground black pepper
	Lemon wedges, for garnish

LEMON DIJON DRESSING

1/2	cup extra virgin olive oil
1/4	cup freshly squeezed lemon juice
1/4	cup minced shallot
2	tablespoons Champagne or white wine vinegar
2	tablespoons Dijon mustard
1	tablespoon packed light brown sugar
1/4	teaspoon salt
1/2	teaspoon freshly ground black pepper

SMOKED SALMON

Not all smoked salmon is created the same. In the Northwest, the classic preparation is hot-smoked salmon, also known as kippered salmon. The rich fish is first cured in a brine of salt and sugar with any number of other seasonings (cracked pepper, orange zest, herbs). The fish is then smoked over very low embers so that the smoky flavor infuses the fish while it slowly cooks. The final product is firm and flaky, with an astounding amount of flavor— pure Northwest!

Wheat Berry Salad with Autumn Dried Fruits

1	cup hard red wheat berries (pearl barley can be substituted)
1/4	teaspoon salt
1/2	cup diced apple or pear tossed with 1 tablespoon freshly squeezed lemon juice
2/3	cup hazelnuts, toasted and skinned
2/3	cup finely diced Gouda cheese (optional)
1/2	cup dried cranberries
1/2	cup coarsely chopped dried cherries
1/2	cup chopped dried apricots
1/2	cup minced celery
3	tablespoons minced fresh parsley

RED ONION DRESSING

1/4	cup vegetable oil
1/4	cup cranberry juice
3	tablespoons raspberry vinegar
1	tablespoon balsamic vinegar
1 1/2	teaspoons Dijon mustard
	Salt and freshly ground black pepper
1/2	cup minced red onion

This earthy but light salad captures the essence of autumn with sweet dried fruits and nutty grain. Grain salads tend to soak up dressings as they rest and may need to be tasted for seasoning again—making slight adjustments—just before serving. Serve after an afternoon of apple-picking with the Pork Tenderloin with Maple Glaze (page 185) and Lemon Roasted Green Beans (page 207).

Bring a medium saucepan of salted water to a boil over high heat. Add the wheat berries, reduce the heat to medium, and cook until tender but still a bit chewy, about 1 hour, stirring occasionally. (The grain should be fully covered by water during cooking; add more boiling water to the pan if needed.) Drain the wheat berries well, set aside in a large bowl, and let cool.

For the dressing, whisk together the oil, cranberry juice, raspberry vinegar, balsamic vinegar, and mustard with a good pinch each of salt and pepper in a medium bowl. Stir in the red onion and set aside for 30 minutes to allow the onion to "pickle" slightly.

Add the apple, nuts, cheese (if using), dried fruits, celery, and parsley to the cooled wheat berries. (The recipe can be prepared to this point a day ahead, the salad and dressing refrigerated separately. Let both come to room temperature before continuing.) Drizzle about two-thirds of the dressing over and toss to mix. Add salt and pepper to taste. Chill for 2 to 3 hours, but not overnight. Toss with the remaining dressing. Serve slightly chilled or at room temperature.

MAKES 6 SERVINGS

◆ The cranberry and dried fruits in this tasty salad are well suited to the ripe berry flavors of zinfandel.

The quiet, suburban area of modern Bothell (near Seattle) was once referred to by native people as "squak" or swampy, forested lowland. The transformation has been radical over the last 100 years, but the first changes came slowly through timber harvesting and farming. A busy network of freeways criss-crosses the landscape today, connecting a burgeoning population.

Middle Eastern Lentil and Orzo Salad

This pasta salad brings in flavors of the Eastern Mediterranean, creating a somewhat sweet-and-sour dish. This is especially good served with grilled chicken.

1	cup French green lentils
1	can (14 ounces) chicken broth
1	bay leaf
4–5	tablespoons olive oil, divided
1 1/2	cups chopped onion
1	teaspoon sugar, if needed
1	tablespoon minced garlic
1/4	cup plus 2 tablespoons balsamic vinegar, divided
8	ounces orzo pasta
1	bunch spinach (about 10 ounces), rinsed, dried, and tough stems removed
2	cups seeded, diced plum tomatoes or halved grape tomatoes
1/2–3/4	cup crumbled feta cheese, to taste
1/2	cup golden raisins
3	tablespoons chopped fresh oregano or 1 1/2 teaspoons dried oregano
1	teaspoon ground cinnamon
1/2	teaspoon ground allspice
1/2	teaspoon ground cardamom
1/2	cup toasted slivered almonds
	Salt and freshly ground black pepper
	Nonfat plain yogurt, for garnish
	Chopped fresh parsley, for garnish

Rinse the lentils in a strainer under cold running water. Combine the lentils, broth, and bay leaf in a small saucepan and bring to a boil over medium-high heat. Reduce the heat to medium-low and simmer uncovered until the lentils are tender but not mushy, 20 to 25 minutes. Drain and let cool to room temperature.

Heat 1 tablespoon of the olive oil in a large skillet over medium heat. Add the onion and sauté until tender and caramelized, 15 to 20 minutes. Add the sugar, if necessary, to facilitate the caramelization. The onions should be very soft, golden brown, aromatic, and sweet. Stir in the garlic, then add 2 tablespoons of the vinegar, scraping up any browned bits from the bottom of the skillet.

Bring a large saucepan of salted water to a boil over high heat. Add the orzo, reduce the heat to medium-high, and cook until the orzo is *al dente* (tender but still with a bite), about 10 minutes.

While the orzo cooks, cut the spinach leaves into thin ribbons and put them in a large bowl. When the orzo is cooked, drain well and pour the hot orzo over the spinach leaves. Let rest for 2 to 3 minutes, then toss gently so the spinach wilts. Add the lentils, caramelized onions, tomatoes, feta cheese, raisins, oregano, cinnamon, allspice, and cardamom and toss gently to thoroughly combine. Let cool to room temperature, about 20 minutes.

Just before serving, stir the remaining 3 or 4 tablespoons of olive oil, remaining 1/4 cup balsamic vinegar, and the almonds to the salad and toss to mix. Taste the salad for seasoning, adding more oil, vinegar, salt, or pepper if needed. Serve chilled or at room temperature, topped with a dollop of yogurt and a sprinkle of parsley.

Makes 6 servings

French green lentils have a uniquely nutty flavor that differs from the earthy flavor of more familiar brown lentils. They also hold their shape better than brown lentils, making them ideal for salads. You can use other types of lentils, but take care to not overcook them.

CURRIED COUSCOUS SALAD

This salad is fabulous the day you make it and saves well for leftovers. Add cubed, roasted chicken from the deli for a heartier entrée salad.

For the yogurt dressing, stir together the yogurt, olive oil, lemon juice, garlic, curry powder, and turmeric in a small bowl and season to taste with salt and pepper. Cover and refrigerate until ready to serve.

Place couscous in a large bowl suitable for serving. Bring the chicken broth to a boil in a small saucepan and pour over couscous, cover, and let stand until the liquid is fully absorbed and the couscous has expanded, about 10 to 15 minutes. Fluff the couscous with a fork to separate the grains, and set aside to cool.

Cut the green beans into 2-inch pieces on the diagonal. Put about 2 inches of water in a medium saucepan and add a collapsible steamer to the pan. Bring the water to a boil and steam the beans until crisp-tender, 2 to 3 minutes. Take the beans from the steamer and set aside to cool.

Combine the green beans, cucumber, onion, carrots, currants, almonds, parsley and dressing with the couscous and toss gently to mix. Season the salad to taste with salt and pepper and serve either slightly chilled or at room temperature.

MAKES 4 TO 6 SERVINGS

1 1/2	cups couscous
1	can (14 ounces) chicken broth
1/2	pound green beans, trimmed
1	cup chopped, seeded cucumber
1/2	cup diced red onion
1/2	cup shredded carrots
1/2	cup dried currants
1/4	cup sliced almonds, toasted
1/4	cup chopped fresh parsley
	Salt and freshly ground black pepper

YOGURT DRESSING

1/2	cup plain yogurt
1/4	cup olive oil
2	tablespoons freshly squeezed lemon juice
1	teaspoon minced garlic
1	teaspoon curry powder
1/2	teaspoon turmeric
	Salt and freshly ground pepper

COUSCOUS

Couscous is a staple in North African and Middle Eastern cuisines. Though commonly believed to be a grain, couscous is actually a pasta-like product made from semolina flour. The style common in North African and many other regions of the Mediterranean has a very fine texture that is traditionally made by pressing the semolina dough through a fine mesh, creating tiny little beads of dough. Israeli couscous, on the other hand, is a larger, pearl-like ball that is cooked in boiling water much like other pastas or pilaf-style as you would rice. Though the two types of couscous may show up in similar types of recipes, they cannot be used interchangeably without modifying the recipe. Look for Israeli couscous in ethnic markets or in the ethnic or bulk section of your supermarket. Orzo, cooked according to the package directions, would be an acceptable substitute.

LEMON GARLIC SHRIMP WITH GREENS

Serrano ham is a dry-cured ham from the Serrano Mountains in Spain, similar to Italian prosciutto. Manchego cheese is a hard Spanish cheese similar to Parmesan but with a nuttier flavor.

Cut the ham into ½-inch-thick strips, about 6 inches long. Wrap each strip snugly around the center of each shrimp.

Heat the olive oil in a large nonstick skillet over high heat until very hot. Add the shrimp and cook until pink and opaque on the outside, about 2 minutes. Turn the shrimp, stir in the garlic and red pepper flakes and cook for about 30 seconds, then stir in the wine and lemon juice. Cook until the liquid is nearly evaporated and the shrimp are opaque through, about 1 minute longer.

Take the pan from the heat and stir in the lemon zest, parsley, and paprika. Put the shrimp in a bowl and refrigerate, uncovered, until chilled, about 30 minutes. If storing for longer than 30 minutes, cover tightly once chilled.

For the salad dressing, stir together the shallot, lemon zest, and lemon juice. Slowly drizzle in the olive oil, whisking constantly, until emulsified (slightly thickened). Season to taste with salt and pepper. Put the lettuces in a large bowl, drizzle the dressing over, and toss. Arrange the salad on individual plates and top with the shrimp arranged in a circular fan. Make thin shavings of the manchego cheese using a vegetable peeler and sprinkle the cheese over the shrimp. Garnish with parsley sprigs and cracked pepper.

MAKES 4 TO 6 SERVINGS

The shrimp should not be too crowded in the skillet or they won't cook as quickly and evenly as they should. If your skillet's not big enough to hold them generously, it would be best to cook the shrimp in 2 batches, splitting the other ingredients between the batches as well.

◆ The refreshing melon flavors of semillon offer a nice contrast to the zest of lemon and paprika.

8	ounces Serrano ham (or prosciutto)
1	pound medium shrimp, peeled and deveined
3 – 4	tablespoons olive oil
2	tablespoons minced garlic
1/2	teaspoon dried red pepper flakes, or to taste
2	tablespoons dry white wine
2	tablespoons freshly squeezed lemon juice
1	tablespoon finely grated lemon zest
1	tablespoon minced fresh parsley
1	teaspoon paprika

SALAD

2	tablespoons minced shallot
1	teaspoon finely grated lemon zest
2	tablespoons freshly squeezed lemon juice
5	tablespoons extra virgin olive oil, or to taste
	Salt and freshly ground black pepper
1	head red or green leaf lettuce, rinsed, dried, and torn into pieces
1	head butter or bibb lettuce, rinsed, dried, and torn into pieces
4	ounces manchego cheese (can substitute with Parmesan or asiago)
	Chopped fresh parsley and cracked pepper, for garnish

ELLIOTT BAY CEVICHE

I	large red onion, quartered
8	ounces halibut fillet, skin and pin bones removed, cut into 1/2-inch pieces
8	ounces small raw shrimp, peeled, deveined, and cut into 1-inch pieces
8	ounces bay scallops, halved
1 1/2	cups freshly squeezed lime juice, more if needed
I	cup freshly squeezed orange juice, divided
1/4	cup extra virgin olive oil
1/2 – I	teaspoon mild Mexican chile paste (optional)
I	tablespoon minced jalapeño chile (optional)
2	teaspoons finely grated lime zest
2	teaspoons finely grated orange zest
8	ounces Dungeness crabmeat
1 1/2	cups seeded, diced tomato
1 1/2	cups diced avocado
1/3	cup chopped fresh cilantro, plus more for garnish
	Salt
	Lime wedges, for garnish
	Tortilla chips, for serving

Freshness is key with seafood that is served raw (this seafood is transformed by the lime juice so that it seems to be "cooked," though it's still raw). It's worth the effort to buy the freshest seafood that you can for this ultimate seafood-lover's treat.

Mince enough of the red onion to make 1/4 cup and set aside. Cut the rest of the quartered onion across into 2-inch pieces.

Combine the halibut, shrimp, scallops, and red onion pieces in a large bowl. Pour the lime juice and 1/2 cup of the orange juice over the seafood, stirring gently to make sure the juice is well incorporated. Add more lime juice if needed to cover the seafood completely. Cover tightly with plastic wrap and refrigerate until the halibut, scallops, and shrimp are opaque throughout, no longer translucent, at least 12 hours. Drain and remove the onion pieces, returning the seafood to the bowl. Cover and refrigerate while making the dressing.

For the dressing, whisk together the olive oil, remaining orange juice, and Mexican chile paste (if using). Stir in the minced red onion, jalapeño (if using), and lime and orange zests. Let rest for 30 minutes to allow the flavors to blend.

Add the crabmeat, tomato, avocado, and cilantro to the marinated seafood, drizzle the dressing over, and gently stir to mix. Season to taste with salt and served chilled, with lime wedges for garnish and tortilla chips alongside to use for scooping up the ceviche.

MAKES 6 TO 8 SERVINGS

If you prefer not to serve the seafood raw, you may lightly poach it. Cook each type of seafood separately in a large pan of boiling water just until barely cooked through, less than a minute. Drain the seafood well and marinate in the lime juice mixture for 6 to 8 hours before tossing with dressing to serve.

◆ Enjoy it with a light Mexican beer or crisp, white wine such as semillon.

MEDITERRANEAN POTATO SALAD

If you love the flavors of the sunny Mediterranean, you'll love this flavorful variation on the classic potato salad. It's an ideal complement to grilled chicken or even a great accompaniment to good old burgers. You can substitute sour cream or mayonnaise for the crème fraîche, though the flavor will be a bit different.

Put the potatoes in a large pot of salted water, bring to a boil, and boil until the potatoes are tender when pierced with the tip of a knife, 10 to 12 minutes. Drain and let rest in the colander for 5 minutes. Transfer the potatoes to a large bowl, drizzle the wine and lemon juice over, and gently toss. Set aside.

For the dressing, combine the vinegar, shallot, mustard, garlic, and a good pinch of salt in a small bowl. Let sit for 15 minutes to allow the shallot to "pickle" slightly. Slowly drizzle in the olive oil, whisking constantly, until emulsified (slightly thickened), then whisk in the crème fraîche.

Scatter the prosciutto, feta cheese, oregano, thyme, parsley, lemon zest, and a good pinch of pepper over the potatoes. Drizzle the vinaigrette over and toss gently to mix thoroughly. Taste for seasoning, adding more salt or pepper to taste.

MAKES 6 TO 8 SERVINGS

1	pound small white potatoes, scrubbed and cut into 1/2-inch dice
1	pound small red potatoes, scrubbed and cut into 1/2-inch dice
2	tablespoons dry white wine
2	tablespoons freshly squeezed lemon juice
6	ounces prosciutto, cut into 1/2-inch dice
3 – 4	ounces feta cheese, crumbled
2	tablespoons finely chopped fresh oregano
2	tablespoons finely chopped fresh thyme
2	tablespoons chopped fresh parsley, plus more for garnish
2	teaspoons finely grated lemon zest

CRÈME FRAÎCHE DRESSING

2	tablespoons Champagne vinegar or white wine vinegar
2	tablespoons minced shallot
1	tablespoon Dijon mustard
1	teaspoon minced garlic
	Salt and coarsely ground black pepper
1/4	cup extra virgin olive oil
2	tablespoons crème fraîche or sour cream

SPICY GREENS WITH MINIATURE WASABI CRAB CAKES

<table>
<tr><td>1/2</td><td>cup thinly sliced green onions, white and green parts</td></tr>
<tr><td>1/4</td><td>cup minced shallots</td></tr>
<tr><td>1/4</td><td>cup mayonnaise</td></tr>
<tr><td>2</td><td>teaspoons seasoned rice vinegar</td></tr>
<tr><td>2</td><td>teaspoons freshly squeezed lemon juice</td></tr>
<tr><td>1</td><td>teaspoon tamari or soy sauce</td></tr>
<tr><td>1/2</td><td>teaspoon finely grated lemon zest</td></tr>
<tr><td>1</td><td>pound Dungeness crabmeat</td></tr>
<tr><td>1</td><td>tablespoon wasabi paste, more to taste</td></tr>
<tr><td>1</td><td>egg, lightly beaten</td></tr>
<tr><td>1 1/2</td><td>cups panko (Japanese bread crumbs) or other dried bread crumbs, divided</td></tr>
<tr><td>1/4</td><td>cup peanut or vegetable oil, more as needed, for cooking</td></tr>
</table>

ingredient list continued on next page

This salad makes a stunning starter for your favorite seafood dinner, but it's also a great luncheon centerpiece or complement to a light Asian soup. Mizuna and tatsoi are Asian greens that make distinctive additions to this salad. If you are unable to find them, you can substitute additional watercress, arugula, or other assertive greens.

For the crab cakes, combine the green onions, shallots, mayonnaise, vinegar, lemon juice, tamari, and lemon zest. Pick over the crabmeat to remove any bits of shell or cartilage and add it to the bowl with the wasabi paste. Stir to mix well, then taste for seasoning, adding more wasabi paste in 1/2 teaspoons, mixing thoroughly between each addition. Cover the bowl and refrigerate for 30 to 60 minutes before cooking the crab cakes. When ready to cook, stir in the egg and 3 to 5 tablespoons of the bread crumbs, a little at a time, just so the mixture holds together. Form the crab mixture into 24 small patties, about 2 inches in diameter and about 1/2 inch thick. Refrigerate, covered, until ready to cook.

Combine the greens and sprouts in a large bowl and toss to mix. Whisk together the rice vinegar, shallot, garlic, ginger, tamari, brown sugar, and wasabi paste. Whisk in the sesame oil until slightly thickened. Stir the mushrooms into the vinaigrette and let sit while preparing the crab cakes.

recipe continued on next page

To cook the crab cakes, preheat the oven to 200°F. Spread the remaining bread crumbs in a shallow dish and coat the crab cakes in the crumbs, patting to remove excess. Heat 2 tablespoons of the peanut oil in a large nonstick skillet over medium heat. Sauté the crab cakes in batches until golden brown and warmed through, 2 to 3 minutes on each side, adding more oil to the skillet as needed. Keep them warm on a baking sheet in the oven while assembling the salad.

Remove the mushrooms from the dressing with a slotted spoon and add them to the salad greens. Reserve ¼ cup of the dressing and toss the remaining dressing with the greens.

Divide the salad among individual plates and sprinkle with sesame seeds. Arrange the crab cakes on top of each salad, drizzle them with the reserved dressing, and serve right away.

MAKES 8 SERVINGS

Panko is a type of Japanese bread crumb that has a coarser, flakier texture than regular, more granular bread crumbs. It is a staple in Japanese cuisine, providing an extra-crispy coating in a variety of different recipes. Look for panko bread crumbs in Asian markets or in the Asian section of well-stocked grocery stores.

◆ Aromatic gewürztraminer's low alcohol won't compete with the peppery flavors in the salad greens.

2	cups lightly packed baby spinach leaves, rinsed and dried
2	cups lightly packed watercress, stems trimmed to ¹/2 inch below leaves, rinsed and dried
1	cup lightly packed mizuna, rinsed and dried
1	cup lightly packed tatsoi lettuce, rinsed and dried
1	cup daikon radish sprouts or other sprouts
¹/4	cup seasoned rice vinegar
2	tablespoons minced shallot
1	tablespoon minced garlic
1	tablespoon minced or grated fresh ginger
2	teaspoons tamari or soy sauce
2	teaspoons packed light brown sugar
1	teaspoon wasabi paste, or to taste
6	tablespoons toasted sesame oil
8	shiitake mushrooms, brushed clean, stemmed, and very thinly sliced
4	teaspoons toasted sesame seeds

GINGERED CHICKEN SALAD WITH HOISIN VINAIGRETTE

This is a delicious update to the popular Asian chicken salad. The hoisin vinaigrette is a particularly refreshing change. It's great for lunch or a light dinner.

For the gingered chicken marinade, whisk together all ingredients, except chicken, in a small bowl. Put the chicken in a resealable plastic bag and add the marinade. Squeeze all the air from the bag and seal tightly. Marinate, refrigerated, for at least 6 hours or overnight.

Preheat an outdoor grill (to high, if using a gas grill) and oil the grill grate. Take the chicken from the marinade, allowing excess to drip off, and grill the chicken breasts until firm to the touch and cooked through, 4 to 6 minutes on each side. Let cool completely, then dice into bite-sized pieces. Refrigerate until ready to serve.

Heat the peanut or canola oil to 400°F in a wok or large sauté pan. Drop 1 rice stick into the oil; if it puffs up immediately, add a small handful of rice sticks to the oil (otherwise, wait for the oil to heat a bit more). The noodles will crackle and puff quickly, just a matter of seconds; turn the rice sticks over to allow the other side to puff up for a few seconds longer. Remove from the wok with tongs or a slotted spoon and drain on paper towels, seasoning lightly with salt. Continue with the remaining rice sticks, in batches, allowing the oil to reheat as needed. Season to taste with salt as each batch is removed from the pan.

recipe continued on next page

2	cups peanut or canola oil
3	to 4 ounces maifun rice stick noodles
	Salt
6	cups shredded Napa cabbage
2	cups shredded red cabbage
1	cup snow peas, sliced on the diagonal and blanched
1	cup thinly sliced green onions, divided
3	tablespoons toasted sesame seeds

GINGERED CHICKEN

1/4	cup minced or grated fresh ginger
3	tablespoons soy sauce
3	tablespoons dry sherry
3	tablespoons hoisin sauce
1	tablespoon toasted sesame oil
1	teaspoon minced garlic
1	teaspoon hot Chinese mustard
1/4	teaspoon five-spice powder
1	pound boneless, skinless chicken breasts

ingredient list continued on next page

HOISIN VINAIGRETTE

1/4   cup seasoned rice vinegar

2   tablespoons hoisin sauce

2   teaspoons soy sauce

2   teaspoons minced or grated fresh ginger

1   teaspoon minced garlic

1/2   teaspoon hot Chinese mustard

1/4   cup toasted sesame oil

For the hoisin vinaigrette, whisk together all ingredients, except the sesame oil. Let rest for about 15 minutes. Slowly drizzle in the sesame oil, whisking constantly, until emulsified.

Combine the cabbages, snow peas, ½ cup of the green onions, chicken, and sesame seeds in a large bowl and toss to mix. Add the dressing, toss well, and mound the salad in a large serving dish. Crumble the maifun noodles over the top and sprinkle with the remaining green onion. Serve right away.

MAKES 4 TO 6 SERVINGS

◆ The Iced Lemon Ginger Cooler expands on the Asian theme of this salad.

ICED LEMON GINGER COOLER

6   cups water

1/2   cup honey

1/2   cup sugar

1   piece (4 inches) ginger, peeled and cut into 1/2-inch slices

     Grated zest of 2 lemons

1   cup freshly squeezed lemon juice

8   lemon slices, for garnish

Combine all ingredients, except the lemon juice, in a medium saucepan over medium heat. Cook, stirring occasionally, just until the sugar is dissolved, about 5 minutes. Take from the heat, cover, and steep for 45 minutes. Uncover and let cool. Strain through a fine sieve and transfer to a pitcher, then stir in the lemon juice. Refrigerate until fully chilled. Serve over ice in tall glasses, with lemon slices for garnish.

MAKES 8 SERVINGS

TRI-COLOR COLESLAW WITH MISO DRESSING

Serve this ultra-simple salad to complement Asian-style barbecue or with Five-Star Asian Ribs (page 183).

Combine the green and red cabbages, carrots, and green onions in a large bowl and toss to mix.

For the dressing, combine the vinegar, miso, ginger, garlic, and cayenne pepper in a blender or food processor and purée until smooth. Add the lemon juice through the chute and then add the peanut and sesame oils slowly, with the motor running, until the dressing is emulsified (slightly thickened).

Pour the dressing over the cabbage mixture and sprinkle with the sesame seeds. Toss to coat thoroughly and let rest about 5 minutes before serving. (Do not dress the coleslaw too far in advance or the cabbage will wilt.)

MAKES 8 SERVINGS

2	cups finely shredded green cabbage
2	cups finely shredded red cabbage
2	cups grated carrots
2/3	cup sliced green onions, white and green parts
2	tablespoons toasted sesame seeds

MISO DRESSING

1/3	cup seasoned rice vinegar
1	tablespoon white miso
1	tablespoon minced or grated ginger
1	tablespoon minced garlic
1/8	teaspoon cayenne pepper
2	tablespoons freshly squeezed lemon juice
1/4	cup peanut oil
1/4	cup toasted sesame oil

MISO PASTE

Miso is a staple ingredient in Japanese cuisine made from dried soybeans that are soaked and crushed, then blended with water and salt. It is then fermented, and a particular type of mold interacts deliciously with the soybean paste. There are many different styles of miso not to mention different colors, and some are aged for years. White miso is a common type and is mild, mellow, and slightly sweet. Look for it in the refrigerated section of Asian markets or in well-stocked grocery stores.

Overlooking the Roses
XIAOGANG ZHU

Roche Harbor in the San Juan Islands is what many people in the Puget Sound envision as the perfect place for a short vacation, just a one or two hour boat ride from home. The local cuisine is a blend of European and Asian influences, from the standard steak to stir-fry, and fresh produce such as local strawberries add a touch of color to everything.

Pasta & Seafood

Wild Mushroom Linguine 114

Noodles with Mushrooms and
Sesame Ginger Broth 115

Citrus Saffron Pasta 117

Confetti Pesto Pasta 118

Nutty Chard with Buttered Noodles 119

Squash, Goat Cheese, and Sage Ravioli
with Hazelnut Butter 120

Gourmet Mac 'n' Cheese 122

Grilled Vegetable and Herb Pasta 123

Sautéed Tortellini
with Prosciutto and Greens 125

Antipasto Pasta 126

Caramelized Onion Lasagna with Pancetta 128

Lasagna Cacciatore 131

Smoked Salmon Shells 132

Pasta alla Vodka 133

Linguine with Mussels in
Chipotle Coconut Milk 134

Jalapeño Capellini with Crab 137

Pacific Rim Pad Thai 138

Champagne Shrimp
with Ginger Butter Sauce 139

Spicy Indian Shrimp with Greens 140

Northwest Microbrew Steamers 141

Halibut with Sake Clam Broth 142

Pecan Crusted Halibut
with Sautéed Apples 145

Halibut with Raspberries 146

Snapper with Papaya and Fresh Herbs 147

Cajun Pacific Snapper Tacos 149

Miso Glazed Salmon 150

Honey Glazed Salmon
with Figs and Cranberry Vinaigrette 151

Grilled Salmon with Red Currant Glaze 153

Northwest Cedar Planked Salmon 154

Martini Trout 155

WILD MUSHROOM LINGUINE

1	ounce dried wild mushrooms (such as porcini, morel, or chanterelle)
2	cups boiling water
4	tablespoons unsalted butter, divided
3	tablespoons all-purpose flour
3/4	cup whipping cream
1	tablespoon finely chopped fresh thyme
1	tablespoon finely chopped fresh rosemary
1	cup chopped onion
8	ounces button mushrooms, brushed clean, stemmed, and sliced
8	ounces shiitake mushrooms, stemmed and sliced
	Salt and freshly ground black pepper
8	ounces dry linguine
1/2	cup freshly grated Romano cheese

A traditional plate of linguine gets dressed up with some delicious wild mushrooms and fresh herbs. Romano cheese gives this dish a slightly nutty flavor.

Put the dried mushrooms in a bowl, pour the boiling water over, and set aside to soften for about 30 minutes. Lift the mushrooms out with your hands and squeeze excess water back into the bowl; coarsely chop the mushrooms (if they aren't already) and set them aside. Strain the mushroom liquid through a fine-mesh sieve lined with cheesecloth or a dampened paper towel. Add water to the liquid as needed so that it measures 2 cups; set aside.

Melt 3 tablespoons of the butter in a large saucepan over medium heat. When bubbling, add the flour and cook, stirring, until the mixture begins to just lightly brown, about 3 minutes. Slowly whisk in the mushroom liquid and continue to cook, whisking constantly, until the mixture bubbles and thickens, 3 to 5 minutes. Stir in the cream, thyme, and rosemary. Reduce the heat to medium-low and simmer gently to allow the flavors to infuse, 25 to 30 minutes, stirring occasionally.

Meanwhile, heat the remaining tablespoon of butter in a large skillet over medium heat. Add the onion and cook until beginning to soften, about 3 minutes. Add the button mushrooms and cook until they release their liquid. Add the shiitakes and reconstituted dried mushrooms, and cook until tender, about 5 minutes. Add the mushroom sauce to the skillet and stir to combine. Season to taste with salt and pepper; keep the sauce warm over low heat.

Bring a large pot of salted water to a rolling boil. Add the pasta and cook until *al dente*, about 8 to 10 minutes. Drain the pasta well and stir the linguine into the mushroom sauce. Serve the pasta in individual shallow bowls and sprinkle with some of the cheese, passing remaining cheese separately.

MAKES 4 TO 6 SERVINGS

◆ Choose a chardonnay with just a kiss of oak to balance the intense flavors of dried mushrooms and the rich cream.

Noodles with Mushrooms in Sesame Ginger Broth

If using soba noodles for this dish, look for noodles that are made with some wheat flour, as 100% buckwheat flour pasta breaks and overcooks easily.

Bring a large pot of salted water to a boil. When the water comes to a rolling boil, add the noodles and cook until *al dente*, about 5 to 7 minutes. Drain well, return the noodles to the pot, and toss with the sesame oil. Cover to keep warm.

In a medium skillet, heat the vegetable oil over medium heat. Add the mushrooms, shallots, and ginger and cook, stirring constantly, until the vegetables begin to soften and turn golden brown, about 2 minutes. Add the broth, soy sauce, and vinegar, and bring to a simmer. Cook until the mushrooms are very tender, about 5 minutes. Add the spinach, chicken or tofu, and green onions, with salt and pepper to taste, and stir to mix.

To serve, divide the noodles among individual shallow soup bowls. Ladle the broth mixture over the noodles and garnish with sesame seeds.

MAKES 4 SERVINGS

8	ounces dry Japanese udon or soba noodles
1	tablespoon toasted sesame oil
1	tablespoon vegetable oil
4	ounces shiitake mushrooms, stemmed and sliced
2	ounces oyster mushrooms
2	shallots, very thinly sliced
1 1/2	tablespoons minced or grated ginger
2	cups chicken broth
1 1/2	tablespoons soy sauce
1	tablespoon rice vinegar
1/2	bunch spinach, rinsed, drained, and tough stems discarded, leaves cut into 2-inch strips (about 3 cups)
1	cup diced cooked chicken or diced firm tofu (or a combination of both)
4	green onions, sliced diagonally into 2-inch pieces
	Salt and freshly ground black pepper
1	teaspoon black sesame seeds or toasted white sesame seeds, for garnish (optional)

GINGER

Fresh ginger packs a distinct, peppery flavor that adds character to a wide range of recipes from sweet muffins to savory stir-fries. Often called a "root," ginger is actually a rhizome, though the common name "ginger root" still remains. Look for ginger that is plump and firm; it should have no soft or dried-out spots. To peel away the thin papery skin, simply scrape it off with the back of a small knife or a small spoon. There are tough fibers that run through ginger, more pronounced in older roots. Special ginger graters—often porcelain—have tiny raised teeth against which you rub the ginger to draw away tender flesh and juice while leaving the fibers intact. You can also grate ginger on the smaller holes of a traditional box grater, but you may pick up more of the tough fiber as well.

CITRUS SAFFRON PASTA

Combine this light, summery dish with a salad and freshly baked bread for a quick weeknight meal that has a distinct touch of elegance.

Combine the butter, drained saffron, ¼ teaspoon salt, and a few pinches pepper in a small bowl and stir well until smooth. Set aside.

Bring a large pot of salted water to a boil for the pasta. While the water is heating, heat the olive oil in a large skillet, and add the shallots, bell pepper, and a good pinch each of salt and pepper. Sauté over medium heat until the peppers are tender, about 5 minutes, stirring occasionally. Add the orange juice and wine and continue to cook over medium heat until the liquid is reduced by half, about 3 minutes.

When the water comes to a rolling boil, add the penne and cook until *al dente*, 8 to 10 minutes. When the pasta is nearly done, add the asparagus to the cooking water for 2 minutes. Add the peas and cook for 1 minute longer. Drain the pasta, asparagus, and peas well in a colander. Add the pasta mixture, orange zest, and ¼ teaspoon salt to the sauce in the skillet. Quickly toss the mixture together, then add the saffron butter. Toss to evenly mix. Transfer the pasta to a serving bowl or individual plates and garnish with chives and Parmesan cheese. Serve right away.

MAKES 4 SERVINGS

◆ Sip a crisp, citrus-accented sauvignon blend to complement the saffron and asparagus.

1/4	cup unsalted butter, at room temperature
1	generous pinch saffron threads, steeped in 1 tablespoon hot water
	Salt and freshly ground black pepper
1	tablespoon olive oil
2	shallots, thinly sliced
1/2	red or yellow bell pepper, cored, seeded, and thinly sliced
	Freshly squeezed juice of 1 orange
1/4	cup dry white wine
8	ounces dry penne
8	ounces asparagus, or green beans, trimmed and cut into 2-inch lengths
3/4	cup fresh shelled or frozen peas
	Grated zest of 1 orange
	Coarsely chopped chives, for garnish
	Freshly grated Parmesan cheese, for serving

Confetti Pesto Pasta

1 tablespoon olive oil

2 boneless, skinless chicken breasts

1 tablespoon unsalted butter

1/4 cup diced red onion

2 cups diced red, orange, yellow,
    and/or green bell pepper

1 cup diced zucchini

1/4 cup finely chopped green onion

1 jalapeño chile, cored, seeded, and
    finely chopped

12 ounces dry gemelli or other
    spiral pasta

   Freshly grated Parmesan cheese

RED PEPPER PESTO

1 cup lightly packed fresh basil leaves

4 cloves garlic

1/2 cup mayonnaise (regular or low-fat)

3 tablespoons extra virgin olive oil

1 cup freshly grated Parmesan cheese

2 red bell peppers, roasted (see
    page 39) and chopped

1/4 – 1/2 teaspoon dried red pepper flakes
    (optional)

   Salt and freshly ground
   black pepper

This versatile, fresh, colorful pasta dish can be served warm or at room temperature as a summer salad. Omit the chicken for a vegetarian entrée or spice it up with additional crushed red pepper and a diced serrano chile.

For the red pepper pesto, combine the basil and garlic in a food processor and pulse to finely chop, scraping down the side as needed. Combine the mayonnaise and olive oil in a medium bowl and stir to blend. Fold in the basil-garlic mixture and Parmesan. Purée the roasted peppers in the food processor until smooth. Add to the bowl and stir to combine. For a spicier pesto, add dried red pepper flakes. Season to taste with salt and pepper. Cover and refrigerate until ready to use (the pesto can be made a day ahead).

Heat the olive oil in a large nonstick skillet over medium heat. Season the chicken breasts with salt and pepper and sauté until cooked through (juices run clear when pierced in the thickest part with the tip of a knife), 4 to 5 minutes per side. Transfer the chicken to a plate and let cool; do not clean the skillet. Dice the chicken into 1/4-inch pieces.

Melt the butter in the skillet over medium heat. Add the onion and sauté until beginning to soften, about 3 minutes. Add the bell pepper, zucchini, green onion, and jalapeño, and cook until beginning to soften, 4 to 5 minutes. Take skillet from the heat.

Bring a large pot of salted water to a boil, add the pasta and cook until *al dente*, about 10 minutes or according to the instructions on the package. Drain the pasta and return it to the pot. Add 1/2 to 3/4 cup of the red pepper pesto depending on how "saucy" you want the dish to be. Add the chicken and vegetables and toss gently to evenly mix. Arrange on individual plates and top each serving with Parmesan.

MAKES 6 SERVINGS

You can substitute orzo for the gemelli pasta and use it to stuff halved bell peppers. Bake and serve as a do-ahead side dish.

Nutty Chard with Buttered Noodles

Whole-wheat pasta is combined with sweet onions and currants, hearty chard, and nutty brown butter to create a tasty and colorful dish to serve as a light entrée or alongside roasted meat. Look for whole-wheat pasta in well-stocked grocery stores, or regular pasta may be substituted, if you prefer.

Melt the butter in a small saucepan over low heat. Simmer until small bubbles appear on the surface. When it begins to smell slightly nutty and turns a rich amber color, in 10 to 12 minutes, take the pan from the heat. Keep the brown butter warm enough to remain liquid.

Put the currants in a small bowl, cover with the hot water, and set aside to plump for about 30 minutes. Cut the chard leaves and stalks into 2-inch wide strips. Bring a large pot of salted water to a boil.

While the water is heating, heat the olive oil in a large skillet over medium heat. Add the onion with salt and pepper to taste and sauté until the onion is tender and aromatic, about 5 minutes. Stir in the garlic, then add the chard and a good pinch of salt. Sauté until the chard is just barely tender, 4 to 5 minutes, then reduce the heat to low to keep warm until ready to serve.

When the water comes to a rolling boil, add the pasta and cook until *al dente*, about 10 minutes. Drain the pasta well and put it in a large bowl. Drain the currants and add them to the pasta with the onion-chard mixture, walnuts, and brown butter. Toss well to evenly mix and season the pasta to taste with salt and pepper. Serve with Parmesan cheese alongside for sprinkling.

MAKES 6 SERVINGS

You can substitute spinach, kale, or other winter greens for the chard. Dried cranberries can be used in place of the currants, as well, for a tasty flavor variation.

2/3	cup unsalted butter
1/3	cup dried currants
1 1/2	cups hot water
2	bunches red or green Swiss chard, rinsed, dried, and ends trimmed
2	tablespoons olive oil
1	medium red onion, thinly sliced
	Salt and freshly ground black pepper
4	cloves garlic, minced
1	pound dry whole-wheat ziti or fettuccine
2/3	cup toasted walnut pieces
	Freshly grated Parmesan cheese, for serving

SQUASH, GOAT CHEESE, AND SAGE RAVIOLI WITH HAZELNUT BUTTER

About 60 wonton wrappers
(one 12-ounce package)

1/2 cup unsalted butter

1/2 cup hazelnuts, toasted, skinned, and
coarsely chopped

Freshly grated Parmesan cheese,
for serving (optional)

SQUASH, GOAT CHEESE, AND
SAGE FILLING

2 pounds acorn or butternut squash,
halved lengthwise and seeded

1 tablespoon unsalted butter

1 medium onion, finely chopped

1 tablespoon finely chopped fresh
sage or 1 1/2 teaspoons ground sage

1 clove garlic, minced

3 ounces fresh goat cheese (such as
Montrachet), crumbled

Salt and freshly ground
black pepper

These elegant ravioli—which use wonton wrappers as a shortcut rather than making fresh pasta—combine fresh Northwest ingredients to create a dish that can be served as a vegetarian main course or an impressive first course. When shopping for fresh wonton wrappers be sure to get the thickest wrappers available. Thin wrappers tend to fall apart when simmering the ravioli.

Preheat the oven to 425°F. Lightly oil a baking sheet.

Put the squash halves, flesh-sides down, on the baking sheet and roast until the flesh is tender, about 30 minutes. When the squash is cool enough to handle, scoop out the flesh into a large bowl and discard the skin. Mash the squash with a fork until smooth.

Melt the 1 tablespoon butter in a medium skillet over medium heat. Add the onion and sage and cook, stirring often, until the onion is tender and aromatic, about 5 minutes. Add the garlic and cook, stirring, for 1 minute. Let the onion mixture cool slightly and add it to the squash. Add the goat cheese and stir to evenly mix. Season to taste with salt and pepper.

Set 1 wonton wrapper on a lightly floured work surface, keeping the remaining wrappers in plastic wrap, and mound ½ tablespoon filling in the center. Lightly brush the edges of the wrapper with water and fold the wrapper in half over the filling, making a triangle, pressing down around the filling to force out any air and seal the edges well. Continue making ravioli with the remaining wrappers and filling, transferring each onto a towel and covering with another towel to keep from drying out. Make sure that the ravioli don't overlap or they will stick together.

Melt the butter with the hazelnuts in a large sauté pan or skillet over medium heat until the butter begins to brown slightly, about 3 minutes. Immediately remove the skillet from the heat (the nuts will continue to cook) and season the hazelnut butter to taste with salt and pepper.

Fill a large pot with salted water and bring to a boil. Reduce the heat to medium and cook the ravioli in batches of about 8 to 12 in gently simmering water, 30 to 45 seconds.

recipe continued on next page

As each batch is cooked, drain them well, then gently add to the hazelnut butter, tossing a bit to coat in butter; keep warm over low heat while cooking the remaining ravioli.

Transfer the ravioli and hazelnut butter to plates and serve, passing the Parmesan cheese separately, if using.

MAKES 6 TO 8 SERVINGS

Fresh goat cheese—often sold in logs—with its soft texture and bright tangy flavor is a better choice for this ravioli filling than drier, aged goat cheese.

◆ Rich in flavor and high in acid, sangiovese marries nicely with the autumnal flavors of these ravioli.

GOURMET MAC 'N' CHEESE

One of those tastes of childhood we never outgrow, macaroni and cheese only gets better when you use a delicious variety of cheeses as with this recipe.

3	tablespoons unsalted butter, plus more for dish
2	shallots, diced
1/4	cup all-purpose flour
2 3/4	cups milk (use whole milk for best results)
1	cup grated Parmesan cheese, divided
3/4	cup grated Gruyère cheese
3/4	cup grated fontina cheese
3/4	cup crumbled Gorgonzola or other blue cheese
3	ounces thinly sliced prosciutto, cut into 1/2-inch pieces
	Pinch cayenne pepper, more to taste
	Salt and freshly ground black pepper
12	ounces dry gemelli or other spiral pasta
1/2	cup fresh or dried bread crumbs
3	tablespoons finely chopped fresh parsley

Preheat the oven to 375°F. Butter an 8-inch square baking dish.

Melt the butter in a large saucepan over medium heat. Add the shallots and sauté until tender and aromatic, about 5 minutes. While the butter is still bubbling, add the flour and cook, whisking constantly, for 1 minute. Slowly whisk in the milk and continue cooking, whisking constantly, until the mixture bubbles and becomes thick, 3 to 5 minutes. Take the pan from the heat and add ¾ cup of the Parmesan with the Gruyère, fontina, and Gorgonzola, whisking to help the cheese melt gently into the sauce. Stir in the prosciutto and cayenne with salt and pepper to taste; set aside.

Bring a large pot of salted water to a boil. Add the pasta, and cook until the pasta is tender outside but still uncooked in the center, about 5 to 7 minutes. Drain the pasta in a colander, rinse under cold running water to stop the cooking, and drain well. Stir the pasta into the cheese sauce and pour into the prepared dish.

Stir together the bread crumbs, parsley, and remaining ¼ cup of the Parmesan cheese and sprinkle the mixture over the pasta. Bake until the pasta is heated through and browned on top, about 30 minutes. If the top is not turning golden brown, put it under the broiler for a few minutes, watching carefully. Transfer the dish to a wire cooling rack and let cool 5 minutes before serving.

MAKES 4 TO 6 SERVINGS

◆ The well rounded finish of a Northwest amber ale with its robust flavor and good balance would be an ideal beverage companion.

GRILLED VEGETABLE AND HERB PASTA

Grilled eggplant, onion, and bell pepper take on flavor from a delicious herb-enhanced marinade before being tossed with pasta, a terrific side dish to serve with roasted or grilled meat or chicken. The vegetables can be marinated up to a day in advance of assembling the pasta dish.

Lay the eggplant slices on a baking sheet and liberally sprinkle both sides with salt; let sit for 15 to 20 minutes (this draws out excess moisture along with any bitterness the eggplant may have). Wipe off the salt and pat dry.

Preheat an outdoor grill (to high if using a gas grill) and oil the grill grate, or preheat the broiler. Grill or broil the eggplant and onion slices until just tender, 6 to 8 minutes, turning occasionally. Let cool slightly, then coarsely chop them. Grill or broil the bell pepper quarters, skin side towards the heat, until the skin becomes charred. Put the peppers in a plastic bag for 10 minutes. Take them from the bag and peel off and discard the skin. Coarsely chop the peppers.

Combine the eggplant, onion, bell pepper, basil, mint, garlic, and red pepper flakes in a large bowl and toss to mix. In a small bowl, whisk together the olive oil and balsamic vinegar and pour over the vegetables. Toss to coat them well and season to taste with salt and pepper. Let stand at least 1 hour.

Just before serving, bring a large pot of salted water to a boil, add the pasta, and cook until *al dente*, 10 to 12 minutes. Drain well and toss the pasta with the grilled vegetable and herb mixture. Spoon onto individual plates and garnish each serving with a small herb sprig.

MAKES 6 SERVINGS

You can add grilled portobello mushrooms to the vegetable mixture for a heartier version of the recipe, which would also make a great vegetarian main course.

2	eggplants (about 2 pounds total), stemmed and cut into 1/2-inch slices
	Salt and freshly ground black pepper
3	red onions or Walla Walla sweet onions, cut into 1/2-inch slices
2	red bell peppers, cored, seeded, and quartered
1/2	cup chopped fresh basil
1/2	cup chopped fresh mint
4	cloves garlic, minced
1/2	teaspoon dried red pepper flakes
1/2	cup extra virgin olive oil
1/4	cup balsamic vinegar
1	pound dry farfalle or rotini pasta
	Fresh sprigs of basil, mint, and/or parsley, for garnish

Sautéed Tortellini with Prosciutto and Greens

From gourmet pasta shops to grocery aisles, there is a growing range of high-quality pastas available now. Tortellini is among the tastiest options, small pillows of pasta that can be stuffed with a variety of fillings, the classic cheese variation used here is particularly versatile.

Bring a large pot of salted water to a boil. When the water is at a rolling boil, add the tortellini and cook 5 minutes (or according to the package instructions). Drain well and set aside.

Heat 2 tablespoons of the olive oil in large skillet over high heat. Add the onion and sauté until tender and aromatic, 2 to 3 minutes. Add the prosciutto and cook 1 minute, stirring to evenly incorporate the prosciutto with the onions. Stir in the tomatoes, basil, and oregano with salt and pepper to taste and cook 1 minute longer, stirring constantly to evenly blend the ingredients. Add the vinegar and taste for seasoning, adding more salt and pepper if needed. Take the skillet from the heat and transfer the onion-prosciutto mixture to a large serving bowl. Lightly wipe out the skillet.

Heat the remaining 3 tablespoons olive oil in the same skillet over medium-high heat. Add the tortellini with a pinch of salt and pepper and sauté until golden brown, about 4 minutes. Add the sautéed tortellini to the bowl and toss with the other ingredients. Add the greens and cheese and toss well, then spoon onto individual plates and pass more cheese alongside.

Makes 6 servings

◆ A spicy-earthy sangiovese would suit this rustic pasta.

18	ounces fresh cheese tortellini
5	tablespoons olive oil, divided
1	medium red onion, halved and sliced
5	ounces prosciutto, thinly sliced
1 1/4	cups seeded, chopped plum tomatoes
1/2	cup chopped fresh basil
1	tablespoon chopped fresh oregano or 1 teaspoon dried oregano
	Salt and freshly ground black pepper
3	tablespoons balsamic vinegar
3 – 4	cups lightly packed mixed salad greens or baby spinach
1/4	cup freshly grated Parmesan cheese, plus more for serving

ANTIPASTO PASTA

1/2 cup coarsely chopped sun-dried tomatoes packed in oil

2 small shallots, quartered

2 cloves garlic, halved

3 tablespoons balsamic vinegar

1 tablespoon fresh thyme or 1 teaspoon dried thyme

1 tablespoon chopped fresh basil or 1 teaspoon dried basil

1/2 cup extra virgin olive oil

Salt and freshly ground black pepper

1 cup chopped cremini or button mushrooms

1/2 cup coarsely chopped, pitted, brine-cured black olives

1/2 cup chopped artichoke hearts

12 ounces dry penne

1 1/2 cups diced cooked chicken breast

1 1/2 cups seeded, chopped tomatoes

1 cup diced fresh mozzarella (optional)

This hearty pasta salad can be served as a vegetarian entrée or as a side salad simply by omitting the chicken. The colorful presentation makes this a great buffet item, too!

Purée the sun-dried tomatoes, shallots, garlic, vinegar, thyme, and basil in a food processor. With the blades running, slowly add the oil through the chute and process until smooth. Add salt and pepper to taste and pulse to blend. Pour the dressing into a medium bowl, add the mushrooms, olives, and artichoke hearts, and stir to coat. Set aside to marinate for at least 30 minutes.

Bring a large pot of salted water to a boil and cook the penne to *al dente*, about 10 to 12 minutes. Drain the pasta in a colander set in the sink and run cold water over to cool the pasta, then drain well and transfer the pasta to a large bowl. Pour the dressing and vegetables over, add the chicken, tomatoes, and mozzarella and toss to evenly mix. Serve right away.

MAKES 6 TO 8 SERVINGS

The pasta salad can be made up to 2 days in advance and refrigerated, though the cheese and tomatoes should be added just before serving. The salad will be more flavorful, too, if allowed to come to room temperature.

Meydenbauer Bay
HEIDI-MARIE BLACKWELL

Living at the edge of the water is a dream for some, but a happy reality for many people in the Puget Sound area. Lake Washington and Lake Sammamish have entire cities perched upon their shores in western Washington, while Lake Chelan in the sunny eastern part of the state is a popular place to own a vacation home.

CARAMELIZED ONION LASAGNA WITH PANCETTA

8   ounces pancetta, or quality regular bacon, minced

15   dry lasagna noodles

1   tablespoon olive oil

12   ounces fresh mozzarella cheese, thinly sliced

     Fresh thyme or parsley sprigs, for garnish

CARAMELIZED ONIONS

1/4   cup unsalted butter

1/4   cup olive oil

5   pounds Walla Walla sweet onions or other sweet onions, halved, and thinly sliced

1   tablespoon sugar

2   teaspoons chopped fresh thyme

BÉCHAMEL SAUCE

1/4   cup unsalted butter

2   shallots, minced

1/4   cup all-purpose flour

2   cups whole milk

1   cup whipping cream

     Salt and freshly ground white pepper

This elegant lasagna is a unique twist on the traditional meat lasagna. The caramelized onions take a bit of time, but the results are well worth it. Caramelizing the onions a day or two before serving this dish cuts down on the preparation time.

For the caramelized onions, heat the butter and olive oil in a large Dutch oven or heavy-bottomed skillet over medium-high heat. Add the onions (the pan will be quite full at first), cover the pan with its lid (or with foil as the pan is too crowded), and cook, stirring occasionally, until the onions are completely limp, 10 to 15 minutes. Reduce the heat to medium, remove the lid, add the sugar, and cook uncovered, stirring often, until the onions are golden brown and sweet, 45 to 55 minutes. Do not let them burn; reduce the heat to medium-low if the onions are browning too fast. About 2 minutes before removing the onions from the heat, stir the thyme into the onions. Transfer the onions to a bowl, let cool, and use immediately, or cover and refrigerate for up to 10 days or freeze for up to 2 months.

For the béchamel, melt the butter in a medium saucepan over medium-low heat. Add the shallots and sauté until soft, about 5 minutes. Add the flour and cook, stirring frequently, for 3 minutes (do not let it brown). Increase the heat to medium and slowly whisk in the milk and cream. Reduce the heat to medium-low and simmer, whisking frequently, until the sauce thickens, 8 to 10 minutes. Remove from the heat and season to taste with salt and white pepper. Use immediately or let cool, cover, and refrigerate for up to 1 day. If using the next day, warm the sauce over low heat before continuing.

Sauté the pancetta in a medium skillet over medium heat until just cooked, 3 to 5 minutes, stirring often. Scoop out onto paper towels to drain; set aside.

Bring a large pot of salted water to a boil. Add the lasagna noodles and olive oil and cook until *al dente* (tender but still with a bite), about 12 minutes, or according to the package instructions. Drain well, rinse under cool water, and drain again.

recipe continued on next page

Preheat the oven to 350°F. Brush a 9- by 13-inch baking dish with olive oil.

Spread ½ cup of the béchamel sauce in the bottom of the baking dish. Cover with 3 lasagna noodles, touching but not overlapping. Spread the noodles with another ½ cup of the béchamel then top with ¼ each of the caramelized onions, pancetta, mozzarella cheese (the cheese won't be a solid layer, just sprinkled over the pancetta), and top with another layer of noodles. Repeat this layering 3 more times. Top with the remaining béchamel sauce. Cover the baking dish tightly with foil and bake for 30 minutes. Remove the foil and bake until the top is just beginning to brown, about 10 minutes more. If the top is not browning, turn on the broiler and cook the lasagna under the broiler until the top begins to brown, about 5 minutes.

To serve, let lasagna sit in the pan for 10 to 15 minutes, then cut into servings and arrange the lasagna on individual plates. Garnish each serving with a thyme or parsley sprig.

MAKES 8 TO 10 SERVINGS

MAKE-AHEAD CARAMELIZED ONIONS

Here's a great technique for caramelizing sweet or regular onions which you could also use for the Walla Walla Onion Soup (page 71).

5	pounds onions, cut into ¼- to ½-inch slices
½	cup unsalted butter
2	teaspoons salt

Put the butter in a 4-quart or larger slow cooker insert. Separate the onion slices into rings and add them to the slow cooker, lightly packing them down. Sprinkle the salt over and cover with the lid (the cooker will be quite full). Cook on high until the onions are very soft and a deep caramel color, about 10 to 12 hours, stirring once or twice. Can be made a day in advance and freezes well.

LASAGNA CACCIATORE

This interesting, make-ahead dish is sure to become a family favorite, combining the aromatic elements of chicken cacciatore with much-loved lasagna.

Heat 2 tablespoons of the olive oil in a large saucepan over medium-high heat. Season the chicken breasts with salt and pepper, add them to the pan, and cook until browned, about 6 minutes. Turn the chicken and cook until tender and cooked through, about 5 minutes longer. Transfer the chicken to a plate and let cool; reserve the saucepan. When the chicken is cool, shred it and set aside.

Heat the remaining 2 tablespoons olive oil in the saucepan over medium heat. Add the onion and sauté until tender and lightly browned, about 15 minutes, stirring occasionally. Stir in the mushrooms and garlic and cook until the mushrooms are tender, about 5 minutes longer. Add the bell pepper and sauté until nearly tender, about 2 minutes. Stir in the tomatoes, parsley, oregano, basil, salt, black pepper, and dried red pepper flakes. Add the chicken, reduce the heat to low and simmer for 10 minutes.

Preheat the oven to 350°F. Oil a 9- by 13-inch baking dish.

Spread ½ cup of the tomato sauce (avoiding large chunks of chicken or vegetables) on the bottom of the dish. Line the dish with 4 cooked lasagna noodles or 3 no-boil lasagna noodles. Spread 1½ cups of the tomato sauce over the pasta and sprinkle with ⅓ of the mozzarella and ⅓ of the Parmesan. Repeat the layering of noodles, sauce, and cheese two more times. (The lasagna can be prepared a few days ahead, covered with plastic, and refrigerated, or covered securely with plastic and foil and frozen for a few weeks.)

Bake the lasagna until the cheese turns golden brown in spots and the sauce is bubbling, about 30 minutes. Transfer the dish to a wire rack and let the lasagna sit for 5 to 10 minutes before serving.

MAKES 8 SERVINGS

You could use roasted chicken from the grocery store as a great shortcut for this recipe. You'll need about 2 cups cooked, shredded chicken with the skin and bones discarded. Using the no-boil type lasagna noodles is a time-saver too.

1/4	cup olive oil, divided
3/4	pound boneless, skinless chicken breasts
	Salt and freshly ground black pepper
2	medium onions, thinly sliced
10	ounces button mushrooms, brushed clean, trimmed, and thinly sliced
4	cloves garlic, minced
1	large red bell pepper, cored, seeded, and cut into 1/2-inch dice
1	can (28 ounces) crushed tomatoes
1/4	cup minced fresh parsley
2	teaspoons dried oregano
2	teaspoons dried basil
1	teaspoon salt
1/2	teaspoon freshly ground black pepper
1/4	teaspoon dried red pepper flakes
1	pound mozzarella cheese, grated
1	cup freshly grated Parmesan cheese
12	cooked lasagna noodles or 9 no-boil lasagna noodles

SMOKED SALMON SHELLS

Oversized pasta shells make an intriguing edible container in which a rich filling of smoked salmon, peas, and leeks are baked.

9	tablespoons unsalted butter, divided
2	leeks, white and light green parts only, rinsed well and finely chopped
1	cup fresh shelled or thawed frozen peas
	Salt and freshly ground black pepper
8	ounces hot-smoked salmon, flaked, skin and bones discarded
4	ounces cream cheese, at room temperature
1/2	cup sour cream
1/4	teaspoon cayenne pepper
6	tablespoons all-purpose flour
2	cups milk
1	cup whipping cream
	Freshly squeezed juice of 1 lemon
3/4	cup freshly grated Parmesan cheese, divided
1	pound dry jumbo pasta shells
1/2	cup dried bread crumbs
6	cloves garlic, very finely minced
1/4	cup minced fresh parsley
1	tablespoon extra virgin olive oil

Melt 3 tablespoons of the butter in a medium skillet over medium heat. Add the leeks and sauté until tender, about 5 minutes. Add the peas and cook until bright green, about 3 minutes. Transfer the peas and leeks to a bowl and season to taste with salt and pepper. Stir in the smoked salmon and set aside. In a medium bowl, stir together the cream cheese, sour cream, and cayenne until smooth. Gently fold in the smoked salmon mixture to evenly combine. Refrigerate until ready to assemble. Preheat the oven to 350°F.

Melt the remaining 6 tablespoons of the butter in a large saucepan over medium heat. When the butter is bubbling, whisk in the flour. Cook, whisking constantly, for 1 minute. Slowly whisk in the milk and continue cooking, whisking constantly, until the mixture bubbles and thickens, 2 to 3 minutes. Take the skillet from the heat and whisk in the cream, lemon juice, and 1/2 cup of the Parmesan with salt and pepper to taste.

Bring a large pot of salted water to a boil. Add the pasta and cook until *al dente*, about 10 to 12 minutes.

While the pasta is cooking, combine the remaining 1/4 cup Parmesan, bread crumbs, garlic, parsley, and olive oil in a small bowl and stir to thoroughly mix; set aside. Stir 1/2 cup of the cream sauce into the smoked salmon and cream cheese mixture. Spread 1 cup of the cream sauce over the bottom of a 9- by-13-inch baking dish.

When the pasta is cooked, drain the shells in a colander and rinse with cold water to stop the cooking. When draining the shells make sure they don't slip inside one another, or some of the shells may tear or lose their shape.

Fill each shell with a heaping tablespoon of the smoked salmon mixture and set them in the baking dish, open-side up so the filling doesn't slip out. Spoon the remaining sauce over the shells and sprinkle the bread crumb mixture evenly over the sauce. Bake until the sauce is bubbling and the top is golden brown, about 30 minutes. Spoon the filled shells onto individual plates and serve.

MAKES 10 TO 12 SERVINGS

Pasta alla Vodka

This spicy, tasty dish is a great weeknight, family-pleasing option that can be prepared in 30 minutes. Round out the meal with a simple green salad and crusty bread.

Heat the olive oil in a large, deep skillet over medium heat. Add the garlic, salt, and red pepper flakes and cook, stirring often, just until the garlic turns golden but not brown, 2 to 3 minutes. Add the tomatoes and stir to blend. Simmer uncovered until the sauce begins to thicken, about 15 minutes.

Meanwhile, cook the sausage in another skillet over medium-high heat, breaking up the meat into smaller pieces as it cooks, until cooked through, about 5 to 7 minutes. Scoop out the sausage with a slotted spoon, allowing any excess fat to drip away, and add it to the tomato sauce.

Bring a large pot of salted water to boil, add the pasta, and cook until *al dente*, about 10 to 12 minutes. Drain the pasta well and add it to the tomato sauce. Add the cream and vodka and toss. Cover the skillet, reduce the heat to low, and let sit for 2 to 4 minutes to allow the pasta to absorb the sauce. Add the parsley and season to taste with salt and pepper. Arrange the pasta on individual plates, passing the Parmesan separately.

Makes 6 to 8 servings

◆ Lots of wineries are making red blends these days—because of the cream in this dish, look for one with soft tannins.

1/4	cup olive oil
5	cloves garlic, minced
1 1/2	teaspoons salt
1/2	teaspoon dried red pepper flakes
1	can (28 ounces) crushed tomatoes in purée
1	pound spicy chicken sausage or Italian sausage, casings removed
1	pound dry penne
1	cup whipping cream
2	tablespoons Finlandia vodka
2	tablespoons chopped fresh parsley
	Salt and freshly ground black pepper
	Freshly grated Parmesan cheese, for serving

Linguine with Mussels in Chipotle Coconut Milk

2	tablespoons vegetable oil
1	cup chopped onion
1/2	cup chopped carrot
1/2	cup chopped celery
1	can (14 ounces) unsweetened coconut milk
1	cup chicken broth
1	cup dry white wine
3	tablespoons chopped garlic
1/4	cup chopped fresh mint
1/4	cup chopped fresh cilantro
1 1/2	teaspoons chopped canned chipotle chiles in adobo
2 1/4	pounds mussels, scrubbed and debearded
12	ounces dry linguine

Chipotle chiles are a dried, smoked version of the common jalapeño chile, available dried or canned in a flavorful sauce, as is used here. Look for chipotles in the ethnic section of most larger supermarkets.

Heat the oil in a large pot over medium heat. Add the onion, carrot, and celery and sauté until the onion is tender, about 5 minutes, stirring occasionally. Stir in the coconut milk, broth, wine, and garlic. Bring to a boil over medium-high heat and boil until reduced to 2 cups, 12 to 15 minutes. While the sauce is reducing, bring a large pot of salted water to a boil for cooking the pasta.

Stir the mint, cilantro, and chipotles into the sauce. Add the mussels, cover the pot, and cook over medium-high heat until the mussels open, about 5 minutes, shaking the pan gently a few times during cooking. (Discard any mussels that do not open.) Keep warm over low heat.

When the water comes to a rolling boil, add the linguine and cook to *al dente*, about 8 to 10 minutes. Drain the pasta well, then divide it among individual large shallow bowls. Spoon the mussels and their cooking liquid over the pasta and serve.

MAKES 6 SERVINGS

Crabs, shellfish and mussels are abundant in the waters of the northern Pacific Coast. The Dungeness crab variety was named after Dungeness Spit in Puget Sound, where drastic tide fluctuations create the ideal environment for shellfish to thrive. Penn Cove mussels, Westcott Bay oysters, and Dungeness crab are shipped around the country from this area.

Jalapeño Capellini with Crab

There's a surprising amount of jalapeño chile in this recipe! The flavor mellows after it is sautéed for a few minutes, though it is still a chile-lover's dish.

Heat the olive oil in a small skillet over medium heat, add the garlic, and sauté until tender but not brown, 2 to 3 minutes. Add the jalapeño, green onions, mustard, cayenne pepper, and black pepper, and cook, stirring occasionally, until the jalapeño is tender, about 2 minutes; keep warm over low heat.

Bring a large pot of salted water to a boil and prepare a bowl of ice water. Blanch the asparagus until tender, 3 to 4 minutes, then scoop out the spears with a slotted spoon or tongs and set aside on paper towels to drain. Return the water to a boil, add the pasta and cook until *al dente*, about 3 to 5 minutes. While the pasta is cooking, pick over the crabmeat to remove any bits of shell or cartilage. Put it in a small saucepan or skillet (with 1 to 2 tablespoons of water if the crab seems dry) and warm gently over medium heat. When the pasta is cooked, drain it, reserving a few tablespoons of the cooking water. Return the pasta to the pot and pour the jalapeño mixture over it. Add the Parmesan cheese and toss to evenly mix; if the pasta seems dry, add 1 to 2 tablespoons of the cooking water to moisten it.

To serve, arrange a bed of pasta on each plate and top with the warmed crab. Scatter the bell pepper and basil over, garnish with the asparagus, and serve right away.

Makes 4 to 6 servings

For a fancier presentation, twist the pasta around 2 forks—holding them about an inch apart in your hand—to form a tidy nest in which the crab can nestle.

◆ Eminently food-friendly, sauvignon blanc's high acids balance rich crab while remaining compatible with the fresh green flavor of asparagus.

1	tablespoon olive oil
3	tablespoons minced garlic
1/3	cup finely minced jalapeño chile
1/2	cup thinly sliced green onions
1/4	cup Dijon mustard
1/2	teaspoon cayenne pepper, more or less to taste
	Freshly ground black pepper
12	spears asparagus, tough ends trimmed
1	pound dried capellini, angel hair, or other long thin pasta
12	ounces Dungeness crabmeat
1 1/2	cups freshly grated Parmesan cheese
1/2	cup minced red bell pepper
1/4	cup chopped fresh basil

PACIFIC RIM PAD THAI

1   package (16 ounces) rice noodles
        (about the width of fettucine)

1/4   cup vegetable oil

        Hot chili oil

2   boneless, skinless chicken breasts,
        cut into 1/2-inch strips

5   cloves garlic, minced

8   ounces medium shrimp, peeled
        and deveined

2   eggs, lightly beaten

1/2   cup Thai fish sauce (*nam pla*)

1/2   cup finely chopped dry
        roasted peanuts

1/4–1/2 cup sugar

2   tablespoons freshly squeezed lime
        juice, more to taste

2   tablespoons rice vinegar

1–2   tablespoons paprika

        Dried red pepper flakes

GARNISH

1–2   carrots, cut into
        2-inch matchsticks

1   cup bean sprouts

1/4   cup chopped fresh cilantro and/or
        cilantro sprigs

1–2   green onions, chopped

        Chopped dry roasted peanuts

        Lime wedges or slices

This popular Thai dish can be spiced up to suit your taste, adding more chili oil and/or red pepper flakes for a five-star kick!

Put the rice noodles in a large bowl, add cold water to generously cover and set aside to soak until tender, about 3 hours. (To speed up the soaking time, use warm water and soak for 1½ to 2 hours.) Drain the noodles, reserving about ½ cup of the soaking liquid.

Heat the vegetable oil and as much of the hot chili oil as you like in a wok or large skillet over medium-high heat. Add the chicken strips and garlic and sauté, stirring constantly, until the chicken is no longer pink on the outside, 3 to 4 minutes. Reduce the heat to medium and stir in the shrimp and eggs. Cook, stirring, until the eggs are cooked, about 2 minutes. Add the fish sauce and simmer for 2 minutes. Add the rice noodles, peanuts, sugar, lime juice, vinegar, and paprika with red pepper flakes to taste. Stir to evenly mix. The noodles will begin to soften and become translucent. Add enough of the soaking liquid to make the mixture slightly saucy, at least ¼ cup. Continue cooking until the noodles have completely softened and all the ingredients are evenly distributed, about 5 minutes. Taste the noodles for seasoning, adding more chili oil, pepper flakes, or lime juice to taste. Transfer the noodles to a large platter and top with any or all of the suggested garnishes.

MAKES 6 TO 8 SERVINGS

◆ Off-dry gewürztraminer has lovely aromas and a weight suited to this dish.

CHAMPAGNE SHRIMP WITH
GINGER BUTTER SAUCE

Champagne makes this simple, elegant sauce truly special. Any good quality, dry sparkling wine can be used as well. Lucky for you, there will be some extra left to sip alongside.

For the sauce, put the champagne, vinegar, shallot, fresh ginger, garlic, and pickled ginger in a small saucepan over medium-high heat. Boil until the liquid has reduced to about ¼ cup, 20 to 30 minutes. Reduce the heat to low and whisk the butter pieces, a few at a time, into the reduced liquid to thicken the sauce. Season to taste with salt and pepper, then strain the sauce and return to the saucepan. Keep the sauce warm over very low heat.

Heat the remaining 1 tablespoon of butter in a medium skillet over medium-high heat. Add the shrimp and cook until pink and just opaque through, tossing occasionally, 3 to 4 minutes. Divide the warm sauce among plates and arrange the shrimp over the sauce in a circle. Garnish with the green onion brushes or pickled ginger.

MAKES 6 SERVINGS

To make a green onion brush, trim a green onion to the white and light green portion, about 3 to 4 inches long. Make a series of slits halfway down the length of the onion, from the outer edges to near the center, careful to leave the center intact. Refrigerate in a bowl of cold water until poofy, about 30 minutes.

◆ Highlight the sauce by pouring sparkling wine with dinner.

1	tablespoon unsalted butter
1½	pounds medium shrimp, peeled and deveined

GINGER BUTTER SAUCE

1	cup champagne or other dry sparkling wine
¼	cup rice vinegar
2	tablespoons chopped shallot
1½	tablespoons minced or grated fresh ginger
4	teaspoons finely chopped garlic
1	teaspoon minced pickled ginger
½	cup unsalted butter, cut into pieces
	Salt and freshly ground black pepper
	Green onion brushes or pickled ginger slices, optional, for garnish

Spicy Indian Shrimp with Greens

I	teaspoon ground cumin
1/2	teaspoon cayenne pepper, more or less to taste
1/2	teaspoon ground ginger
1/2	teaspoon salt
1/4	teaspoon ground turmeric
2	teaspoons cider vinegar
I	pound large shrimp, peeled and deveined
2	tablespoons vegetable oil
2	teaspoons toasted sesame oil, divided
I	cup thinly sliced onion
1/4	cup orange juice concentrate, divided
I	large bunch spinach (about I pound)
2	cups lightly packed arugula, or more fresh spinach
	Salt and freshly ground black pepper
	Orange slices, for garnish (optional)

Given the vivid color and flavor of this dish—aromatic with cumin, ginger, and sesame oil—simple steamed white rice is a perfect accompaniment.

Combine the cumin, cayenne, ginger, salt, and turmeric in a medium bowl and stir to mix. Stir in the vinegar until evenly blended, then add the shrimp and gently stir to coat. Set aside while preparing the onions.

Heat the vegetable oil and 1 teaspoon of the sesame oil in a large nonstick skillet over medium heat. Add the onion and cook until lightly browned and aromatic, 8 to 10 minutes, stirring occasionally. Increase the heat to high and add the shrimp with the seasonings and 2 tablespoons of the orange juice concentrate. Cook until the shrimp are just opaque, stirring occasionally, about 3 minutes; reduce the heat to low and keep warm.

Put the spinach and arugula in a medium skillet (with the rinse-water still clinging to the leaves, or add 1 to 2 tablespoons water) and cook over medium-high heat, stirring, just until evenly wilted, 1 to 2 minutes. Drain away any remaining liquid and toss with the remaining 2 tablespoons orange juice concentrate and the remaining 1 teaspoon sesame oil. Season to taste with salt and pepper.

Divide the greens among individual plates and top with the shrimp and any extra sauce. Garnish with the orange slices and serve.

Makes 4 servings

If you are unable to find arugula, you can simply use more of the fresh spinach in its place.

◆ Aromatic and flavorful, dry riesling has enough oomph to meet these exotic flavors head-on.

Northwest Microbrew Steamers

Serve these delicious and aromatic steamed clams with lots of crusty bread for soaking up the sauce. An ideal accompaniment would be more chilled bottles of the same beer with which you steamed the clams.

Melt the butter in a large pot with a tight-fitting lid over medium heat. Add the beer, garlic, shallot, tarragon, thyme, and pepper. Bring to a boil over medium-high heat.

Add the clams, cover the pot, and steam until most of the shells have opened, 5 to 7 minutes, shaking the pot gently a few times during cooking. Scoop the clams out with a slotted spoon and put them in individual shallow bowls (discard any clams that did not open). Pour the cooking liquid over, sprinkle with parsley and chives, and serve right away.

MAKES 6 SERVINGS

◆ Choose a flavorful, robust ale, such as Redhook IPA (India Pale Ale) or BridgePort's Blue Heron Pale Ale for this recipe.

1	cup unsalted butter
1	bottle (12 ounces) Northwest ale
12	cloves garlic, minced
1	tablespoon minced shallot
2	teaspoons chopped fresh tarragon
2	teaspoons chopped fresh thyme
1	teaspoon freshly ground black pepper
2	pounds clams, scrubbed
1/2	cup chopped fresh parsley
1/2	cup chopped fresh chives

CLAMS

Clams are among the most distinctive foods of the Northwest. The most prominent hardshell clam is the Manila clam, which is a transplant from Japan that has taken beautifully to our local waters. These clams are farmed throughout the Puget Sound region and are readily available year-round. The littleneck clam is native to the region but is less commonly available in stores, though its slightly more pronounced flavor is favored by long-time locals. Clams need little preparation before cooking: simply put them in a colander and toss gently under cold running water for a few seconds, scrubbing as needed. Clams should never sit submerged in fresh water, or they will die.

HALIBUT WITH SAKE CLAM BROTH

1/4 cup white miso

1 tablespoon sugar

1 cup sake, divided

4 halibut fillet pieces (about 6 ounces each), skin and pin bones removed

3 cups chicken broth

12 clams, scrubbed

2/3 cup orzo

1 carrot, trimmed and thinly sliced on the diagonal

1 baby bok choy, trimmed and cut into 1-inch pieces

1 cup frozen petite peas

1 cup halved cherry tomatoes

1/3 cup thinly sliced green onions

The slightly sweet, yet earthy flavor of sake (Japanese rice wine) is an ideal ingredient to complement seafood, another tasty marriage of local products with Asian culinary influences.

Preheat the oven to 450°F. Lightly butter or oil a shallow baking dish large enough to hold the halibut pieces generously.

Whisk together the miso, sugar, and 1 tablespoon of the sake. Coat the fish with the miso mixture and set the pieces slightly apart in the baking dish. Bake the fish until just opaque through but still moist in the center of the thickest part, 8 to 12 minutes depending on the thickness of the fish.

While the halibut is baking, bring the broth and remaining sake to a boil in a large saucepan over medium heat. Add the clams, orzo, and carrot; cover, and cook until the clams open, 5 to 10 minutes. As the clams open, scoop them out with a slotted spoon into a small bowl, discarding any clams that do not open.

Continue cooking the orzo until it is *al dente*, tender but with a bite, about 5 minutes longer. Stir in the bok choy and peas and bring just to a boil.

To serve, ladle the orzo and vegetables into individual shallow bowls. Set a piece of fish in the center and surround it with the clams and tomatoes. Sprinkle with the green onions and serve.

MAKES 4 SERVINGS

Brown miso cannot be substituted for white in this recipe. See page 111 for information about miso.

PECAN CRUSTED HALIBUT WITH SAUTÉED APPLES

This is a luxurious treatment for halibut fillet, the nutty crust adding texture and flavor. The more finely you chop the pecans, the better they will adhere to the fish. The nut crust can be prepared up to one day in advance.

Preheat the oven to 425°F. Lightly oil a baking sheet. Put the pecans and parsley in a food processor and pulse to finely and evenly chop (avoid overworking or the mixture will turn to a paste). Spread the mixture in a large shallow dish.

Stir together the melted butter, orange juice, orange zest, mustard, salt, and cayenne in a shallow dish. Coat both sides of each halibut piece with some of the melted butter mixture. Press both sides of the fillets into the nut mixture, patting gently to remove excess. Set the halibut on the prepared baking sheet and bake until the fish is just opaque through, about 8 to 12 minutes depending on the thickness of the fish.

Meanwhile, prepare the sautéed apple garnish. Whisk together the apple juice, mustard, and sugar in a small bowl and season to taste with salt. Melt the butter in a small skillet over medium heat. Add the diced apple and apple juice mixture and cook, stirring occasionally, until the apple is just soft, about 4 minutes. Stir in the green onion and parsley.

Spoon the sautéed apples over the halibut pieces and garnish with parsley.

MAKES 4 SERVINGS

1 1/2	cups pecans (about 8 ounces) or almonds, walnuts or hazelnuts
2	tablespoons minced fresh parsley, plus more for garnish
4	tablespoons unsalted butter, melted
2	tablespoons freshly squeezed orange juice
1	teaspoon grated orange zest
1	teaspoon Dijon mustard
1	teaspoon salt
1/4	teaspoon cayenne pepper
4	halibut fillet pieces (8 ounces each), skin and pin bones removed

SAUTÉED APPLES

2	tablespoons apple juice
1	teaspoon Dijon mustard
1	teaspoon sugar
	Salt
1	tablespoon unsalted butter
1	red apple, cored and cut into 1/4-inch dice
2	tablespoons thinly sliced green onion, white and light green parts only
1	tablespoon minced fresh parsley

HALIBUT WITH RASPBERRIES

Vibrant red berries make a dashing contrast to the snow-white color of the Northwest's prized halibut. It is a surprising marriage of flavors that play beautifully off one another.

1 cup dry white wine

1/2 cup raspberry vinegar

1 tablespoon chopped shallot

1 teaspoon whole black peppercorns

1 cup whipping cream

6 halibut fillet pieces
(about 6 ounces each)

Salt and freshly ground
black pepper

1/2 cup unsalted butter, cut into
1/2-inch pieces

6 sprigs watercress, for garnish

1 1/2 cups fresh raspberries
(about 8 ounces), divided

Preheat the oven to 400°F. Lightly butter or oil a shallow baking dish large enough to hold the halibut pieces generously.

Combine the wine, vinegar, shallot, and peppercorns in a small saucepan over medium-high heat. Bring to a boil and simmer until reduced to a syrupy consistency, about 20 minutes. Add the cream and reduce by half, 12 to 15 minutes.

While the cream is reducing, season the halibut fillet pieces lightly with salt and pepper, set them in the baking dish, and cover the dish with foil. Bake the fish until it is opaque through the thickest part, 10 to 14 minutes, depending on the thickness of the pieces.

When the cream has reduced, whisk in the butter 1 piece at a time. Strain the sauce and keep warm over low heat until ready to serve.

Transfer the halibut to a platter or individual plates. Pour a little of the sauce over the halibut, sprinkle a few raspberries over each fillet, and garnish with the watercress. Add the remaining raspberries to the remaining sauce and pass it separately.

MAKES 6 SERVINGS

◆ Pinot noir with lots of berry and some tannin will suit both the raspberries and peppercorns.

SNAPPER WITH PAPAYA AND FRESH HERBS

The rich buttery-yellow color of papaya accented with vibrant fresh herbs makes for a colorful—not to mention delicious—embellishment to pan-sautéed fillets of flaky snapper.

Season the fish with salt and pepper and drizzle with the lime juice. Melt 2 tablespoons of the butter in a nonstick skillet over medium heat. Add the fish and cook until opaque through the thickest part, about 3 minutes per side. Transfer the fish to plates, cover with foil, and keep warm in a low oven.

Add the green onions to the skillet and cook over medium heat for 1 minute, stirring. Add the papaya, mint, dill, and tarragon and sauté for 1 minute longer. Stir in the wine and Worcestershire sauce and boil over medium-high heat until the liquid is reduced by half, about 2 minutes. Cut the remaining ¼ cup of butter into small pieces and whisk them into the sauce 1 piece at a time. Spoon the sauce over the fish and garnish with the lime slices.

MAKES 4 SERVINGS

This recipe would also be delicious made with halibut fillet pieces or even pan-fried shrimp, tossing together the shrimp and papaya-herb sauce just before serving.

◆ Highlight papaya's tropical flavor with a fruity chenin blanc.

4	skinless snapper fillets (about 6 ounces each), pin bones removed
	Salt and freshly ground white or black pepper
3	tablespoons freshly squeezed lime juice
1/4	cup plus 2 tablespoons unsalted butter, divided
1/2	cup minced green onions
1	large papaya, peeled, seeded, and diced
2	tablespoons chopped fresh mint
1	tablespoon chopped fresh dill
1	tablespoon chopped fresh tarragon
1/3	cup dry white wine
1	teaspoon Worcestershire sauce
1	small lime, thinly sliced, for garnish

Turn Point
KRISTY GJESME

*T*urn Point lighthouse stands guard over the shipping lanes separating Washington State from Vancouver Island in Canada. This area is not only popular with boaters, but also migrating whales who come to feed here. "Whale watching" boat trips are a popular way to observe the splashy, majestic giants up close.

CAJUN PACIFIC SNAPPER TACOS

There are dozens of types of rockfish found along the Pacific coast. You'll find rockfish fillets, often called "snapper" or "red snapper" fillets; most are easily interchangeable.

For the sauce, stir all ingredients together and add hot pepper sauce to taste. Set aside.

Stir together the paprika, thyme, oregano, salt, cayenne pepper, black pepper, and white pepper in a small bowl. Brush both sides of each fillet with oil and coat 1 side with the spice mixture. Heat 2 tablespoons of the oil in a large nonstick skillet over high heat. When hot, add the fish to the skillet spice side down and cook until nicely browned, 3 to 4 minutes. Turn the fish and cook until firm and opaque through, but not dry, 3 to 4 minutes longer. Add more oil if needed during cooking.

Put 3 tortillas on each plate, overlapping only slightly. Break the fish into bite-sized pieces and divide it among the tortillas. Spoon some of the sauce over the fish, top with the lettuce, tomatoes, and salsa, if using. Serve with lime wedges alongside for diners to squeeze to taste over the tacos, passing any extra sauce alongside.

MAKES 4 SERVINGS

◆ The spiciness of these tacos would pair well with a Northwest microbrew such as India Pale Ale.

1	tablespoon paprika
2	teaspoons dried thyme
2	teaspoons dried oregano
1 1/2	teaspoons salt
1/4	teaspoon cayenne pepper, or to taste
1/2	teaspoon coarsely ground black pepper
1/2	teaspoon coarsely ground white pepper
4	skinless snapper fillets (about 6 ounces each), pin bones removed
1/4	cup canola oil, more for brushing
12	soft corn tortillas, lightly steamed
2	cups packed shredded iceberg lettuce
2	cups seeded, chopped tomatoes
	Salsa (optional)
2	limes, quartered

SAUCE

1	cup sour cream
	Finely grated zest of 1 lime
2	tablespoons freshly squeezed lime juice
2	tablespoons chopped fresh cilantro
1/4	teaspoon salt
	Dash hot pepper sauce, more to taste

Miso Glazed Salmon

I	cup white miso
1/4	cup sake
1/4	cup seasoned rice vinegar
3	tablespoons packed light brown sugar
4	salmon fillet pieces (about 8 ounces each), pin bones removed
3	tablespoons white sesame seeds
3	tablespoons black sesame seeds
I	tablespoon peanut oil, more if needed
I	tablespoon toasted sesame oil, more if needed

For a particularly striking presentation to show off the distinctive color of the salmon, serve this with sticky white rice and braised bok choy on a stark white plate.

Whisk together the miso, sake, vinegar, and brown sugar in a small bowl. Spread a thin layer in the bottom of a shallow dish and add the fish, skin-side down. Spread the remaining marinade evenly over the fish. Cover with plastic wrap and refrigerate for at least 4 hours or overnight. (If you prefer less salty flavors, marinate for no more than 8 hours.)

Toast the sesame seeds in a dry skillet over medium-high heat, stirring occasionally, until lightly browned and aromatic, about 5 minutes. Let cool.

Scrape the marinade from the fish and coat the top and sides of the salmon pieces with the sesame seeds.

Heat 1 tablespoon each of the peanut and sesame oils in a large nonstick skillet over medium-high heat. When the skillet is hot, add the salmon skin side up and cook until golden brown and lightly caramelized, 4 to 5 minutes. Carefully turn and cook until the fish is just barely translucent in the center, 3 to 4 minutes, adding more oil if needed. Use tongs to very carefully hold the fish on its edges to lightly brown the sides, just 30 seconds to 1 minute. Serve immediately.

Makes 4 servings

◆ Because of its lower tannins and fruity character, pinot noir is one of the rare reds that work with Asian seasonings.

Honey Glazed Salmon with Figs and Cranberry Vinaigrette

Tangy cranberries and sweet figs accent the rich, honey glazed salmon.

For the cranberry vinaigrette, combine the juices, vinegar, shallots, rosemary, parsley, and honey. Whisk in the olive oil and season to taste with salt and pepper. Stir in the cranberries and let sit at room temperature for 4 hours or refrigerate overnight.

Cut the figs into halves or quarters, depending on their size, and put them in a medium bowl. Season with a little salt and pepper, toss with 1 tablespoon of the vinaigrette, and set aside at room temperature.

Shortly before serving, preheat the broiler and set the top oven rack about 4 inches below the element. Oil a broiler pan. Season the salmon with salt and pepper and set the fish flat side down on the broiler pan. Stir together the honey, butter, powdered mustard, and cayenne in a small bowl and brush about half the mixture on the fish.

Broil the salmon for 4 to 5 minutes. Take the pan from the oven and brush the remaining honey mixture on the fish. Scatter the fig pieces around the salmon on the broiler pan and continue broiling until the salmon has just a touch of translucence in the center of the thickest part and the figs are warmed, about 2 to 3 minutes longer.

Arrange the salmon in the center of individual plates and surround with the figs. Spoon the vinaigrette around the salmon, sprinkle with parsley, and serve.

MAKES 4 SERVINGS

8 – 12	fresh figs
4	salmon fillet pieces (about 8 ounces each), skin and pin bones removed
2	tablespoons honey
2	teaspoons unsalted butter, melted
1	teaspoon powdered mustard
1/4	teaspoon cayenne pepper
2	tablespoons chopped fresh parsley

CRANBERRY VINAIGRETTE

1	tablespoon cranberry juice
1	tablespoon freshly squeezed lemon juice
1	tablespoon red wine vinegar
1	tablespoon finely chopped shallot
1	tablespoon minced fresh rosemary
1	tablespoon chopped fresh parsley
1	teaspoon honey
1/3	cup olive oil
	Salt and freshly ground black pepper
1/4	cup fresh cranberries, coarsely chopped

CRANBERRIES

Not all Northwesterners realize that the state of Washington is a prime grower of ruby-red cranberries, not the largest quantities in the country, but among the best quality. The tart berries are grown in bogs in the cool, damp climate of the Pacific coast near the Long Beach Peninsula. Bogs are flooded during harvest time in the fall, the berries floating to the top of the water for easy collection. An annual festival in Ilwaco, Washington, celebrates this annual harvest tradition, and there's even a cranberry museum in the area. Cranberries freeze quite well, so when bags are plentiful during the fall, buy extra to pop into the freezer for use over the following months. Cranberries require little preparation, aside from picking over them to remove any that may be soft.

GRILLED SALMON WITH RED CURRANT GLAZE

The slightly tangy sweetness of red currant jelly is a tasty complement to the rich flavor of salmon, not to mention a pretty color contrast in the rosy sauce that's served alongside the grilled fish.

Preheat an outdoor grill (to high if using a gas grill) and oil the grill grate.

Melt ½ cup of the jelly in a small saucepan over low heat. Season the salmon with salt and pepper and brush both sides with the melted jelly. Grill the salmon until the fish is just opaque through the thickest part, 5 to 8 minutes, depending on the thickness of the fish, turning the pieces halfway through.

While the salmon is cooking, melt the remaining ½ cup jelly over low heat. Add the lemon juice, vinegar, and mustard. Whisk in the olive oil and season to taste with salt and pepper. Keep warm.

Set the grilled salmon on individual plates, spoon the sauce partly over and around the fish, and garnish with the fruit (if using).

MAKES 4 SERVINGS

You could use raspberry jam in place of the red currant jelly, though because of the tiny seeds in the jam, you might want to press it through a fine sieve after warming it over low heat.

1	cup red currant jelly, divided
4	salmon steaks or skinless, boneless fillet pieces (8 ounces each)
	Salt and freshly ground black pepper
1	tablespoon freshly squeezed lemon juice
2	teaspoons balsamic vinegar
2	teaspoons Dijon mustard
1	tablespoon olive oil
	Fresh raspberries, currants, or cherries, for garnish (optional)

NORTHWEST SALMON

If there is one food from the Northwest that is most prominently associated with the region, it is surely salmon. Native tribes have revered salmon for countless generations, and newer arrivals to the region are also undeniably drawn to the rich, flavorful, magnificent fish. There are five species of wild salmon native to the northern Pacific waters. Also known by its Native American name, Chinook, king salmon is the largest. This is the most prized, as well, because of its deep red color and moderately high fat levels that make for supremely delicious eating. Sockeye (also known as "red") salmon is another of the more prized salmon, even deeper in color than king and just a touch less rich. These two varieties are most commonly featured on top restaurant menus and in seafood markets around Seattle. Silver ("coho"), chum, and pink salmon are also abundant in Northwest waters, though much of this is processed into frozen fillets or canned, so these varieties are less common in fresh markets than are king and sockeye salmon.

NORTHWEST CEDAR PLANKED SALMON

1   large or 2 small cedar baking planks

      Vegetable oil

1   tablespoon unsalted butter, at room
      temperature

1   tablespoon finely grated lemon zest

1/2   teaspoon sugar

1/4   teaspoon salt

1/4   teaspoon freshly ground
      black pepper

1/4   teaspoon powdered mustard

4   salmon fillet pieces (about 8 ounces
      each), skin and pin bones removed

8   large cremini mushrooms, halved

      SPICY WINE SAUCE

1   cup dry white wine

1/4   cup minced shallot

1/4   cup freshly squeezed lemon juice

1/2   cup whipping cream

6   tablespoons unsalted butter,
      cut into pieces

1   teaspoon hot pepper sauce

      Salt and freshly ground
      black pepper

1/4   cup chopped fresh parsley,
      for garnish

Salmon and wood are a marriage made in Northwest heaven. This dish is especially dramatic if served directly on the planks.

For the sauce, combine the wine, shallot, and lemon juice in a small saucepan. Bring to a boil over medium-high heat and boil until reduced to ¼ cup, 5 to 8 minutes. Add the cream and simmer until slightly thickened, about 3 minutes. Reduce the heat to medium-low and whisk in the butter, 1 piece at a time, until thoroughly incorporated. Remove the sauce from heat and stir in the pepper sauce with salt and pepper to taste. Keep warm over low heat until ready to serve; do not allow the sauce to boil or it will turn oily.

Rub the top of the cedar planks with a little vegetable oil. Put the planks in a cold oven and preheat the oven to 350°F for about 15 minutes.

Combine the butter, lemon zest, sugar, salt, pepper, and powdered mustard, stirring to make a smooth paste. Rub the seasoning on both sides of the salmon pieces.

Take the planks from the oven and immediately set the salmon on top. Surround the salmon with the mushrooms and return the planks to the oven. Bake until the salmon is just barely translucent in the center, 18 to 20 minutes, depending on the thickness of the fish, turning once halfway through.

To serve, drizzle the sauce over the salmon and mushrooms and sprinkle with parsley.

MAKES 4 SERVINGS

There are several types of cedar and alder planks that can be used for the oven or the grill. Thicker planks are made with the oven in use in mind, easy to clean and re-use many times. Other types of cedar cooking planks are made for the outdoor grill, to set directly on the grill grate for infusing intensive woody aroma to food during grilling. These tend to be one-time-use given the intensity of the grill heat.

Cedar and alder baking planks are available by mail-order and in gourmet shops. Made in Washington offers planks on their website at www.madeinwashington.com. Noted local chef, John Howie, offers them at www.plankcooking.com.

MARTINI TROUT

A splash of dry vermouth and a touch of olives hint at the martini nature of this trout dish. The only gin is whatever you serve in a glass alongside! Filleting trout is a simple job, but to save time, ask your fish retailer to do it for you.

Combine the cornmeal, paprika, and pepper in a shallow dish and stir to mix; set aside.

Heat the oil in a large nonstick skillet over medium heat. While the oil is heating, dredge the fish in the cornmeal mixture, patting to remove excess. Add the fish to the skillet and cook until nicely browned, 3 to 4 minutes. Turn the fillets and cook until the fish is just opaque through, 2 to 3 minutes longer. Transfer the fish to a baking sheet, cover with foil, and keep warm in a low oven; wipe out the skillet with a paper towel.

For the sauce, whisk together the vermouth, olives, capers, parsley, lemon juice, and garlic with a pinch of salt and pepper in a small bowl. Add the mixture to the skillet and bring to a boil over medium-high heat. Reduce the heat to medium-low and whisk in the butter a piece at a time. Do not allow the sauce to boil or it will turn oily. Taste the sauce for seasoning, adding more salt and pepper to taste.

To serve, set the trout fillets on individual plates, spoon the sauce over, and garnish with the parsley sprigs.

MAKES 4 SERVINGS

◆ Steely pinot gris refreshes just like a classic martini.

1/2	cup cornmeal
1	teaspoon paprika
1/2	teaspoon freshly ground black pepper
1	tablespoon olive oil
4	trout fillets, skin removed
4	sprigs parsley, for garnish

MARTINI SAUCE

1/2	cup dry vermouth
2	tablespoons chopped green or kalamata olives
2	tablespoons drained capers, rinsed
2	tablespoons chopped fresh parsley
2	teaspoons freshly squeezed lemon juice
1/2	teaspoon minced garlic
	Salt and freshly ground black pepper
4	tablespoons unsalted butter, cut into pieces

Spring Rain
WILLIAM HEWSON

Although rain is the most well-known characteristic of the mild climate in Western Washington, the average rainfall in Seattle is only thirty seven inches, much less than many East Coast cities. Seattle is known as the "Emerald City" precisely for its lush, verdant parks and gardens which are fed by the rainwaters.

Poultry & Meat

Balsamic Chicken and Peppers 158

Lemon Herb Stuffed Chicken Breasts 159

Hearty Chicken Sandwiches
with Roasted Cherry Tomatoes 160

Gnocchi with Chicken, Sun-Dried Tomatoes,
Prosciutto, and Blue Cheese 162

Blue Cheese and Lemon Chicken 163

Grilled Chicken with Wild Mushroom Salsa 164

Grilled Chicken
with Black Bean and Mango-Pineapple Salsa 166

Mediterranean Herb Baked Chicken 167

Sun-Dried Tomato Capered Chicken 168

Rustic Chicken
with Mushrooms, Tomatoes, and Olives 170

Chicken with Apple, Cranberry, and Bacon 171

Sesame Chicken in Acorn Squash 172

Elegant Chicken with Pears 174

Herb Garden Roasted Chicken
with Baked Shallots 175

Hazelnut Chicken Breasts
with Cranberry Cherry Sauce 176

Orange Thyme Game Hens 177

Five-Spice Lacquered Duck
with Mango Salsa 179

Pork and Scallion Skewers 180

Five-Star Asian Ribs 183

Honey Mustard Pork Roast with Rosemary 184

Pork Tenderloin with Maple Glaze 185

Bing Cherry Chops 186

Prosciutto Stuffed Pork Tenderloin 188

Cumin Scented Pork
with Dried Pineapple Salsa 189

Lamb Chops with Garlic Mint Vinaigrette 191

Herbed Sausage and Feta Burger 192

Tuscan Veal Piccata 193

Beer-Marinated Steaks
with Peppercorn Sauce 194

Margaritaville Steak 196

Winter Roast with
Portobello Mushrooms and Cranberry 197

Beef Tenderloin with Shiitake Cream Sauce 198

BALSAMIC CHICKEN AND PEPPERS

6   boneless, skinless chicken breasts
     (1 1/2 to 2 pounds), flattened to
     1/4 inch thick

     BALSAMIC BELL PEPPERS
1   tablespoon olive oil
3   large red bell peppers, cored,
     seeded, and cut into 1/2-inch strips
1/3 cup currants or raisins
1/4 cup balsamic vinegar
1 1/2 teaspoons sugar
     Salt and freshly ground
     black pepper
1/4 cup toasted slivered almonds

1/4 cup dried bread crumbs
1/4 cup freshly grated Parmesan cheese
1/4 cup all-purpose flour
2   egg whites, lightly beaten
3   tablespoons olive oil, divided
3   tablespoons balsamic vinegar
3   tablespoons water

Saffron Basmati Rice Pilaf (page 215) would be an ideal side dish for this recipe, the golden tones playing off the deep red of the bell peppers.

For the bell peppers, heat the olive oil in a medium skillet over medium-high heat. Add the peppers and sauté until tender and lightly browned, about 6 minutes. Add the currants and sauté 1 minute. Add the vinegar and sugar with salt and pepper to taste, and cook for 1 minute longer. Take the skillet from the heat and stir in the almonds. Keep warm over very low heat.

Combine the bread crumbs and cheese in a shallow dish and stir to mix well. Put the flour in a separate shallow dish, and the egg whites in a third shallow dish. Dredge each chicken piece in flour, pat to remove excess, then dip in the egg whites, allowing excess to drip off. Dredge each in the bread crumb mixture, shaking off the excess.

Heat half of the olive oil in a large heavy skillet over medium-high heat. Add half of the chicken and sauté until cooked through, 2 to 3 minutes on each side. (The chicken should fit comfortably without overlapping; cook 2 breasts at a time if your skillet isn't large enough.) Transfer the chicken to a serving platter or individual plates and heat the remaining oil in the skillet for cooking the remaining breasts.

Spoon the bell pepper mixture over the chicken breasts. Add the vinegar and water to the skillet over medium heat and stir to loosen any browned bits. Spoon over the chicken and serve.

MAKES 6 SERVINGS

An easy way to flatten a chicken breast is to put it in a large freezer bag (not sealed) and use a meat mallet, rolling pin, or the bottom of a small heavy saucepan to gently pound the breast to flatten it.

LEMON HERB STUFFED CHICKEN BREASTS

Set off the lemony snap of this lightly stuffed chicken breast with simple rice or mashed potatoes. Lemon thyme has a delightful citrusy-herbal tone, though regular thyme will be equally delicious in this stuffing.

Preheat the oven to 400°F. Loosen the skin slightly from each chicken breast by sliding a finger gently beneath 1 edge, leaving the opposite edge attached. Set aside.

Heat 1 tablespoon of the oil in a medium skillet over medium heat. Add the shallots and garlic and cook until tender and aromatic, but not browned, 3 to 5 minutes. Take the pan from the heat and stir in the lemon zest, thyme, sage, and prosciutto with salt and pepper to taste. Carefully stuff ¼ of the shallot-herb mixture under the skin of each chicken breast.

Heat the remaining 2 tablespoons of the olive oil in a large nonstick skillet over medium-high heat. Cook the chicken, skin-side down, until well browned, about 4 minutes. Turn and cook another 4 minutes. Transfer the breasts to a baking sheet and bake until the juices run clear when pierced with the tip of a knife in the thickest part, about 10 minutes.

While the chicken is baking, make the sauce. Melt the butter in a small skillet over medium-low heat, shaking the pan gently so the butter melts evenly. Watch carefully as the butter begins to foam, then take the pan from the heat when the butter becomes light brown and smells slightly nutty. Stir in the parsley and lemon juice. Season to taste with salt and pepper, plus more lemon juice if needed.

Put the chicken on a serving platter or individual plates, spoon the sauce over, and serve.

MAKES 4 SERVINGS

◆ Sauvignon blanc with a touch of citrus will accent the fresh flavors in this chicken dish.

4	large skin-on chicken breasts, bone-in or boneless (1½ to 2½ pounds total)
3	tablespoons olive oil, divided
¼	cup minced shallots
2	tablespoons minced garlic
1	tablespoon grated lemon zest
1	tablespoon minced fresh lemon thyme or regular thyme
1	tablespoon minced fresh sage
¼	cup finely chopped prosciutto (may substitute cooked, crumbled bacon)
	Salt and freshly ground black pepper

LEMON BUTTER SAUCE

4	tablespoons unsalted butter
2	tablespoons finely chopped fresh parsley
1	tablespoon freshly squeezed lemon juice, more to taste

HEARTY CHICKEN SANDWICHES WITH ROASTED CHERRY TOMATOES

3	bone-in chicken breasts (about 2 pounds), skin on
1	tablespoon vegetable oil
	Salt and freshly ground black pepper
1	tablespoon plus 2 teaspoons olive oil, divided
2	cups halved cherry tomatoes (about 1 pound)
2	tablespoons plus 1 teaspoon balsamic vinegar, divided
1	tablespoon chopped fresh thyme
1/4	cup mayonnaise (regular or low-fat)
1	tablespoon whole-grain Dijon mustard
1	clove garlic, minced
2	cups lightly packed baby spinach (may substitute fresh basil or arugula)
6	large sandwich rolls, dense but with a soft crust, or focaccia
3	ounces Brie cheese, sliced

You can take a shortcut for this bountiful sandwich by using a deli-roasted chicken (you need 4 cups shredded cooked chicken breast) and pre-washed baby spinach.

Preheat the oven to 400°F. Put the chicken on a foil-lined baking sheet, brush with the vegetable oil, and sprinkle generously with salt. Roast until the juices run clear when pierced with the tip of a knife, 30 to 35 minutes. Let the chicken cool, then discard the skin and bones, and shred the meat with your fingers into bite-sized pieces. Reduce the oven temperature to 300°F.

Heat 1 tablespoon of the olive oil in a large nonstick, ovenproof skillet over medium-high heat. Add the tomatoes and cook until just beginning to soften, about 4 minutes, stirring once. Take the skillet from the heat and stir in 2 tablespoons of the vinegar. Sprinkle with the thyme and salt and pepper to taste. Put the skillet in the oven and bake until aromatic and the tomatoes are lightly roasted, about 15 minutes. Take the skillet from the oven and cover with foil to keep warm.

While the tomatoes are cooking, combine the mayonnaise, mustard, and garlic in a small bowl and mix together. In a large bowl, whisk together the remaining 2 teaspoons olive oil, 1 teaspoon vinegar, and salt to taste. Add the spinach and toss gently to coat.

Preheat the broiler. Split the rolls open or halve the focaccia and brush the cut sides lightly with olive oil. Put them on a baking sheet, cut sides up, and broil until lightly toasted, about 2 minutes, watching carefully to avoid burning.

To make the sandwiches, spread the mayonnaise mixture evenly over the toasted sides of each roll. Arrange the Brie on the bottom half of each roll and top with the chicken. Toss the tomatoes with the spinach and arrange over the chicken. Replace to top half of each sandwich and serve.

MAKES 6 SERVINGS

GNOCCHI WITH CHICKEN, SUN-DRIED TOMATOES, PROSCIUTTO, AND BLUE CHEESE

2 tablespoons sun-dried tomato oil, divided

2 boneless, skinless chicken breasts, cut into 1/2-inch pieces

1 pound gnocchi or small shell pasta

4 cloves garlic, minced

3/4 cup chicken broth

1/2 cup oil-packed sun-dried tomatoes, drained and chopped

1/2 cup whipping cream

1/2 cup crumbled blue cheese

1/4 cup chopped prosciutto

Salt and freshly ground black pepper

1/2 cup chopped fresh basil

1/4 cup toasted pine nuts

Gnocchi are tender pillow-like dumplings that are typically made with potato, though sometimes with flour. If you are unable to find fresh or vacuum-packed gnocchi, you can use other pasta—such as shells or bowties.

Heat 1 tablespoon of the sun-dried tomato oil in large, heavy skillet over medium-high heat. Add the chicken and sauté until just cooked through, about 3 minutes, stirring occasionally. Transfer the chicken to a plate and tent with foil to keep warm; reserve the skillet.

Bring a large pot of salted water to a boil. Add the gnocchi and cook until tender, about 12 minutes for gnocchi or 8 to 10 minutes for shell pasta. While the pasta is cooking, heat the remaining 1 tablespoon of the sun-dried tomato oil in the same skillet over medium-high heat. Add the garlic, and sauté until tender and aromatic, about 1 minute. Add the chicken with the broth, sun-dried tomatoes, cream, cheese, and prosciutto and bring to a boil. Let the sauce reduce until it thickens slightly, 3 to 5 minutes.

When the pasta is cooked, drain it well and transfer to a large serving bowl. Add the sauce to the pasta and toss to coat, seasoning to taste with salt and pepper. Top with the basil and pine nuts and serve.

MAKES 4 SERVINGS

◆ Creamy, starchy dishes such as this call for a wine with some weight as well as acid for refreshment; try a sauvignon blanc-semillon blend.

BLUE CHEESE AND LEMON CHICKEN

This is a treat for blue cheese lovers. Choose a mild blue cheese such as Oregon Blue or Gorgonzola.

Preheat the oven to 350°F. Lightly butter or oil a baking dish large enough to hold the chicken breasts in a single layer.

Stir together the sour cream, blue cheese, lemon zest, lemon juice, and parsley in a medium bowl and set aside. Combine the flour, rosemary, salt, and pepper in a shallow dish and stir to mix. Dredge the chicken in the flour mixture, coating the breasts evenly and patting to remove excess flour.

Heat the butter and oil in a large skillet over medium-high heat until it is just starting to brown. Add the chicken and cook until browned, about 4 minutes per side (cook the chicken in batches if they don't easily fit in the skillet; the skillet should not be crowded). Transfer the chicken to the baking dish, skin side up if using breasts with skin. Spread the blue cheese mixture evenly over the chicken.

Combine the bread crumbs, melted butter, and Parmesan cheese in a medium bowl and stir to mix. Sprinkle the bread crumb mixture over the chicken and bake until the topping is nicely browned and the chicken is cooked through (juices run clear when pierced in the thickest part with the tip of a knife), about 20 minutes.

MAKES 6 SERVINGS

◆ The strong flavors of blue cheese and rosemary need a wine of equal power—cabernet would be a good choice here.

1 1/3	cups sour cream
6	ounces mild blue cheese, crumbled (about 1 heaping cup)
1	tablespoon grated lemon zest
1/4	cup freshly squeezed lemon juice
3	tablespoons minced fresh parsley
1/2	cup all-purpose flour
2	teaspoons dried rosemary, crumbled
1	teaspoon salt
1	teaspoon freshly ground black pepper
6	boneless, skinless chicken breasts (about 2 1/2 to 3 pounds)
3	tablespoons unsalted butter
3	tablespoons olive oil
2	cups fresh bread crumbs
1/2	cup unsalted butter, melted
1/2	cup freshly grated Parmesan cheese

GRILLED CHICKEN WITH WILD MUSHROOM SALSA

4   boneless chicken breasts (1 1/2 to 2 pounds total), skin on or off

4   thick slices bread, cut from a crusty artisan loaf

      Extra virgin olive oil, for brushing

      Salt and freshly ground black pepper

SPICE RUB

4   teaspoons fennel seeds

3/4   teaspoon coriander seeds

1/2   teaspoon white peppercorns

1   teaspoon salt

WILD MUSHROOM SALSA

1   pound mixed large mushrooms such as shiitake, morel, chanterelle, and button, brushed cleaned and stemmed

3/4   cup olive oil, divided

2   teaspoons finely chopped fresh thyme, divided

1   tablespoon minced garlic

1/2   cup diced tomato

2   tablespoons sherry vinegar

2   tablespoons finely chopped fresh parsley

1   tablespoon minced shallot

The simple spice rub that seasons these chicken breasts would also be delicious rubbed on pork or lamb before grilling or roasting. The mushroom salsa would make a tasty topping for bruschetta, served as an appetizer. Peppery arugula tossed with your favorite vinaigrette will be a great finish, served alongside the chicken.

For the spice rub, put the fennel, coriander, and peppercorns in a small heavy skillet over medium heat. Toast, watching carefully, shaking the pan frequently, until the seeds are light brown and fragrant, 3 to 5 minutes, then pour them onto a plate to cool. When cool, finely crush the spices with a mortar and pestle or finely grind them in a clean coffee grinder. Put the spices in a small bowl and stir in the salt.

Coat the chicken with the spice rub and set aside until ready to grill (refrigerate if longer than 30 minutes). Brush the bread on both sides with olive oil, season to taste with salt and pepper, put on a baking sheet, and set aside.

Heat an outdoor grill (to medium-high if using a gas grill) and oil the grill grate. Grill the bread slices around the outer edge of the grill until brown and crispy on both sides but still soft inside, about 5 minutes total.

For the mushroom salsa, leave the mushrooms whole and toss in a large bowl with 1/2 cup of the olive oil, 1 teaspoon of the thyme, the garlic, and salt and pepper to taste. Grill the mushrooms, turning at least once, until browned and cooked through, about 5 minutes. As the mushrooms are done, return them to the marinade bowl. When cool, remove them from the marinade, finely chop them, and return them to the marinade again. Add the tomato, vinegar, parsley, shallot, the remaining teaspoon thyme, and salt and pepper to taste. Toss well and add the remaining 1/4 cup olive oil if the salsa looks dry. Toss well again. (The mushroom salsa can be made a day ahead, covered, and refrigerated, and then returned to room temperature before serving.)

Grill the chicken over medium-high heat, skin side down if skin-on breasts, and cook until browned, about 5 minutes. Turn the chicken over, move it to the edge of the grill, away from direct heat, and continue to cook until the juices run clear when pricked at its thickest point with the tip of a knife, about 7 minutes. Set aside on a plate.

recipe continued on next page

Put a grilled bread slice on each plate. Slice the chicken breasts crosswise and arrange on top of the bread. Pour any accumulated chicken juices into the mushrooms and stir. Spoon the mushrooms over and alongside the chicken and serve immediately.

MAKES 4 SERVINGS

When grilling mushrooms, take care to lay them perpendicular to the grill lines to help them avoid falling through to the fire below. A grill basket or rack laid over the grill grate will make grilling easier, or thread the mushrooms onto a skewer to grill.

◆ Mushrooms and chardonnay are natural partners; with the smokiness from the grill, choose one with a bit of toasty oak.

GRILLED CHICKEN WITH BLACK BEAN AND MANGO-PINEAPPLE SALSA

4 boneless, skinless chicken breasts (about 1¹/₂ to 2 pounds total)

MARINADE

¹/₄ cup plus 2 tablespoons olive oil

¹/₄ cup white wine vinegar

1¹/₂ tablespoons coarsely grated ginger

1¹/₂ tablespoons Dijon mustard

1¹/₂ teaspoons ground coriander

1¹/₂ teaspoons ground cumin

Freshly ground black pepper

SALSA

2 ripe mangoes, peeled, pitted, and cut into ¹/₂-inch pieces

1 can (15 ounces) black beans, rinsed and drained

1 cup chopped fresh pineapple, in ¹/₂-inch pieces

¹/₂ cup finely diced red onion

¹/₄ cup chopped fresh cilantro, plus optional sprigs for garnish

3 tablespoons freshly squeezed lime juice

2 teaspoons minced garlic

¹/₂ jalapeño chile, cored, seeded, and minced

Dried red pepper flakes

Salt

With sweet and exotic mangos now available year-round, this is a dish that can brighten up dinner with sunny island flavors any time.

For the marinade, whisk together the oil, vinegar, ginger, mustard, coriander, and cumin in a small bowl and add pepper to taste. Put the chicken in a large resealable plastic bag and pour all but 2 tablespoons of the marinade over the chicken. Securely seal the bag and turn to evenly coat the chicken in the marinade. Refrigerate 1 to 2 hours, turning the bag occasionally. Set aside the reserved marinade for basting the chicken on the grill.

For the salsa, combine the mangoes, black beans, pineapple, onion, cilantro, lime juice, garlic, and jalapeño with red pepper flakes to taste. Mix gently but thoroughly, season to taste with salt, cover with plastic, and refrigerate until ready to serve.

Preheat an outdoor grill (to high, if using a gas grill) and oil the grill grate. Take the chicken from the marinade, allowing excess to drip off, and grill it over medium-high heat, basting each side with the reserved marinade, turning only once. Grill until the chicken is cooked through (juices run clear when pierced with the tip of a knife in the thickest part), 10 to 12 minutes total. Take the chicken from the grill and cut each breast diagonally into ¹/₂-inch strips.

To serve, spread the salsa on a serving platter or individual plates and arrange each breast on top in a fan shape. Garnish with sprigs of cilantro.

MAKES 4 SERVINGS

This colorful, vibrant salsa would also be delicious served with grilled or broiled halibut or swordfish.

◆ The mango salsa will shine with a tropical chardonnay.

MEDITERRANEAN HERB BAKED CHICKEN

This dish is very easy to make and serves up an exotic aroma from the selection of spices used. The chicken can be marinated for up to 8 hours before baking. Steamed couscous is the ideal pairing for this weeknight entrée.

Combine the parsley, cilantro, garlic, cumin, turmeric, and paprika in a 9- by 13-inch baking dish, stirring to blend. Add the chicken, turning to coat, and arrange in an even, single layer.

In a medium bowl, combine the tomatoes and their juices, chicken broth, olives, capers, lemon zest, lemon juice, and salt to taste. Pour the mixture around the chicken pieces, taking care not to disturb the herb coating. Cover the dish with foil and marinate in the refrigerator for up to 8 hours.

Preheat the oven to 400°F. Bake the chicken (still covered with foil) for 40 minutes, remove the foil, and continue baking until the chicken juices run clear when the meat is pierced in the thickest part with the tip of a knife, about 20 minutes longer. Spread the couscous on individual plates, top with the chicken and cooking juices, and garnish with the cilantro sprigs for serving.

MAKES 4 SERVINGS

Moroccan-style couscous could not be a better last-minute side dish for harried dinners. The tiny little pasta-like beads are simply added to boiling water (check the box for proportions) and set aside, covered, for about 5 minutes. Fluff the couscous with a fork and it's ready to serve.

1/2	cup chopped fresh parsley
1/4	cup chopped fresh cilantro, plus whole sprigs for garnish
4	cloves garlic, finely chopped
1	teaspoon ground cumin
1	teaspoon ground turmeric
1	teaspoon paprika
3	pounds skinless chicken thighs (bone in) or chicken pieces
1	can (14 1/2 ounces) chopped plum tomatoes
1/2	cup chicken broth
1/2	cup chopped green olives
1	tablespoon capers, rinsed
1	tablespoon grated lemon zest
2	teaspoons freshly squeezed lemon juice
	Salt
4	cups hot couscous (optional)

SUN-DRIED TOMATO CAPERED CHICKEN

6   boneless, skinless chicken breasts (about 2¹/₂ to 3 pounds)

2   cups sliced button mushrooms

3   tablespoons unsalted butter

2   tablespoons all-purpose flour

2   tablespoons chopped fresh parsley

SUN-DRIED TOMATO CAPER MARINADE

1¹/₂   cups chicken broth

¹/₂   cup dry white wine

¹/₄   cup diced sun-dried tomatoes, dry or oil-packed

3   tablespoons Dijon mustard

2   tablespoons chopped fresh basil

2   tablespoons capers

1   tablespoon caper liquid

A bed of fettuccini or spaghetti will be the ideal base for serving this robust chicken dish. You can make a green salad while the chicken is marinating and you will have a hearty, healthy meal.

For the marinade, whisk all ingredients together and pour into a large bowl or resealable plastic bag. Add the chicken breasts, turn to evenly coat, cover, and marinate in the refrigerator for up to 1 hour.

Preheat the oven to 170°F. Put a baking dish in the oven to hold the chicken while you finish the sauce.

Take the chicken from the refrigerator and pour the chicken and the marinade into a large sauté pan or deep skillet. Add the mushrooms and simmer over medium heat until the juices run clear when the chicken is pierced at the thickest point with a knife, 20 to 25 minutes. Remove the chicken from the marinade and keep warm in the oven. Keep the cooking liquids warm over low heat.

In a small skillet over medium-low heat, melt the butter until the foam recedes. Add the flour, mix well, and cook for 2 minutes. Slowly whisk the flour mixture into the marinade, whisking and simmering over medium-low heat until the sauce thickens.

To serve, arrange the chicken breast on individual plates, pour the sauce over, and sprinkle with the parsley.

MAKES 6 SERVINGS

◆ Tomatoes and an earthy red wine such as sangiovese are well-paired in this Italian-accented chicken.

Stunning Skagit Valley
ANN RUTTER

$\mathcal{E}$ach spring, colorful tulip blooms carpet the fields of the Skagit Valley, just north of Seattle. The annual Tulip Festival is a visual treat and heralds the coming of sunnier days. This valley is an ideal location for growing tulips, daffodils and irises, thanks to the mild climate, evenly distributed rainfall and fertile soil.

RUSTIC CHICKEN WITH MUSHROOMS, TOMATOES, AND OLIVES

2 tablespoons olive oil, more if needed

3 1/2–4 pounds chicken legs and thighs

1 onion, sliced

1 tablespoon minced garlic

1 large portobello mushroom, brushed clean, stemmed, and cut into 1/4-inch slices

Salt and freshly ground black pepper

1/2 cup dry white wine

1 can (14 ounces) diced tomatoes, with juices

1/2 cup chicken broth

1/4 cup kalamata olives, pitted and halved

2 tablespoons balsamic vinegar

2 teaspoons minced fresh rosemary, divided

The Rosemary Bread (page 82) would be an ideal accompaniment— itself rustic and full of aroma and flavor—for this delicious chicken dish.

Heat the olive oil in a large sauté pan or skillet over medium-high heat. Add as many of the chicken pieces, skin side down, as will fit without crowding. Brown the chicken on all sides, about 3 to 4 minutes per side. Transfer to a plate and brown the remaining chicken pieces, adding more olive oil to the pan as needed. Remove the chicken from the pan and set aside.

Reduce the heat to medium, add the onion, and sauté until tender and aromatic, about 5 minutes. Add the garlic and cook, stirring often, about 2 minutes longer. If the pan is dry, add another tablespoon of olive oil. Add the mushroom slices and cook until they release their juices and begin to brown, about 5 minutes. Season to taste with the salt and pepper.

Add the wine and scrape up any browned bits from the bottom of the pan. Return the chicken pieces to the pan and simmer until the wine is reduced by half, about 3 minutes.

Add the tomatoes and their juices, broth, and olives, and reduce the heat to low. Simmer the chicken, uncovered, turning occasionally, until it is cooked through and tender, about 30 to 40 minutes.

Transfer the chicken pieces to a platter or individual plates and cover with foil to keep warm. Add the balsamic vinegar and 1 teaspoon of the rosemary to the pan, and boil for 2 minutes. Pour the sauce over the chicken, sprinkle the remaining rosemary over, and serve right away.

MAKES 4 SERVINGS

◆ A rustic sangiovese suits the simplicity of this savory chicken.

CHICKEN WITH APPLE, CRANBERRY, AND BACON

This Northwest dish is a real crowd-pleaser. Serve with crusty bread to soak up the delicious sauce.

Preheat the oven to 175°F. Warm a heatproof dish or plate in the oven to hold the chicken while you make the sauce.

Fry the bacon in a large skillet over medium heat until browned and crisp, about 5 minutes. Scoop out the bacon with a slotted spoon and drain on paper towels. Pour about 2 tablespoons of the bacon drippings into a small dish and set aside; reserve the skillet with the remaining 2 tablespoons or so of bacon drippings for cooking the chicken.

Combine the flour, cinnamon, and poultry seasoning in a shallow dish and stir to mix. Dredge the chicken breasts in the seasoned flour, coating them well and patting to remove excess. Add the oil to the skillet and heat over medium heat. Add the chicken breasts and cook until nicely browned and cooked through (juices run clear when pierced with a knife), turning once, 5 to 8 minutes per side, depending on the thickness. Transfer the chicken to the warmed dish in the oven and reserve the skillet.

Peel, core, and quarter the apple, then cut each quarter into 3 even slices. Melt the butter in a small skillet over medium heat. Add the apple and sauté until it just begins to soften, about 4 minutes, turning the slices once. Take the skillet from the heat and set aside.

Heat the reserved bacon fat in the large skillet over medium heat. Add the shallots and cook until tender and aromatic, about 5 minutes, stirring occasionally. Add the apple juice, wine, chicken broth, and cranberries with salt and pepper to taste, stirring to scrape up the browned bits from the bottom of the pan. Boil over medium-high heat until reduced by almost half, about 10 minutes. Add the cream and bacon, and gently stir in the apple slices. Add the chicken and any liquid that has accumulated in the dish, turning to coat the breasts with the sauce. Cook just until the chicken is warmed through, stirring gently. Taste the sauce for seasoning, adding salt or pepper to taste. Transfer the chicken and sauce to a serving platter or individual plates and sprinkle with the parsley.

MAKES 4 SERVINGS

4	slices bacon, diced
1/2	cup all-purpose flour
1/2	teaspoon ground cinnamon
1/2	teaspoon poultry seasoning
4	boneless, skinless chicken breasts (1 1/2 to 2 pounds total)
2	tablespoons olive oil
1	Granny Smith apple
1	tablespoon unsalted butter
1/3	cup minced shallots
2/3	cup apple juice
2/3	cup dry white wine
2/3	cup chicken broth
1/4	cup dried cranberries
	Salt and freshly ground black pepper
1/4	cup whipping cream
2	tablespoons chopped fresh parsley

SESAME CHICKEN IN ACORN SQUASH

4	boneless, skinless chicken breasts (about 1 1/2 to 2 pounds total), cut diagonally into 3/4-inch strips

SOY SESAME MARINADE

1/2	cup rice vinegar
1/4	cup soy sauce
2	tablespoons toasted sesame oil
3	cloves garlic, thinly sliced
1	piece (1 inch) fresh ginger, peeled and thinly sliced
1	teaspoon chili powder
	Pinch dried red pepper flakes

2	acorn squash, halved and seeds removed
3	carrots, cut into 1/4-inch slices
20	snow peas
1	cup small broccoli florets
1/2	cup all-purpose flour
1/4	cup sesame seeds
3	tablespoons unsalted butter

Lovely, rich fall colors make this a particularly striking entrée. The chicken can be marinated up to a day in advance, the recipe finished just before serving.

For the marinade, whisk all ingredients together and pour into a large bowl or resealable plastic bag. Add the chicken and gently mix to evenly coat the chicken pieces in marinade. Let marinate in the refrigerator at least 30 minutes or overnight, stirring or turning the bag occasionally.

recipe continued on next page

Preheat the oven to 350°F. Put the squash halves, cut side down, in an oiled baking pan. Add ½ inch water to the pan and bake until the squash is tender, 30 to 40 minutes.

While the squash is baking, bring a large saucepan of salted water to boil. Blanch the carrots until the color brightens and the carrots are tender, about 5 minutes. Scoop out the carrots with a slotted spoon and drain. Keep the water boiling, add the snow peas and blanch until bright green and just tender, about 2 minutes. Scoop out the peas with a slotted spoon. Add the broccoli to the boiling water and blanch until bright green and just tender, about 2 minutes, scoop out, and drain. Set the vegetables aside. (The vegetables may be blanched earlier and refrigerated until ready to use.)

Combine the flour and sesame seeds in a shallow dish. Remove the chicken from the marinade, reserving ¼ cup of the marinade. Roll the chicken strips in the flour mixture and set aside.

Melt the butter in a large skillet over medium heat. Working in batches so that the skillet's not overcrowded, sauté the chicken until golden on all sides and cooked through, 4 to 5 minutes total. Take the chicken from the skillet and set aside. Pour off the excess butter and crumbs from the skillet. Strain the reserved marinade and add it to the skillet. Bring the marinade to a boil, scraping up any browned bits, then add the carrots, snow peas, and broccoli, and cook, stirring gently, just enough to warm the vegetables. Add the chicken strips and toss well.

Set the acorn halves on individual plates and spoon the chicken and vegetable mixture into the acorn, spilling out over the sides.

MAKES 4 SERVINGS

◆ A full-bodied Northwest amber ale or a seasonal winter brew complements many poultry dishes.

ELEGANT CHICKEN WITH PEARS

2	tablespoons finely chopped toasted and skinned hazelnuts
2	tablespoons minced fresh parsley
2¹/2	teaspoons grated lemon zest
4	boneless chicken breasts (1¹/2 to 2 pounds total), skin on or off
¹/4	teaspoon ground coriander
¹/4	teaspoon ground cardamom
	Salt and freshly ground black pepper
2	Bosc or Anjou pears, peeled, cored, and cut lengthwise into 8 wedges
¹/2	cup pear nectar
¹/3	cup dry white wine
1¹/2	tablespoons freshly squeezed lemon juice
2	tablespoons unsalted butter
1	tablespoon vegetable oil
¹/3	cup thinly sliced green onions (white part only) or minced shallots
2	teaspoons minced garlic
¹/3	cup pear brandy or eau-de-vie
1	cup whipping cream

This sophisticated dish will impress even your most discerning friends.

Preheat the oven to 170°F. Warm a serving dish in the oven to hold the chicken while you make the sauce. Stir together the hazelnuts, parsley, and lemon zest in a small bowl; set aside.

Season both sides of the chicken breasts with the coriander, cardamom, and salt and pepper to taste. Set aside while cooking the pears.

Put the pears, pear nectar, wine, and lemon juice in a medium skillet. Simmer over medium-low heat until the pears are just beginning to soften but are still slightly crisp, about 10 minutes. Take the skillet from the heat and cover to keep warm.

Melt the butter with the oil in heavy large skillet over medium-high heat. Add the chicken, skin-side down if using skin-on chicken, and cook until browned, about 10 minutes. Turn the chicken and cook 5 minutes longer. Reduce the heat to medium and add the green onions or shallots and garlic and continue cooking until the chicken is cooked through (juices run clear when pierced at the thickest part with the tip of a knife). Pour the brandy in at one side of the skillet and use a long match to carefully ignite the brandy, taking care to avoid the flames that will rise high from the skillet. Very gently shake the skillet until the flames subside. Transfer the chicken to the warm dish in the oven.

Drain the pear cooking liquids into the skillet and boil over high heat until reduced by half, scraping up any browned bits, 5 to 7 minutes. Add the cream and boil until reduced by half again, 5 to 7 minutes. Season the sauce to taste with salt and pepper. Take the chicken from the oven, arrange it on a platter or individual plates, and spoon the sauce over the chicken. Garnish with pear slices, sprinkle with the hazelnut mixture, and serve.

MAKES 4 SERVINGS

Flambéing is a dramatic technique that allows you to quickly burn off the alcohol from spirits, leaving the distinctive flavor behind. Use a long match to light the liquor, leaning your face back from the skillet to avoid the initial whoosh of flames that rise up. Keep easily flammable things—dish cloths, long flowing sleeves—away from the area around the skillet.

HERB GARDEN ROASTED CHICKEN WITH BAKED SHALLOTS

The gentle flavor of the baked shallots with this aromatic bird elevates the weeknight baked chicken to good-enough-for-company fare. The garlic that roasts alongside the chicken would be delicious whisked into mashed potatoes to serve alongside, or simply spread on toasted bread.

1	roasting chicken, 5 to 6 pounds, rinsed and dried
3	tablespoons freshly squeezed lemon juice, rind reserved
	Salt and freshly ground black pepper
10	sprigs fresh thyme, divided
6	sprigs fresh rosemary, divided
6	sprigs fresh sage, divided
2	tablespoons unsalted butter, melted
16	shallots, peeled and left whole
6	cloves garlic, unpeeled
1/2	cup dry white wine

Preheat the oven to 400°F. Rub the inside of the chicken with the lemon juice, ½ teaspoon salt, and ¼ teaspoon pepper. Fill the cavity with half of the fresh herb sprigs and the lemon rind halves. Truss the bird, or at least tie the legs together.

Put the chicken, breast side up, in a shallow heavy roasting pan. Rub the chicken with the butter and season the skin with salt and pepper. Roast for 15 minutes.

After 15 minutes, put the shallots and garlic around the chicken, add most of the remaining herb sprigs to the pan, leaving a few for garnish. Pour the white wine over the shallots and garlic and return the pan to the oven. Roast until the juices run clear when the thickest part of a thigh is pricked with a sharp knife, 45 minutes to 1 hour.

Arrange the chicken on a heated serving platter. Peel the garlic and distribute the shallots and garlic around the chicken. Decorate with the remaining herbs and serve right away.

MAKES 4 SERVINGS

Add 1½ pounds of small red potatoes, tossed with 1 tablespoon olive oil, around the chicken with the shallots and garlic to fill out the menu.

◆ A soft, fruity merlot suits the caramelized shallots and mellow herbs of this dish.

HAZELNUT CHICKEN BREASTS WITH CRANBERRY CHERRY SAUCE

4   boneless, skinless chicken breasts
    (about 1 1/2 to 2 pounds total)

2   tablespoons Dijon mustard

1   tablespoon finely chopped
    fresh oregano

1   tablespoon finely chopped
    fresh thyme

    Salt and freshly ground
    black pepper

CRANBERRY CHERRY SAUCE

2   cups dry marsala wine

1/2 cup dried tart cherries

12 ounces cranberries, fresh or frozen

12 ounces frozen pitted dark sweet
    cherries, halved (about 2 2/3 cups)

1   cup packed light brown sugar

2   teaspoons minced fresh rosemary

HAZELNUT CRUST

1   cup all-purpose flour

1   teaspoon salt

1/4 teaspoon freshly ground
    black pepper

1   egg

2   tablespoons milk

1   cup finely chopped toasted and
    skinned hazelnuts

Both the chicken breasts and the cranberry sauce should be made at least 3 hours in advance, which makes this a great make-ahead recipe for a dinner party. It will take only a few minutes to coat the chicken in its hazelnut crust for baking just before serving. This cranberry sauce would also be delicious alongside roast pork or with your holiday turkey.

For the cranberry sauce, bring the marsala and dried cherries to a boil in a large saucepan. Simmer until the liquid has reduced by ⅔ cup, about 8 minutes. Stir in the cranberries, sweet cherries, brown sugar, and rosemary. Return the mixture to a boil, stirring occasionally. Reduce the heat to medium, cover the pan, and simmer until the cranberries burst and the sauce thickens, stirring occasionally, about 8 minutes. Transfer to a bowl and let cool to room temperature, then cover and refrigerate until cold, about 3 hours. The sauce can be prepared up to 1 week ahead.

Put the chicken breasts in a shallow dish and spread them evenly on both sides with the mustard. Sprinkle both sides with oregano, thyme, and salt and pepper to taste. Cover the dish with plastic and refrigerate for at least 2 hours or overnight.

Preheat the oven to 450°F. Lightly oil a baking dish large enough to hold the chicken breasts without crowding.

For the hazelnut crust, put the flour, salt and pepper in a shallow dish and stir to blend. In another shallow dish, lightly beat together the egg and milk. Put the hazelnuts in a third shallow dish. First dip a chicken breast in the flour to evenly coat, patting to remove the excess. Then dip it in the beaten egg, allowing excess to drip off, then coat it evenly with the hazelnuts. Set the breast in the baking dish and repeat with the remaining breasts. Bake until the juices run clear when pierced with the tip of a knife, 12 to 15 minutes. To serve, put chicken on individual plates, spoon some of the cranberry sauce (chilled or at room temperature) over, and serve right away, passing extra sauce separately.

MAKES 4 SERVINGS

ORANGE THYME GAME HENS

Brining is a very easy technique that lightly seasons the game hens while helping ensure that they remain juicy and moist when fully cooked. Take note that the birds need to sit in the brine for several hours before baking, so plan accordingly.

Add the salt to 5 quarts of cold water in a large pot or bowl and stir until fully dissolved. Add the hens, breast side down, and refrigerate for 2 to 3 hours. Take the hens from the brine and rinse thoroughly. Use heavy kitchen shears to cut down both sides of the backbone and remove it. Flatten the bird with the palms of your hands, breast side facing up, then cut down the middle of the breast.

Preheat the oven to 450°F. In a small bowl, stir together the shallots, parsley, thyme, and orange zest. Set aside ⅓ of the mixture for the sauce. Slide your fingertips under the skin of the hen halves to loosen it, then spread the herb mixture under the skin. Rub the skins with 3 tablespoons of the butter and season with salt and pepper. Put the hen halves in a shallow roasting pan that can later be placed on a burner when it is time to complete the sauce.

Roast the hens for 10 minutes, then add the broth to the pan and baste them with the broth. Continue roasting, basting every 10 minutes, until the hen halves are golden brown and the juices run clear when they are pierced in the thigh with the tip of a knife, about 25 minutes longer. Transfer the hen halves to a serving platter or individual plates and cover with foil to keep warm. Put the roasting pan on the stove over medium heat. Add the orange juice, sherry, and reserved herb mixture. Boil for 2 minutes, scraping up browned bits from the bottom of the pan. Whisk in the remaining tablespoon butter so that it melts gently into the sauce, then season to taste with salt and pepper. Spoon the sauce over the hen halves, garnish with the orange slices, and serve.

MAKES 6 SERVINGS

◆ Choose a white blend with viognier or pinot gris to pump up the citrus.

2	cups kosher or 1 cup table salt
3	Cornish game hens (about 1¼ pounds each)
⅓	cup minced shallots
¼	cup chopped fresh parsley
3	tablespoons chopped fresh thyme
2	tablespoons grated orange zest
4	tablespoons unsalted butter, at room temperature, divided
	Salt and freshly ground black pepper
1	cup chicken broth (preferably low-salt)
½	cup freshly squeezed orange juice
¼	cup dry sherry
6	thin orange slices, for garnish (optional)

FIVE-SPICE LACQUERED DUCK WITH MANGO SALSA

Plan ahead, since the duck must marinate for 2 days before roasting, but the wait is definitely worth it! The depth of delicious flavor matches the deep brown color of the roasted duck. An ideal partner alongside will be the Shiitake Pilaf (page 215).

For the marinade, whisk all ingredients together. Put the duck in a large resealable plastic bag and pour in the marinade mixture. Securely seal the bag and turn to evenly coat the duck in the marinade. Refrigerate for 2 days, turning the bag occasionally.

When ready to cook the duck, preheat the oven to 400°F. Drain the duck well and discard the marinade. Use paper towels to dry the duck inside and out. Put the duck breast side up in a rack set on a large roasting pan to catch the fat during cooking. Roast the duck for 45 minutes.

For the salsa, combine all ingredients together and stir to evenly mix. Set aside until ready to serve.

Take the roasting pan from the oven, pour off the fat, and turn the duck over. Return the pan to the oven and roast until glazed a deep brown, about 15 minutes. An instant-read thermometer inserted in the thickest part of the breast should read 140° for medium-rare. (If you prefer your duck cooked medium or medium-well, put the duck back in the breast-side-up position and roast to your taste.) When the duck is done, take it from the oven, insert a long wooden spoon into the cavity of the duck, and tilt to drain off the fat. Transfer the duck to a platter, tent it with foil, and let it rest for 15 minutes before carving. Pass the salsa separately to serve alongside.

MAKES 4 SERVINGS

◆ For a unique pairing, try chenin blanc to accent the anise flavor in this recipe.

1	duck (about 5 pounds), thawed if frozen, rinsed well

MARINADE

1	cup soy sauce
2	tablespoons dry sherry
2	tablespoons mirin (sweet Japanese cooking wine)
2	tablespoons packed dark brown sugar
2	tablespoons honey
2	tablespoons hoisin sauce
1	tablespoon minced garlic
1	tablespoon minced or grated ginger
1	tablespoon toasted sesame oil
1	teaspoon five-spice powder
1/2	teaspoon cayenne pepper

MANGO SALSA

2	mangoes, peeled, pitted, and cut into 1/4-inch dice
1/2	red bell pepper, cored, seeded, and cut into 1/4-inch dice
1/4	cup diced Walla Walla Sweet onion or other sweet onion
1	teaspoon finely grated lime zest
1 1/2	teaspoons freshly squeezed lime juice
3/4	teaspoon chili garlic sauce, or to taste
3	cloves garlic, finely minced
1	teaspoon minced or grated ginger
2	tablespoons chopped fresh mint or fresh cilantro or 1/4 cup chopped fresh basil

PORK AND SCALLION SKEWERS

2	pork tenderloins (12 to 14 ounces each), trimmed of excess fat
12	green onions, root ends trimmed
1/2	cup soy sauce
1/4	cup honey
2	teaspoons minced garlic
2	teaspoons minced or grated ginger
	Freshly ground black pepper
1/3	cup orange marmalade
1/3	cup seasoned rice vinegar
	Dash hot chili oil (optional)
	Rice (optional)
	Lettuce leaves (optional)
	Toasted coconut (optional)

Satays are quite popular skewers of meat and/or vegetables that can be used in many ways. You could serve them as small bites for appetizers, cocktail party fare, or as a main course like in this recipe.

Cut the pork into ½-inch slices, place them in a glass baking dish or resealable plastic bag, and set aside. Slice the white parts of the green onions, then cut the remaining green tops into 1½-inch lengths and set aside.

Combine the sliced green onions, soy sauce, honey, garlic, and ginger in a food processor with pepper to taste. Process until smooth. Pour the mixture over the pork and turn to evenly coat the meat. Cover the dish tightly, or securely seal the bag, and let the meat stand at room temperature for 15 minutes, or refrigerate it for up to 4 hours.

Preheat an outdoor grill (to medium-high, if using a gas grill) and oil the grill grate, or preheat the broiler. Take the pork from the marinade, reserving the marinade. Thread the meat onto 12-inch skewers so that the slices lie relatively flat, threading 1 green onion piece perpendicular to the skewer between each meat slice. Grill or broil the skewers until just cooked through, about 3 minutes per side.

Meanwhile, put the reserved marinade, marmalade, and vinegar in a medium saucepan and bring to a boil over medium-high heat; boil for 2 minutes. Season to taste with the hot oil (if using). If the sauce is too strong, dilute it with water.

Serve the skewers with a drizzle of the sauce. If using, place a spoonful of rice and a piece of meat on a lettuce leaf, top with sauce and toasted coconut, and wrap up to eat.

MAKES 4 TO 6 SERVINGS

◆ Sake's deep flavors complement the soy and honey flavors in this dish.

Heart of Seattle
MARSHALL JOHNSON

*H*istoric Pioneer Square reigns over the oldest section of the city of Seattle, where settlers rebuilt their commercial buildings after the Great Fire of 1889. The ornate iron and glass pergola sits next to a handsome carved Totem Pole in the heart of this area. Pioneer Square is known today for its restaurants, clubs and contemporary art galleries. An evening each month is dedicated to a popular "art walk" through the galleries and glass blowing studios of this area.

FIVE-STAR ASIAN RIBS

These are not your ordinary ribs; the flavor has a distinctive East-meets-West style that is particularly delicious! There will be lots of tasty sauce to serve alongside, perhaps with steamed rice and the Tri-Color Coleslaw with Miso Dressing (page 111). Even kids have been known to lick their fingers, so pass the napkins.

Preheat the oven to 300°F. Lightly oil a 9- by 13-inch baking dish.

For the marinade, whisk all ingredients together. If you like spicy flavors, you can add more chili sauce and/or dried red pepper flakes to taste.

Spread a very thin layer of the marinade in the bottom of the dish and arrange the ribs on top. Pour the remaining marinade over the ribs, turning if necessary to coat them thoroughly. This can be done up to a day ahead.

Cover the dish tightly with foil and bake for 3 hours. Remove the foil, increase the oven temperature to 350°F. After 30 minutes of baking, turn the ribs once very carefully and bake for 30 minutes longer. Total baking time is 4 hours.

Transfer the ribs to a platter, tent with foil and let rest for 10 to 15 minutes. Spoon the sauce from the baking dish into a serving bowl, passing it alongside the ribs for serving.

MAKES 4 TO 6 SERVINGS

◆ Serve with imported Asian beer or a fruity red wine, such as pinot noir or a zinfandel.

4	pounds country-style pork ribs
	MARINADE
1	cup hoisin sauce*
1/2	cup plum sauce*
1/3	cup oyster sauce*
1/3	cup chopped green onions
1/3	cup seasoned rice vinegar*
1/4	cup freshly squeezed orange juice
1/4	cup honey
1/4	cup minced garlic
1/4	cup minced or grated ginger
2	tablespoons soy sauce*
2	tablespoons dry sherry
1	tablespoon Asian chili sauce*, or to taste
1	tablespoon toasted sesame oil*
1	tablespoon grated orange zest
3/4	teaspoon five-spice powder*
1/4	teaspoon dried red pepper flakes, or to taste

*Such as Sun Luck brand

Among the most cherished shopping destinations in Seattle is Uwajimaya, a distinctive Japanese grocery in the city's International District. The spacious, family-owned store offers a dizzying array of Japanese and Asian products, from exotic fruits and vegetables, to countless spices, to fish so fresh that it comes out of huge saltwater tanks. The shelves are lined with every kind of sauce you could need for your Asian recipes, including many from their private label, Sun Luck. The store also features distinctive gifts and housewares, cooking demonstrations, and a food court with take-out. To learn more about Uwajimaya, see www.uwajimaya.com.

HONEY MUSTARD PORK ROAST WITH ROSEMARY

1 boneless pork loin roast
(about 3 pounds)

1/2 cup whipping cream

Salt and freshly ground
black pepper

MARINADE

3/4 cup beer, such as a Northwest
microbrew blonde or golden ale

1/2 cup Dijon whole-grain mustard

1/4 cup honey

2 tablespoons minced fresh rosemary

2 tablespoons minced garlic

MUSTARD RUB

1/4 cup whole-grain mustard

2 tablespoons minced garlic

2 tablespoons olive oil

2 tablespoons balsamic vinegar

1 tablespoon minced fresh rosemary

If you happen to have any leftovers from the flavorful pork roast, they will make an excellent sandwich, sliced thin and served on a bun slathered with the mustard sauce, topped with sliced red onion and watercress or lettuce.

For the marinade, whisk all ingredients together. Pour the marinade into a glass baking dish or resealable plastic bag, and add the meat, turning to evenly coat the roast. Cover the dish tightly, or securely seal the bag, and refrigerate at least 1 hour or overnight, turning occasionally. Preheat the oven to 350°F.

For the rub, stir all ingredients together. Take the pork from the marinade and set it in a roasting pan; reserve the marinade. Spread the rub mixture over the top and sides of the pork. Roast until a thermometer inserted into the center registers at least 150°F, about 1 hour 30 minutes. Remove the roast from the oven and let it rest, tented with foil to keep warm, while making the sauce.

Put the reserved marinade in a medium saucepan with the cream and any juices from the roasting pan. Boil until the liquid has reduced and thickened, about 15 minutes. Season the sauce to taste with salt and pepper. Slice the pork about ½ inch thick and arrange the slices on a platter or individual plates. Drizzle with the sauce, passing any extra sauce separately.

MAKES 6 TO 8 SERVINGS

◆ Dijon mustard and white burgundy (a.k.a. chardonnay) have the same origins—maybe that's why they are such a great match!

PORK TENDERLOIN WITH MAPLE GLAZE

This is a great autumn dish, as the aromatic maple, sage, and mustard create a unique seasonal treatment for pork. Consider sautéing some apple slices in butter—maybe with a pinch of sage as well—to serve alongside.

2	pork tenderloins (12 to 14 ounces each), trimmed
2	tablespoons minced fresh sage, divided or 2 teaspoons dried sage
	Salt and freshly ground black pepper
2	tablespoons unsalted butter, divided
1	tablespoon olive oil
1/4	cup chopped shallots
1	cup chicken broth
3	tablespoons maple syrup
3	tablespoons cider vinegar
1	tablespoon Dijon mustard

Rub the pork tenderloins with 1 tablespoon of the fresh sage (or all of the dried sage, if using) and season them with salt and pepper. Heat 1 tablespoon of the butter and the olive oil in a large skillet over medium-high heat until sizzling. Add the pork and brown on all sides, about 4 minutes. Reduce the heat to medium-low, cover, and cook until the pork registers about 150°F in the center of the thickest part, turning the tenderloins occasionally, about 15 minutes. Transfer the pork to a platter and tent with foil to keep warm.

Add the shallots to the skillet and cook over medium heat until they begin to soften, about 30 seconds. Add the broth, maple syrup, vinegar, and mustard, and scrape up any browned bits from the bottom of the skillet. Simmer until the liquid is reduced by one-quarter and has thickened enough to coat the back of a spoon, 8 to 10 minutes, stirring often. Whisk in the remaining tablespoon of butter until well blended, then season the sauce with the remaining tablespoon of fresh sage (if using) and salt and pepper to taste. Return the pork and any accumulated juices to the skillet and turn the pork to coat with the glaze.

Remove the pork from the skillet, slice the tenderloins into ½-inch strips and arrange them, overlapping, on a serving platter or individual plates. Drizzle the meat with additional sauce and serve.

MAKES 4 TO 6 SERVINGS

Real maple syrup gives by far the best results in this recipe, both in flavor and in consistency of the sauce. If using maple-flavored pancake syrup, don't reduce the sauce too much or it will become quite sticky.

◆ Chardonnay and pinot noir both have an affinity for mustard and sage. Open a bottle of each and decide which you prefer.

BING CHERRY CHOPS

4	boneless pork loin chops, about 1 inch thick
	Salt and freshly ground black pepper
1/2	cup all-purpose flour
4	tablespoons unsalted butter, divided
I	tablespoon olive oil
1/2	cup ruby port
1/4	cup dried Bing cherries (about 1 1/2 ounces)
I	tablespoon minced fresh rosemary
I	tablespoon red currant jelly

This recipe is simple enough for every day, but special enough for company—or even a romantic Valentine's Day dinner. Complete your meal by adding a side dish of couscous made with chicken stock, with dried cherries and sliced green onions stirred in before serving.

Season the chops on both sides with salt and pepper, dredge them in the flour, and pat to remove the excess. Heat 2 tablespoons of the butter and the olive oil in a large skillet over medium-high heat. Add the chops and cook to medium-well (only the slightest hint of pink remains in the center), about 4 minutes per side.

While the chops are cooking, stir together the port, cherries, rosemary, and jelly in a small bowl. When the chops are done, transfer them to a plate and set aside, covered with foil to keep warm. Add the port mixture to the skillet and stir to scrape up any browned bits from the bottom of the skillet. Simmer until the mixture has reduced to about 1/4 cup, 3 to 4 minutes. Swirl in the remaining 2 tablespoons butter until incorporated. Season the sauce to taste with salt and pepper. Arrange the chops on individual plates and drizzle the sauce and cherries over the chops.

MAKES 4 SERVINGS

You can substitute dried cranberries for the dried cherries, if you prefer. You can also double the amount of the sauce ingredients, for a little more generous service of sauce.

◆ Bump up the fruit flavor with a cherry-laden pinot noir.

PROSCIUTTO STUFFED PORK TENDERLOIN

1/2   cup fresh bread crumbs

2   tablespoons finely diced shallot

2   tablespoons freshly grated
       Parmesan cheese

1   tablespoon minced fresh
       rosemary, divided

1   tablespoon minced fresh
       thyme, divided

2   tablespoons olive oil, divided

2   pork tenderloins (12 to 14 ounces
       each), trimmed

8   slices prosciutto

1   teaspoon salt

1/2   teaspoon freshly ground
       black pepper

This fancy twist on roast pork is certainly suitable for company, especially since the pork roast can be prepared up to a day in advance and cooked just before serving.

Stir together the bread crumbs, shallot, Parmesan, 1 teaspoon of the rosemary, and 1 teaspoon of the thyme. Add 1 tablespoon of the olive oil and stir to evenly blend.

Arrange the tenderloins side by side on a clean work surface with the thick end of one next to the thin end of another. Slightly overlap the prosciutto slices crosswise down the length of the pork so all the pork is covered (the prosciutto will hang over both sides of the pork). Sprinkle the crumb mixture down the center of the prosciutto along the length of the pork. Fold the prosciutto over to cover the stuffing, and then roll the second tenderloin on top of the first: the 2 tenderloins will have the crumb-stuffed prosciutto sandwiched between them. Tuck the ends of the prosciutto underneath so the filling will not fall out during cooking. Use kitchen string to tie the tenderloins and the stuffing together in 4 places to create a cylindrical roast.

Combine the remaining 2 teaspoons rosemary and 2 teaspoons thyme with the salt and pepper in a small bowl. Rub the mixture all over the outside of the roast. Press firmly to help the herbs and spices adhere evenly. Let the roast sit for 30 minutes. (At this point, the roast can be covered and refrigerated for up to 24 hours before continuing.)

Preheat the oven to 350°F. Heat the remaining tablespoon olive oil in a large ovenproof skillet over medium-high heat until hot. Add the roast and brown it on all sides, about 6 minutes. Transfer the skillet to the oven until the meat registers at least 150°F in the thickest part, 25 to 35 minutes. Transfer the roast to a cutting board and let rest 5 minutes, tented with foil to keep warm. Remove the strings and cut the roast into ½-inch slices. To serve, overlap the slices on individual plates or a serving platter.

MAKES 4 TO 6 SERVINGS

◆ Look for a pinot gris in the Italian style (crisp, light and dry) to accent the rich flavors of the pork and prosciutto.

Cumin Scented Pork with Dried Pineapple Salsa

The flavorful cumin and garlic rub is a tasty accent for meaty pork chops, which are capped off by a colorful, slightly sweet salsa with dried pineapple. It is the makings for a perfect summertime barbeque.

Stir together the olive oil, garlic, cumin, salt, and pepper in a small bowl. Rub the spice mixture evenly on both sides of the pork chops. Set them on a plate, cover with plastic wrap, and refrigerate while making the salsa. (The chops can be cooked right away, or they can marinate in the refrigerator for up to 24 hours.)

For the salsa, combine all ingredients together. Stir to evenly mix and set aside for the flavors to blend for at least 15 minutes or up to 1 hour.

Preheat an outdoor grill (to medium-high heat if using a gas grill) and oil the grill grate, or preheat the broiler. Grill or broil the pork until medium-well (only the slightest hint of pink remains in the center), about 4 minutes per side. Serve each chop with a generous spoonful of salsa on top.

MAKES 4 SERVINGS

The Dried Pineapple Salsa will also be delicious served with simple grilled halibut.

◆ Rich in texture and low in acid, semillon will contrast beautifully with the dried pineapple salsa.

1	tablespoon olive oil
1	teaspoon minced garlic
1	teaspoon ground cumin
1	teaspoon salt
1	teaspoon freshly ground black pepper
4	boneless or bone-in pork loin chops, about 1 inch thick

DRIED PINEAPPLE SALSA

1	cup diced red bell pepper
1	cup diced dried pineapple
1/4	cup chopped fresh cilantro
1/4	cup freshly squeezed lime juice
2	teaspoons finely diced jalapeño chile
1	teaspoon olive oil
1/4	teaspoon salt

Lamb Chops with Garlic Mint Vinaigrette

Lamb chops are always a winner for a special dinner treat, made even more spectacular if cooked in a whole rack rather than individual chops. The simple vinaigrette sauce is quick, but also has a depth of flavor. Herbs used in the vinaigrette could be varied to serve with other meats, such as thyme in place of mint for beef steaks, or use sage instead of mint for pork chops.

1	cup chicken broth
1	tablespoon olive oil
2	teaspoons minced garlic
1/4	cup balsamic vinegar
2	tablespoons unsalted butter
1	tablespoon chopped fresh mint
1	tablespoon chopped fresh parsley
	Salt and freshly ground black pepper
8	lamb chops (3/4 inch thick, about 2 1/2 pounds total)

Simmer the broth in a medium skillet over medium-high heat until reduced by half, 5 to 8 minutes. Pour the broth into a small bowl and set aside. Return the skillet to the heat, add the olive oil and garlic and sauté until the garlic is golden brown and aromatic, about 1 minute, being careful not to burn it. Add the reduced broth and vinegar and boil until the liquid is reduced by half, about 5 minutes. Whisk in the butter, mint, and parsley, stirring constantly to evenly blend. Season to taste with salt and pepper. The sauce can be prepared several hours ahead and reheated gently before serving. If making ahead, add the fresh herbs just before serving to maintain the fresh green color.

Preheat an outdoor grill (to medium-high if using a gas grill) and oil the grill grate, or preheat the broiler. Season the lamb chops generously with salt and pepper. Grill or broil the chops to medium-rare, 3 to 5 minutes on each side, or longer to suit your taste. Transfer the chops to a serving platter or individual plates, spoon the warm sauce over, and serve.

MAKES 4 SERVINGS

You could use this recipe with racks of lamb in place of the lamb chops, cooking 2 trimmed racks of lamb (1¼ pounds each) and increasing the cooking time to about 15 minutes. Before cooking, cut a diagonal crisscross pattern onto the outside layer of fat of each rack.

◆ Lamb and merlot both have an inherent sweetness, making them classic companions.

Herbed Sausage and Feta Burger

1/2 cup fresh bread crumbs

1/3 cup half-and-half

8 ounces ground beef

8 ounces bulk pork sausage

1/2 cup minced fresh parsley

1/4 cup freshly grated Parmesan cheese

1 tablespoon minced fresh basil or 1 teaspoon dried basil

1 teaspoon minced fresh sage or 3/4 teaspoon dried sage

1 teaspoon minced garlic

1 teaspoon salt

1/2 teaspoon minced fresh rosemary or 1/4 teaspoon dried rosemary

1/4 teaspoon freshly ground black pepper

1 red bell pepper, cored, seeded, and cut into 8 rings (or use purchased roasted red peppers)

4 hamburger buns, Kaiser rolls, or other soft rolls

FETA CHIVE SPREAD

1/2 cup crumbled feta cheese

1/4 cup mayonnaise

2 tablespoons minced fresh chives

2 tablespoons milk, more if needed

1/2 teaspoon freshly ground black pepper

The sausage that is blended with the ground beef in these burgers adds a surprising burst of richness and moisture, while the herbs, garlic, and Parmesan add to the intriguing flavor.

Combine the bread crumbs and half-and-half in a large bowl and set aside to soak until all the liquid is absorbed, about 5 minutes. Add the ground beef, sausage, parsley, Parmesan, basil, sage, garlic, salt, rosemary, and pepper. Mix together gently but thoroughly to evenly blend all the ingredients. Shape the mixture into 4 patties about 1 inch thick; refrigerate until ready to cook.

For the feta chive spread, stir together the feta cheese, mayonnaise, chives, milk, and pepper in a small bowl.

Preheat an outdoor grill (to medium-high, if using a gas grill) and oil the grill grate, or preheat the broiler. Cook the burgers until cooked through and browned, 4 to 6 minutes per side. Grill or broil the red peppers alongside the burgers until tender, 5 to 7 minutes. Lightly toast the buns around the outer edge of the grill, away from direct flames, or under the broiler.

To serve, spread a thin layer of the feta chive spread (if it's too thick to easily spread, add another 1 to 2 teaspoons milk) on the toasted bun bottoms, top with the burgers and red peppers, and finish with another dollop of the feta chive spread. Add the top bun and serve.

Makes 4 servings

The craft of beer making has been practiced in the Northwest since the mid-1800s, but it took a new wave of brewers in the early 1980s to create a renewed interest in local brewing. Redhook Ale Brewery was a leader in this microbrewing movement, creating full-bodied ales with a freshness of flavor. The portfolio of Redhook beer styles includes ESB, IPA, Blonde, Blackhook and three seasonal varieties. Many Seattle neighborhoods boast numerous pubs that offer a great selection of local ales, plus tasty beer-friendly fare that makes for a perfect casual meal out.

Tuscan Veal Piccata

Classic veal piccata gets a bit of a twist with the addition of prosciutto. This recipe can be prepared with any thinly sliced meat such as turkey, pork, or chicken.

Put the flour in a shallow dish, dredge the veal in the flour, and pat to remove the excess.

Heat a large skillet over medium-high heat, add 1 tablespoon of the olive oil and 1 tablespoon of the butter, and swirl to coat the pan. When sizzling, add the veal to the pan in a single layer (do this in batches) and sauté until lightly browned, about 1 minute per side. Transfer the veal to a platter or individual plates and keep warm in a low oven. Repeat with the remaining veal cutlets, adding more butter and oil to the skillet with each batch.

Add the prosciutto and shallot to the skillet and sauté until tender and aromatic, scraping up remaining browned bits from the pan, about 30 seconds. Add the broth and wine and bring to a boil, then simmer to reduce the liquid to about ⅓ cup, about 3 minutes. Add the lemon juice and capers and reduce again to about ⅓ cup, about 3 minutes. Swirl in the remaining 3 tablespoons butter and parsley and stir until evenly blended and the sauce thickens slightly. Spoon the sauce over the veal and serve right away.

Makes 4 servings

◆ A blend of semillon and sauvignon blanc will play well against the sharpness of lemon and caper.

1/2	cup all-purpose flour
1	pound veal cutlets, pounded to 1/4-inch thick
2	tablespoons olive oil, more if needed
5	tablespoons unsalted butter, divided, more if needed
2	ounces prosciutto, julienned
1	tablespoon minced shallot
3/4	cup chicken broth
1/4	cup dry white wine
1/4	cup freshly squeezed lemon juice
2	tablespoons capers, drained and rinsed
3	tablespoons minced fresh parsley

BEER-MARINATED STEAKS WITH PEPPERCORN SAUCE

The beer marinade and peppercorn sauce are equally flavorful if used separately, but treating your favorite steak to both provides an amazing flavor impact. A tasty accompaniment for this showstopper entrée would be mashed potatoes embellished with a tablespoon or two of horseradish whisked in.

6 New York steaks or other steak

BEER MARINADE

1 bottle (12 ounces) full-bodied Northwest microbrew amber ale

1/2 cup packed light brown sugar

5 tablespoons freshly squeezed lime juice

2 tablespoons Worcestershire sauce

2 tablespoons whole-grain mustard

2 tablespoons olive oil

1 tablespoon minced garlic

1/2 teaspoon hot pepper sauce

PEPPERCORN SAUCE

1/2 cup dry white wine

2 tablespoons coarsely crushed peppercorns (preferably a 4-color blend, or use a scant 2 tablespoons of black peppercorns)

1 tablespoon minced shallot

1 can (14 ounces) chicken broth

1 can (14 ounces) beef broth

1/2 cup whipping cream

1 tablespoon unsalted butter

1 tablespoon all-purpose flour

For the marinade, whisk all ingredients together and pour into a glass baking dish or resealable plastic bag. Add the steaks and turn to coat them evenly. Cover the dish tightly, or securely seal the bag, and refrigerate overnight, turning occasionally.

For the sauce, combine the wine, peppercorns, and shallot in a medium saucepan and bring to a boil over medium-high heat. Reduce the heat to medium and simmer until the liquid has reduced by half, about 5 minutes. Add the chicken broth and beef broth and boil until reduced to about 2 cups, 25 to 30 minutes. Add the cream and simmer until the sauce begins to thicken further, about 10 minutes. Stir together the butter and flour in a small bowl to make a smooth paste. Add the butter mixture to the sauce, whisking constantly. Let the sauce simmer briefly until it thickens and coats the back of a spoon. The sauce can be made up to 2 hours ahead and reheated gently just before serving.

Preheat an outdoor grill (to medium-high if using a gas grill) or the broiler. Take the steaks from the marinade and discard the marinade. Grill the steaks about 4 minutes per side for medium-rare, or longer to suit your taste. While the steaks are grilling, gently reheat the peppercorn sauce over low heat. Transfer the steaks to a platter or individual plates. To serve, drizzle some of the sauce over the steaks and pass additional sauce at the table.

MAKES 6 SERVINGS

◆ For a casual dinner, a Northwest microbrew pilsner or ale works well, or open a robust red such as zinfandel. You could also offer a wine with a cabernet-merlot blend, as the peppercorns can stand up to the tannins in the cabernet while bringing out the fruit in the merlot.

Ten Minutes to Coleman Dock
MARSHALL JOHNSON

Many people live on the bucolic islands surrounding Seattle and commute daily on the ferry to jobs in the city. The population has swelled to over a million people in the Seattle metropolitan area now, but the quality of life remains high, thanks to a vibrant cultural environment, low crime, excellent sports opportunities, many universities, and of course, great food!

MARGARITAVILLE STEAK

2	flank steaks (about 1 1/2 pounds each), trimmed

MARINADE

2	teaspoons grated lime zest
1/2	cup freshly squeezed lime juice
1/2	cup chopped fresh cilantro
1/4	cup olive oil
1/4	cup soy sauce
1/4	cup tequila
1	tablespoon chopped garlic
2	teaspoons ground cumin
2	teaspoons dried oregano
	Freshly ground black pepper

This steak is just crying out for a margarita to be served alongside, though a Mojito (page 44) would be a great option as well! Grill up some assorted peppers and onions and serve with warmed flour tortillas, your favorite salsa, and guacamole for a new twist on fajitas. Any leftovers will make for a great steak sandwich the next day.

For the marinade, whisk all ingredients together. Use a small sharp knife or fork to pierce the meat all over. Pour the marinade into a large glass baking dish or 2 resealable plastic bags, and add the meat, turning to evenly coat the steaks. Cover the dish tightly, or securely seal the bags, and refrigerate at least 2 hours or overnight, turning occasionally.

Preheat an outdoor grill (to medium-high heat, if using a gas grill) and oil the grill grate, or preheat the broiler. Take the steak from the marinade, let the excess drip off, and discard the marinade. Grill or broil the steaks to medium-rare, about 4 minutes per side, or longer to suit your taste. Transfer the steaks to a cutting board and let stand 10 minutes tented with foil to keep warm. To serve, slice thinly on a diagonal across the grain.

MAKES 8 SERVINGS

Other cuts of meat, such as tri-tip steak or New York strip, could be used in place of the flank steak.

WINTER ROAST WITH PORTOBELLO MUSHROOMS AND CRANBERRY

This roast can be prepared up to 2 days in advance, making it a great do-ahead dish for a casual wintertime dinner party—or when you know the snow is about to begin falling! An ideal side dish would be Mount Rainier Chantilly Mashers (page 219).

Preheat the oven to 300°F. In a large roasting pan, combine the wine, broth, onion, ½ cup of the cranberry juice cocktail concentrate, rosemary, and garlic. Season the beef with salt and pepper and then place fat-side up in the roasting pan. Cover the pan tightly with aluminum foil and bake for 3½ hours, basting with pan juices every hour. (The roast can be prepared up to 2 days in advance to this point).

Take the beef from the liquid and slice it across the grain. Lay the slices in a large shallow roasting pan or baking dish. Use a slotted spoon to lift the onions from the liquid and put them on top of the meat. Strain the remaining braising liquid and reserve. Preheat the oven to 400°F.

Melt 3 tablespoons of the butter in a large skillet over medium-high heat, add the mushrooms, and sauté until tender, about 5 minutes, then add to the roasting pan with the beef, retaining the accumulated juices in the skillet. Add the remaining 2 tablespoons butter to the mushroom liquid in the skillet and bring to a simmer over medium heat. Whisk in the flour and cook until the mixture is smooth, 2 to 3 minutes. Whisk in the reserved beef braising liquid, ½ cup at a time, allowing the mixture to thicken before adding more. Continue to cook a few more minutes and add the remaining 3 tablespoons cranberry juice cocktail concentrate. Bring to a boil again, add the cranberries, and cook until they begin to plump, about 2 minutes. Season to taste with salt and pepper. Pour the sauce over the meat and the mushrooms, cover the pan with foil, and bake until hot and bubbly, 15 to 20 minutes, or up to 45 minutes if refrigerated. Remove the sliced beef and mushrooms to a platter, and spoon the sauce over it. Garnish with the parsley and serve.

MAKES 6 TO 8 SERVINGS

◆ A soft, earthy pinot noir is a perfect match for the melt-in-your-mouth brisket.

1	cup dry red wine
1	cup beef broth
1	large onion, sliced
½	cup plus 3 tablespoons cranberry juice cocktail concentrate, divided
2	tablespoons minced fresh rosemary
2	teaspoons minced garlic
2	tri-tip roasts (about 2 pounds each) or 1 flat-cut brisket (about 4 pounds)
	Salt and freshly ground black pepper
5	tablespoons unsalted butter, divided
3	large portobello mushrooms, stemmed, gills scraped, and cut into ¼-inch slices
¼	cup all-purpose flour
1½	cups dried cranberries
½	cup chopped fresh parsley

BEEF TENDERLOIN WITH SHIITAKE CREAM SAUCE

1 beef tenderloin roast (about 2 pounds), trimmed

Cilantro sprigs, for garnish (optional)

MARINADE

1/3 cup hoisin sauce

1/4 cup oyster sauce

2 tablespoons Finlandia vodka

2 tablespoons honey

1 tablespoon minced or grated ginger

1 teaspoon hot chili oil

SHIITAKE CREAM SAUCE

1 cup whipping cream

1/2 cup dry sherry

1 tablespoon soy sauce

1 tablespoon toasted sesame oil

1 teaspoon grated orange zest

1/4 teaspoon hot chili oil

1/4 cup unsalted butter

1 tablespoon minced or grated ginger

1 1/2 cups sliced, stemmed shiitake mushrooms

This rich, elegant dish is sure to be a crowd-pleaser; an ideal choice for impressing your boss or for any other special occasion.

For the marinade, whisk all ingredients together. Pour the marinade into a glass baking dish or resealable plastic bag, and add the meat, turning to evenly coat the roast. Cover the dish tightly, or securely seal the bag, and refrigerate at least 2 hours or overnight, turning occasionally.

Preheat the oven to 450°F. Take the meat from the marinade and put it on a rack in a roasting pan. Roast the beef until the internal temperature at the thickest part registers 130°F for medium-rare, about 25 minutes, or longer to suit your taste. When the meat is done, remove it from the oven and tent it with foil. The meat temperature will rise to 140 to 150°F while resting.

For the sauce, combine the cream, sherry, soy sauce, sesame oil, orange zest, and chili oil in a small bowl and set aside. Melt the butter in a large skillet over medium-high heat, add the ginger, and cook, stirring, until very fragrant but not browned, about 1 minute. Add the mushrooms and cook until they are tender, 2 to 3 minutes. Add the cream mixture and boil until the sauce begins to brown and thicken, about 4 minutes.

Slice the beef tenderloin into medallions about ½ inch thick. Spoon the mushroom sauce over and garnish with cilantro (if using).

MAKES 6 SERVINGS

◆ Pinot noir, with its affinity for both mushrooms and Asian spices, would be an elegant wine choice.

Summer Picking
Pierce Milholland

$\mathcal{A}$pples hold a special place in the heart of every Washingtonian. They are used in a multitude of recipes and even symbolize the biggest football game in the state — the annual "Apple Cup" match between rivals University of Washington and Washington State University. Apples are principally grown in the Yakima Valley and are enjoyed year-round.

Side Dishes

ASPARAGUS WITH SUN-DRIED TOMATO VINAIGRETTE

3	pounds asparagus, tough ends trimmed and stalks peeled if necessary
1/2	cup sun-dried tomatoes in oil, drained and finely chopped
2	tablespoons balsamic vinegar
2	tablespoons grated lemon zest, in long shreds, divided
1/4	cup finely chopped shallots
1/4	cup capers, rinsed, drained, and chopped
1/4	cup chopped fresh parsley
1/3	cup diced red bell pepper
1	tablespoon freshly squeezed lemon juice
1/2	cup olive oil, more if needed
	Salt and freshly ground black pepper

With its beautiful colors and zippy flavor, this is a perfect dish in a spring or summer buffet. It can be prepared in advance and served at room temperature. Use thick or thin asparagus, but it is best to use spears of equal size for even cooking.

Bring a large saucepan of salted water to a boil and prepare a large bowl of ice water. Add the asparagus and blanch until crisp-tender, 1 to 3 minutes, depending on the thickness of the spears. Drain and refresh immediately in ice water. Drain again and pat the asparagus dry on paper towels.

Combine the sun-dried tomatoes and balsamic vinegar in a small bowl. Mince about two-thirds of the grated lemon zest and reserve the rest for garnish. Add the minced lemon zest, shallots, capers, parsley, red pepper, and lemon juice to the tomatoes. Whisk in the olive oil to make an emulsion. Season the vinaigrette to taste with salt and pepper, adding a bit more olive oil, if desired.

Arrange the asparagus on a serving platter or individual plates, pour the vinaigrette over the spears, and garnish with the remaining lemon zest. Serve right away, at room temperature.

MAKES 8 TO 10 SERVINGS

ASPARAGUS

The Yakima Valley and Columbia Basin of Washington State produce a large amount of asparagus annually, second only to California in production value. Local asparagus season typically begins in April, locals relishing the first appearance of the vivid green spears, which means that spring is upon us. Though pencil-thin spears are considered more delicate and desirable, it is actually the fatter spears that tend to be more flavorful. To trim asparagus, bend the spear near the thicker stem end and the spear will naturally break at the point where the tough end gives way to tender spear. You can use a vegetable peeler to peel away the skin from the lower portion of the stalk, if you like.

SWEET AND SPICY GINGERED CARROTS

This same preparation could also be done with green beans, quartered Brussels sprouts, broccoli florets, or other vegetables. You may need to alter the cooking time according to the size and density of the vegetable used.

Melt the butter in a large, heavy skillet over medium heat. Add the ginger, curry, and garlic and sauté until aromatic, about 1 minute.

Stir in the broth and preserves. Add the carrots, cover the skillet (if you don't have a lid, use foil), and simmer until the carrots are crisp-tender and coated with sauce, about 6 to 8 minutes, stirring occasionally. Season to taste with salt and pepper, and stir in the cilantro just before serving.

MAKES 4 SERVINGS

3	tablespoons unsalted butter
1	teaspoon minced or grated ginger
3/4	teaspoon curry powder
1	clove garlic, minced
1/4	cup chicken broth
2	tablespoons apricot preserves
1	pound carrots, cut diagonally into 1/4-inch slices
	Salt and freshly ground black pepper
3	tablespoons chopped fresh cilantro

THREE PEA MEDLEY

If you're unable to find all 3 types of peas, the recipe will be equally tasty with just 1 or 2 kinds! Serve with the Beef Tenderloin with Shiitake Cream Sauce (page 198).

Stir the butter in a small bowl until creamy, then add the orange zest and sugar with salt to taste and stir until smooth. Wrap butter tightly in plastic wrap, and refrigerate until firm. (The orange butter can be made up to a day ahead.)

Bring a large pot of salted water to a boil and blanch each variety of pea separately until just tender, no longer than 3 or 4 minutes. Scoop the peas out and drain in a colander, then toss them together in a serving bowl. While the vegetables are still hot, add the orange butter and toss until the butter is melted and evenly coats the peas. Serve immediately.

MAKES 6 SERVINGS

2	tablespoons unsalted butter, at room temperature
1/2	teaspoon grated orange zest
	Pinch sugar
	Salt
5	ounces snow peas, strings removed
5	ounces sugar snap peas, stemmed and strings removed
3/4	cup shelled English peas or frozen petite peas

Recipe pictured on page 199

Corn Cakes Topped with Bacon and Goat Cheese

There's something really delicious about corn and bacon together; the melding of bacon's rich, smoky character is a tasty contrast to the sweetness of corn. Here, the two come together in a side dish of pan-fried corn cakes, embellished with tangy goat cheese and a good peppery bite from cayenne.

5	thick slices bacon, cut into 1/2-inch pieces
4	tablespoons vegetable oil, divided
1	package (10 ounces) frozen corn kernels, thawed
1	cup chopped onion
3/4	cup buttermilk
1	egg
5	ounces fresh goat cheese (such as Montrachet), crumbled, plus more for serving
1	cup yellow cornmeal
2	teaspoons baking powder
1	teaspoon salt
1/2	teaspoon baking soda
1/4	teaspoon cayenne pepper
1/4	cup thinly sliced green onions, for serving

Cook the bacon in a large skillet over medium heat until lightly browned and crisp. Scoop out onto paper towels to drain. Pour off all but 2 tablespoons of the drippings from the skillet. Add 1 tablespoon of the oil to the drippings and warm over medium heat. Add the corn and onion and sauté over medium heat until the onion is lightly browned. Set aside.

In a large bowl, whisk together the buttermilk and egg to blend, then whisk in the goat cheese. Add the cornmeal, baking powder, salt, baking soda, and cayenne and mix well. Stir in the corn-onion mixture. Heat 1 tablespoon of the oil in the same skillet over medium heat. Working in batches, drop the batter by scant ¼ cupfuls into the skillet. Cook until browned on the bottom, about 1 minute. Turn the corn cakes and cook until the other side is brown, about 1 minute longer. Transfer to a baking sheet and keep warm in a low oven while cooking the remaining cakes, adding more oil to the skillet as needed.

Arrange the corn cakes on a serving platter or individual plates. Top each with a generous ½ teaspoon goat cheese, sprinkle with the bacon and green onions, and serve.

Makes 6 servings

◆ Serve with a chilled Northwest microbrew such as Redhook Ale.

CRISP AND SPICY CORN ON THE COB

1/2   cup mayonnaise

2   tablespoons grated lime zest

2   tablespoons chopped fresh cilantro

    Juice of 1 lime

1   jalapeño chile, cored, seeded, and diced

1   teaspoon salt

1/4   teaspoon freshly ground black pepper

4   cups fresh sourdough bread crumbs

4   tablespoons unsalted butter, melted

6   ears tender sweet corn, husks and silk removed

This unique way to serve corn is great for a crowd—with tender sweet kernels coated in a zesty mayonnaise and topped off with crisp bread crumbs.

Preheat the oven to 375°F. In a small bowl, stir together the mayonnaise, lime zest, cilantro, lime juice, jalapeño, salt, and pepper. Spread the bread crumbs on a shallow rimmed platter. Drizzle the bread crumbs with the melted butter and toss to coat.

Generously brush an ear of corn with the mayonnaise mixture, roll it in the bread crumbs, and place it on a baking sheet lined with foil. Repeat with the remaining ears of corn. Bake until browned and crisp, about 30 minutes. Serve right away.

MAKES 6 SERVINGS

FIRECRACKER GREEN BEANS

1/2   cup walnut pieces

    Vegetable spray or 1 teaspoon vegetable oil

1/2   teaspoon cayenne pepper

3/4   pound slender green beans, stemmed and cut into 3-inch pieces

2   tablespoons soy sauce, regular or low sodium

1   tablespoon red wine vinegar

2   tablespoons vegetable oil

Delicious served right away, these green beans are also tasty cold, served as part of a picnic spread or summertime luncheon.

Put the walnuts in a small skillet and spray evenly with vegetable spray, or drizzle the vegetable oil over and toss gently to evenly coat the walnuts. Sprinkle the cayenne pepper over and toss again to evenly coat. Toast the walnuts over medium-low heat, stirring often, until the walnuts are lightly browned and aromatic, about 4 to 5 minutes. Set aside to cool.

Whisk together the soy sauce and vinegar in a large bowl, then whisk in the oil. Bring a large saucepan of salted water to a boil over high heat. Add the green beans to the boiling water and reduce the heat to medium, cooking until the beans are just crisp-tender and bright green, about 3 to 5 minutes. Drain well and add the beans to the soy mixture, tossing to evenly coat. Let the beans cool and toss the walnuts in just before serving.

MAKES 4 SERVINGS

LEMON ROASTED GREEN BEANS

Don't let your diners know about the anchovies—watch them try to discover the surprising source of the unique flavors!

Preheat the oven to 500°F. Put a large rimmed baking sheet in the oven to preheat at the same time. Toss the whole beans with the olive oil, thyme, and garlic in a large bowl. Spread the beans in a single layer on the hot baking sheet and bake for 2 minutes. Shake the pan to reposition the beans. Cook the beans until they begin to brown and just start to shrivel, another 5 to 7 minutes. Be careful not to overcook; you may want to remove smaller beans earlier, as they are done.

While the beans are cooking, mash the anchovies with a fork in a large bowl. Add the lemon zest and juice, and stir well. Take the beans from the oven and add them to the bowl, tossing them with the anchovy and lemon mixture. Season to taste with pepper. (Salt only if needed; anchovies are usually salty enough.) Serve the beans hot or at room temperature.

MAKES 4 SERVINGS

This recipe would also be delicious prepared with asparagus spears in place of the green beans.

1	pound green beans, stemmed
1/4	cup extra virgin olive oil
4	sprigs fresh thyme
2	cloves garlic, crushed
2	anchovy fillets, rinsed and dried, or 1/2 teaspoon anchovy paste
	Grated zest of 1 lemon
	Juice of 1/2 a lemon, or to taste
	Salt and freshly ground black pepper

EGGPLANT ENVELOPES

For this recipe, four lengthwise slices of eggplant are broiled until tender, then folded around a feta-tomato-basil filling. The outer slices with a good deal of skin will not be used here but can be saved for another recipe.

1 pound eggplant, stem end trimmed and cut lengthwise into 1/3-inch slices

2 teaspoons salt, more if needed

4 tablespoons olive oil, divided

   Freshly ground black pepper

2 plum (Roma) tomatoes, seeded and diced

3 tablespoons minced fresh parsley, divided

1/4 cup crumbled feta cheese

2 large fresh basil leaves, finely shredded

Preheat the broiler and set the rack about 3 inches below the element. Working with 4 inner eggplant slices, rub the salt onto both sides of each slice and let the eggplant drain in a colander for 10 minutes. Rinse the eggplant and pat dry with paper towels. Brush both sides of the eggplant slices with 3 tablespoons of the olive oil and set them on a baking sheet. Lightly pepper the top of each slice and broil the eggplant until golden and tender, about 6 to 8 minutes, turning the slices once.

While the eggplant is cooking, heat the remaining 1 tablespoon of olive oil in a small skillet over medium heat. Add the tomato and sauté until soft, about 4 minutes. Stir in 1½ tablespoons of the parsley; set aside.

When the eggplant is ready, set the baking sheet on a wire rack. Turn the eggplant slices over so the peppered side is facing up. Spread 1 tablespoon of feta cheese on each slice and top with the tomato mixture. Sprinkle the basil evenly over the tomato mixture. Then fold the eggplant slices in thirds (like folding a letter), beginning with the wider, base end, then folding the narrower, stem end over that. Sprinkle with the reserved parsley and serve right away.

MAKES 4 SERVINGS

Balsamic Roasted Walla Walla Onions

These tangy onions pair well with the Bing Cherry Chops (page 186).

Preheat the oven to 450°F. Oil a 9- by 13-inch baking dish, choosing a lidded dish if you have one. Cut each onion into 6 wedges (from top to root). Stir together the vinegar, olive oil, thyme, and basil in a large, wide bowl and season generously with salt and pepper. Add the onion wedges and toss gently to coat. Arrange the wedges, flat side down, in the baking dish. Pour the remaining liquid over the onions. Cover with the lid, or cover securely with foil, and bake the onions for 25 minutes. Take the dish from the oven, remove the lid, and baste the onions with a pastry brush. They will fan open slightly as you do this. Baste again so the vinegar mixture seeps in between the onion layers. Return the dish to the oven, and bake, uncovered, until the onions are tender, about 10 minutes longer.

Transfer the onions to a warm platter or individual plates and garnish with fresh herbs.

MAKES 6 SERVINGS

3	large Walla Walla sweet onions (about 3 pounds total), peeled with root ends intact
1/4	cup plus 2 tablespoons balsamic vinegar
1 1/2	tablespoons olive oil
2	teaspoons chopped fresh thyme or 1 teaspoon dried thyme
2	teaspoons chopped fresh basil or 1 teaspoon dried basil
	Salt and freshly ground black pepper
	Fresh basil and/or thyme sprigs, for garnish

Recipe pictured on page 187

Zucchini with Parmesan Crust

This is one way to get children to eat their vegetables.

Preheat the broiler. Melt the butter in a large ovenproof skillet over medium-low heat. Add the garlic and cook until aromatic, about 30 seconds. Put the zucchini halves cut side down in the skillet and season with salt and pepper. Increase the heat to medium-high, and sauté until the zucchini are just slightly tender when pierced with the tip of a knife.

Turn the zucchini over and sprinkle generously with the Parmesan cheese. Cook for 1 to 2 minutes longer, then broil until the cheese is melted and golden brown, about 2 to 3 minutes.

MAKES 4 SERVINGS

1	tablespoon unsalted butter
2	teaspoons minced garlic
4	small, slender zucchini (about 6 inches long), halved lengthwise
	Salt and freshly ground black pepper
1/2	cup freshly grated Parmesan cheese

BOUNTIFUL BAKED TOMATOES

Whole tomatoes make a striking presentation as an edible container for this vegetable side dish. The trick is in finely chopping the vegetables for the stuffing, so they cook quickly without overcooking the tomato.

Preheat the oven to 350°F. Lightly oil a baking dish just large enough to hold the tomatoes. Slice the top quarter from the stem end of each tomato. Trim and finely chop the tops; set aside. Scoop out the insides of the tomatoes and sprinkle the interior of each tomato shell with ¼ teaspoon of the salt. Set the tomatoes upside down on a few layers of paper towel to drain while preparing the stuffing.

Heat 2 tablespoons of the oil in a medium skillet over medium heat. Add the zucchini, onion, eggplant, green pepper, sugar, and reserved chopped tomato tops and cook until tender, about 5 minutes, stirring occasionally. Stir in the garlic and cook for 1 minute longer. Transfer to a medium bowl.

Wipe out the skillet and add the remaining tablespoon of oil. Add the bread crumbs and sauté over medium heat until golden brown, about 2 minutes. Add the toasted bread crumbs to the vegetables and toss to mix. Stir in 2 tablespoons of the parsley, basil, and vinegar with salt and pepper to taste.

Use a paper towel to soak up any liquid remaining in the tomato shells and fill them with the vegetable mixture. Bake until the tomatoes are tender and the stuffing is heated through, but the tomatoes are still firm enough to hold their shape, about 25 to 30 minutes. Take the tomatoes from the oven and sprinkle them with the remaining 1 tablespoon parsley to garnish. Serve right away, at room temperature or slightly chilled.

MAKES 4 SERVINGS

4	firm medium tomatoes (about 1 ⅓ pounds total)
1 3/4	teaspoons salt, divided
3	tablespoons olive oil, divided
1/2	cup finely chopped zucchini
1/3	cup finely chopped onion
1/3	cup finely chopped eggplant
2	tablespoons finely chopped green bell pepper
1/4	teaspoon sugar
1/2	teaspoon minced garlic
1	tablespoon fresh bread crumbs
3	tablespoons minced fresh parsley, divided
2	tablespoons minced fresh basil
1	teaspoon red wine vinegar
	Freshly ground black pepper

COUSCOUS CROWNS

1/4   cup dried currants

3/4   cup chicken broth

1   tablespoon unsalted butter

1/2   cup couscous

1/3   cup thinly sliced green onions, light and dark green parts only

1/4   cup shelled pistachios, toasted and finely chopped

1   tablespoon minced fresh parsley

    Salt and freshly ground black pepper

3   tablespoons olive oil

1 1/2   tablespoons freshly squeezed lemon juice

    Pinch cinnamon

Recipe pictured on page 190

This recipe is easily doubled or tripled for company. If you don't have small molds, this exotic side dish will be just as delicious simply spooned onto the plate.

In a small bowl, cover currants with hot water until plump, about 15 minutes. Then drain and set aside.

In a medium saucepan, combine the broth and the butter and bring to a boil. Stir in the couscous, cover and remove from heat. Let sit, covered, for 5 minutes. Fluff the couscous with a fork, breaking up any lumps. Stir in the currants, green onions, pistachios, and parsley and season to taste with salt and pepper. In a small bowl, whisk together the olive oil, lemon juice, and cinnamon, then toss with the couscous mixture.

Pack the couscous into two ¾-cup custard cups or interesting gelatin molds with the back of a spoon. Unmold the couscous onto individual plates—it easily pops right out and holds its shape. Serve immediately.

MAKES 2 SERVINGS

Sweet Grass Ranch
BARBARA VANDYKE SHUMAN

*F*armlands east of the Cascade Mountains are still of pioneer proportions — and need large amounts of water for the successful production of their crops. Fortunately, the Columbia River is a bountiful source of irrigation water, in addition to furnishing hydroelectric power from several dams along its span.

MIRACULOUS MICROWAVE RISOTTO

1 1/2   tablespoons olive oil

1   shallot, finely chopped

1   cup Arborio rice

1/3   cup dry white wine

3   cups chicken broth

1/2   cup crumbled blue cheese

2   tablespoons minced fresh parsley

    Salt and freshly ground
black pepper

This is a very versatile recipe with plenty of room for adaptation. Try stirring in a combination of dried cranberries and chopped pecans or sautéed mushrooms in place of the blue cheese. The tasty variations are endless!

Heat the olive oil in a large skillet over medium heat. Add the shallot and sauté until tender and aromatic, but not browned. Add the rice and stir to evenly coat with the oil and cook, stirring until the rice is golden, 1 to 2 minutes. Stir in the wine and simmer until it has been absorbed. Add the chicken broth and stir to loosen the rice from the bottom of the pan. Pour the mixture into a microwaveable 3-quart container and cover it.

Microwave at 80 percent power for 10 minutes. Stir the risotto and re-cover the dish. Cook for 10 minutes longer. Remove the dish from the microwave and keep the lid on for a minute or two. (Don't worry if your risotto looks slightly liquid. The rice will absorb the remaining chicken stock as it rests.) Stir in the blue cheese and parsley, season to taste with salt and pepper, and serve.

MAKES 4 TO 6 SERVINGS

ARBORIO RICE

Arborio rice is an Italian short-grain rice from the Piedmont region that has high levels of starch, much higher than that of regular long-grain rice. When Arborio is cooked in preparations such as risotto—its classic use—the starch is released in the gentle cooking and constant stirring, creating the distinctive silky-creamy texture of the finished dish. Carnaroli is another Italian variety of short-grain rice that also works well in risotto recipes.

SAFFRON BASMATI RICE

This pilaf is an ideal accompaniment to entrées with spicy Indian or Asian flavors.

Heat the oil in a medium saucepan over medium-high heat. Add the cinnamon stick, cardamom, and cloves. Sauté until the spices are aromatic, about 1 minute, then scoop them out with a slotted spoon and discard. Add the rice to the pan and cook, stirring, until the rice is evenly coated in oil and beginning to toast, 1 to 2 minutes. Add the water, sugar, salt, and saffron to the pan and bring to a boil over medium-high heat, then reduce the heat to medium-low and partially cover the pan. Simmer 10 minutes, then fully cover the pan, and cook until the water is fully absorbed, about 10 minutes more. Take the pan from the heat and let stand 5 minutes without removing lid. Fluff with a fork and stir in the pistachios just before serving.

MAKES 4 SERVINGS

1	tablespoon vegetable oil
1	cinnamon stick
5	green cardamom pods
5	whole cloves
1	cup white basmati rice
1 1/3	cups water
5 – 7	tablespoons sugar
1/2	teaspoon salt
	Pinch saffron
1/4	cup shelled pistachios, toasted

SHIITAKE PILAF

Put the mushrooms in a small bowl and cover with 1 cup boiling water to soften, about 20 minutes. Drain the mushrooms, reserving the soaking water and adding enough water so that you have a total of 3 cups liquid. Trim the stems from the mushrooms and thinly slice the caps; set the mushrooms and mushroom liquid aside.

Heat the oil in a medium saucepan over medium heat. Add the mushrooms and onion and cook until tender, about 5 minutes. Add the reserved mushroom liquid and bring to a boil. Stir in the wild rice, reduce the heat to low, and cook, covered, for 40 minutes.

Stir the long-grain rice into the wild rice. Cover the pan and cook until both rices are tender and all of the liquid has been absorbed, about 20 minutes longer. Take the pan from the heat and stir in the soy sauce. Spoon the pilaf onto individual plates, sprinkle with sesame seeds, and serve.

MAKES 6 TO 8 SERVINGS

1	ounce dried shiitake mushrooms
3/4	cup wild rice
1	tablespoon toasted sesame oil
1/2	cup finely chopped onion
3/4	cup long-grain rice
3	tablespoons soy sauce
2	tablespoons toasted sesame seeds, for garnish

Recipe pictured on page 178

CEDAR PLANKED VEGETABLES

Roasting is a nice alternative to steaming or boiling vegetables for dinner; the dry oven heat helps retain their natural moisture and flavor. Here the roasting is done on a cedar plank for added woody essence, a technique borrowed from Northwest natives.

Rub the top of the cedar plank with a little vegetable oil. Put the plank in a cold oven and preheat the oven to 350°F for about 15 minutes. Then, whisk together the olive oil, garlic, herbs, and vinegar with salt and pepper to taste in a large bowl. Add the zucchini, onion, bell pepper, squash, green beans, and carrot, and toss to coat them with the marinade. Spread the vegetables evenly onto the plank, and roast until tender, about 30 minutes.

MAKES 4 SERVINGS

1	large or 2 small cedar baking planks
1	tablespoon olive oil
2	cloves garlic, thinly sliced
1 – 2	tablespoons minced fresh herbs (basil, oregano, tarragon, thyme, parsley, and/or rosemary) or 1 1/2 teaspoons mixed dried herbs
1 1/2	tablespoons balsamic vinegar
	Salt and freshly ground black pepper
1	medium zucchini, cut into 1/2-inch slices
1	medium onion, peeled and quartered
1	red bell pepper, cored, seeded, and cut into 1-inch squares
1	medium yellow squash, cut into 1/2-inch slices
3	ounces green beans, cut into 1-inch lengths
1	medium carrot, cut into 1/4-inch slices

GOAT CHEESE AND THYME POTATO CAKE

Goat cheese that is a bit aged and firmer will be easier to grate, so it is the best choice for this recipe. If you can only find softer goat cheese, cut it into small pieces or finely crumble it.

1 1/2	pounds small red potatoes, scrubbed and cut into 1/4-inch slices
1/2	cup sour cream
6	tablespoons unsalted butter, at room temperature
1/2	cup grated goat cheese (about 4 ounces)
2	eggs
	Salt and freshly ground black pepper
1	teaspoon chopped fresh thyme

Preheat the oven to 375°F. Generously oil or butter a 9-inch square baking pan and line it with a 14- by 8-inch piece of parchment paper so that the ends of the paper hang out over the ends of the pan. Rub the bottom of the paper in the pan's oil or butter, then flip the paper over, greased side up.

Bring a large pan of salted water to a boil, add the potato slices, and cook until tender when pierced with the tip of a knife, about 8 minutes. Drain them in a colander and let cool for 15 minutes.

Whisk together the sour cream and butter in a large bowl until smooth. Whisk in the goat cheese and eggs. Add the potatoes, tossing gently, and then season to taste with salt and pepper. Transfer the mixture to the baking pan and use a spatula to smooth the top and spread the potatoes evenly. Sprinkle the top with thyme. Bake until the top is golden brown, about 35 minutes. Serve warm.

MAKES 6 SERVINGS

MOUNT RAINIER CHANTILLY MASHERS

Chantilly is a term for light and fluffy whipped cream, typically sweet, but here the whipped cream is flavored with Gruyère cheese before topping rich mashed potatoes.

Preheat the oven to 500°F. Peel and cube the potatoes and put them in a large pot of salted water with the garlic. Bring the water just to a boil over high heat, then lower the heat to medium and simmer until the potatoes are tender when pierced with the tip of a knife, about 20 to 25 minutes. Drain the potatoes well, then return them to the pot. Add the butter and milk and gently mash with a potato masher or a large, sturdy whisk until smooth and soft, adding a bit more milk if the potatoes are quite thick. Season to taste with salt and pepper. Spoon the mashed potatoes into a large, well-buttered baking dish, spread them out evenly, and sprinkle the herbs over; set aside.

Whip the cream with an electric mixer at high speed until soft peaks form. Fold in the Gruyère cheese and spoon the mixture over the mashed potatoes. Sprinkle the Parmesan cheese over the top and bake until the potatoes are heated through and the topping is golden brown, about 10 minutes.

MAKES 6 SERVINGS

The potatoes can be boiled and mashed, spread in the gratin dish and refrigerated (covered with foil) for up to a day before serving. Warm the potatoes in the oven while chopping the herbs and preparing the whipped cream, then proceed as directed.

6	russet potatoes (about 3 pounds total)
1	clove garlic, quartered
1/4	cup unsalted butter, at room temperature
3/4	cup milk, warmed, more if needed
	Salt and freshly ground black pepper
1	tablespoon minced fresh herbs (such as chives, sage, rosemary, and/or parsley)
3/4	cup whipping cream, well chilled
1	cup grated Gruyère cheese, chopped to form short strands
3	tablespoons freshly grated Parmesan cheese

Quartermaster Docks
TED KUTSCHER

Boats are such a passion in the Pacific Northwest that this area holds the distinction of having the highest per capita number of boat owners in the nation. From Puget Sound to the many lakes and rivers in this region, boating is the perfect way to enjoy the tranquil, salmon-laden waters. Meals are frequently enjoyed while afloat, and depending on whether there is a galley aboard, the offerings can vary from high cuisine to simply drinks and dessert.

Desserts

CHOCOHOLIC'S MACAROONS

3   cups semisweet chocolate chips

4   egg whites

1   cup sugar

2   teaspoons instant espresso powder
dissolved in 2 teaspoons hot water

1   teaspoon vanilla extract

1/2   teaspoon salt

3   cups sweetened shredded coconut

Preheat the oven to 325°F. Line a baking sheet with parchment paper. Melt the chocolate chips in a medium heatproof bowl set over a saucepan of barely simmering water, stirring occasionally, until just melted and smooth. Set aside to cool. Beat the egg whites with an electric mixer at medium-high speed until foamy. Gradually add the sugar, dissolved espresso powder, vanilla, and salt and beat until well blended. Fold the melted chocolate into the egg white mixture, then fold in the coconut.

Drop the batter in 2-inch mounds onto the baking sheet, allowing at least 2 inches between the cookies. Bake the macaroons until set, 20 to 25 minutes. Let the cookies cool on the baking sheet for 5 minutes, then transfer them to a wire rack to cool.

MAKES ABOUT 30 MACAROONS

LEMON BOUTIQUE COOKIES

1   cup unsalted butter,
at room temperature

2   cups granulated sugar, divided

1   egg yolk

1   tablespoon grated lemon zest

1   teaspoon lemon extract

1/4   teaspoon salt

2 1/2   cups all-purpose flour

2   cups powdered sugar

Recipe pictured on page 227

Preheat the oven to 375°F. Lightly grease 2 baking sheets or line them with parchment paper. Cream the butter and ½ cup of the granulated sugar with an electric mixer at medium speed until light and fluffy. Add the egg yolk, lemon zest, lemon extract, and salt, and beat until evenly blended. Gradually add the flour, and continue mixing just until well combined.

Fill a small bowl with water and another with the remaining 1½ cups granulated sugar. Roll the dough into 1-inch balls. Dip each ball into the water and then roll in the granulated sugar. Set the balls about 2 inches apart on the prepared baking sheets. Use the bottom of a glass to slightly flatten each ball to about ½ inch thick.

Bake the cookies about 11 to 13 minutes. Put the powdered sugar in a shallow bowl. Take the cookies from the oven, then roll each cookie in the powdered sugar while still warm. Let the cookies cool on a wire rack. When they are completely cool, roll them in the powdered sugar again before serving.

MAKES ABOUT 30 COOKIES

Hazelnut Butter Cookies

The delicious simplicity of a fresh-baked butter cookie is embellished here with the addition of hazelnuts and a dip in chocolate.

Sift the flour and salt into a medium bowl; set aside. In another bowl, cream together the butter and brown sugar with an electric mixer at medium speed until light and fluffy. Beat in the egg yolks and Frangelico or vanilla, scraping down the sides of the bowl. Add the flour mixture and beat gently just until well blended. Stir in ¾ cup of the hazelnuts by hand until evenly blended. (This dough is quite stiff; you may need to blend the dough by hand with a large wooden spoon if you don't have a large stand mixer to do the job.)

Turn the dough out onto a lightly floured work surface. Divide the dough in half and roll each half into a log 8 inches long and 1½ inches wide. Wrap each log in waxed paper and freeze until firm, about 30 minutes.

Preheat the oven to 350°F. Unwrap the dough logs and cut into ⅓-inch slices. Put the slices 1 inch apart on 2 ungreased baking sheets. Bake until the cookies are light golden around the edges, about 15 minutes. Transfer the cookies to a wire rack to cool.

Melt the chocolate chips and shortening in a heatproof bowl set over a pan of barely simmering water, stirring until smooth. Dip ½ of a cookie into the chocolate, set it on a piece of parchment paper or waxed paper and immediately sprinkle it with a bit of the remaining hazelnuts. Repeat with the remaining cookies. Let the chocolate completely set on the cookies before serving or storing them in an airtight container.

Makes 48 cookies

2	cups all-purpose flour
½	teaspoon salt
1	cup unsalted butter, at room temperature
½	cup plus 2 tablespoons packed light brown sugar
2	egg yolks
1	teaspoon Frangelico or vanilla extract
1¼	cups toasted chopped hazelnuts, divided
2	cups semisweet chocolate chips
1	tablespoon shortening

Nanaimo Bars

1/2	cup unsalted butter, cut into small pieces
1/3	cup unsweetened cocoa powder
1/4	cup sugar
1	egg, beaten
1	teaspoon vanilla extract
2	cups graham cracker crumbs
1	cup sweetened shredded coconut
1/2	cup finely chopped walnuts

FILLING

3	ounces white chocolate, finely chopped
1/4	cup unsalted butter, cut into small pieces
2	tablespoons cornstarch
2	tablespoons milk
2	egg yolks
	Pinch salt
1	teaspoon vanilla extract
2	cups powdered sugar, sifted if lumpy

GLAZE

2	ounces unsweetened chocolate, chopped
1	tablespoon unsalted butter

These sweet, dense bars are a classic favorite, great for holiday sharing or serving on a buffet table. They can be made up to 3 days in advance and refrigerated, or frozen for 2 weeks (if frozen, thaw slowly in the refrigerator before serving).

Lightly grease an 8- or 9-inch square pan.

Combine the butter, cocoa powder, sugar, egg, and vanilla in a medium saucepan over low heat. Cook, stirring constantly, until it begins to thicken, about 5 minutes. Take the pan from the heat and stir in the graham cracker crumbs, coconut, and walnuts, using your hands if the mixture is too thick to stir with a spoon. Pat the crust mixture into the prepared pan and refrigerate until firm.

For the filling, melt the white chocolate and butter together in a heatproof bowl set over a pan of barely simmering water, stirring until smooth. Combine the cornstarch, milk, egg yolks, and salt in a small bowl and whisk to mix. Add the cornstarch mixture to the white chocolate mixture and cook over the simmering water until steaming, about 5 minutes, whisking often. Whisk in the vanilla, then whisk in the powdered sugar until smooth (the mixture will be thick). Pour the filling over the chilled crust and smooth the top, working quickly. Refrigerate until firm.

For the glaze, melt the chocolate and butter together in a heatproof bowl set over a pan of barely simmering water, stirring until smooth. Working quickly, pour the glaze over the filling, tilting the pan and spreading the chocolate to evenly cover. Score into 24 bars and refrigerate until the glaze is firmly set, about 1 hour, then cut into bars along the score marks for serving.

MAKES 24 BARS

HEAVENLY CRANBERRY BARS

There's a festive, wintry quality to these delicious bar cookies, the snowy white frosting contrasted by red bits of dried cranberry and the distinctive aroma of orange zest.

Preheat the oven to 350°F. Lightly butter an 11- by 15-inch jelly roll pan or rimmed baking sheet. Whisk together the brown sugar, butter, eggs, and vanilla in a large bowl until smooth. Whisk in the flour, baking powder, and salt until well blended, then stir in the white chocolate chips, cranberries, pecans, and orange zest. Spread the mixture evenly in the prepared pan (it will be quite stiff) and bake until golden brown, about 20 to 22 minutes. Set aside on a wire rack to cool.

For the frosting, cream together the cream cheese, powdered sugar, butter, 1 tablespoon of the orange zest, and vanilla with an electric mixer at medium speed until smooth and fluffy. Spread the mixture over the cooled base. Stir together the remaining 2 tablespoons orange zest with the dried cranberries in a small bowl and sprinkle the mixture over the frosting. Melt the white chocolate in a small heatproof bowl set over a pan of simmering water, stirring until smooth. Drizzle the white chocolate over the bars and let sit until the chocolate is set. Cut the bars into 3-inch squares and then diagonally into triangles.

MAKES 48 BARS

These bars can be baked in a buttered 9- by 13-inch baking dish, increasing the baking time to about 30 minutes.

For **Heavenly Toffee Bars,** *omit the dried cranberries, orange zest, and frosting. Decrease the white chocolate chips to 1 cup. Into the batter, stir 5 chocolate-covered English toffee bars (1.4 ounces each), coarsely chopped, and ½ cup chocolate chips along with the pecans.*

1 1/2	cups packed light brown sugar
1	cup unsalted butter, melted and cooled
2	eggs
2	teaspoons vanilla extract
2 1/4	cups all-purpose flour
1	teaspoon baking powder
1	teaspoon salt
1 3/4	cups white chocolate chips
1 1/2	cups dried cranberries, coarsely chopped
1	cup toasted chopped pecans
1/4	cup grated orange zest

WHITE CHOCOLATE FROSTING

8	ounces cream cheese, at room temperature
1	cup powdered sugar
1/2	cup unsalted butter, at room temperature
3	tablespoons grated orange zest, divided
2	teaspoons vanilla extract
1/3	cup dried cranberries, coarsely chopped
6	ounces high quality white chocolate, coarsely chopped

Recipe pictured on page 227

TRIPLE CHOCOLATE BISCOTTI

3/4 cup sugar

1/2 cup unsalted butter,
at room temperature

2 eggs

2 tablespoons amaretto, Frangelico,
Kahlúa, or double-strength coffee

2 cups plus 2 tablespoons
all-purpose flour

1/3 cup unsweetened cocoa powder

1 1/2 teaspoons baking powder

1/4 teaspoon salt

2/3 cup milk chocolate chips

2/3 cup toasted hazelnuts

4 ounces high quality white
chocolate, chopped

Biscotti are always a treat. With chocoholics in mind, our dark chocolate dough is dotted with milk chocolate chips and finished with melted white chocolate.

Preheat the oven to 325°F. Grease and flour a large baking sheet. Cream together the sugar and butter with an electric mixer at medium speed until light and fluffy. Beat in the eggs, 1 at a time, followed by the liqueur or coffee, and beat until smooth. Combine the flour, cocoa powder, baking powder, and salt in a medium bowl and stir to mix. Add the dry ingredients to the creamed mixture and beat at low speed just until blended. Using a wooden spoon, stir in the chocolate chips and hazelnuts.

Divide the dough in half and form the dough into 2 logs that are 14 inches long, 1/2 inch high and 1 1/2 inches wide. Arrange the logs on the baking sheet and bake until lightly browned and set, about 25 minutes. Set the baking sheet on a wire rack to cool; leave the oven on. Cut the logs with a serrated knife into 1/2-inch slices on a 45° angle. Lay the slices cut-side up on the baking sheet and return them to the oven to dry slightly, about 10 to 12 minutes. Dryness is a personal preference, so the crunchier you like biscotti, the longer they need to bake. Transfer the biscotti to a wire rack to cool.

Melt the white chocolate in a small heatproof bowl set over a saucepan of barely simmering water. Stir occasionally, until melted and smooth, then use a small spatula to spread the chocolate over 1 full side of each biscotti. Let them cool until the chocolate is set before serving.

MAKES 3½ TO 4 DOZEN BISCOTTI

CHERRY SORBET

1   pound pitted dark sweet cherries,
     fresh or frozen

1 1/2 cups water

1   cup ruby port

1/2 cup sugar

Though this sorbet will be its very best with summer's fresh cherries, frozen cherries are a great off-season alternative.

Combine the cherries, water, port, and sugar in a large saucepan and bring to a boil over high heat. Lower the heat to medium and simmer until the cherries are soft, about 15 minutes. Purée the mixture in batches in a blender until smooth, then strain through a sieve to remove bits of cherry skin. Refrigerate the purée until thoroughly chilled, at least 2 hours. When chilled, pour the mixture into an ice cream maker and freeze according to the manufacturer's instructions. Transfer the sorbet to an airtight container and freeze until set, at least 2 hours.

MAKES 1½ PINTS

TOFFEE COFFEE SUNDAES

1/3   cup plus 2 tablespoons water, divided

4   teaspoons instant espresso powder

1 1/3 cups sugar

2/3   cup whipping cream

3   tablespoons unsalted butter,
      cut into small pieces

      Pinch salt

1   pint vanilla ice cream

1   pint coffee ice cream

1 1/2 cups coarsely chopped or crushed
      English toffee bars or Almond Roca

This caramel sauce features an extra kick of flavor from espresso.

Stir together 2 tablespoons of the water and the espresso powder in a small dish until dissolved; set aside. Combine the remaining ⅓ cup water and sugar in a heavy medium saucepan. Stir over medium heat until the sugar dissolves, about 5 minutes. Increase the heat to high and boil without stirring until the syrup turns a deep amber color, watching carefully and occasionally washing down the sides of the pan with a wet pastry brush to wash the sugar crystals into the syrup, about 8 minutes. Take the pan from the heat and slowly add the cream, espresso, butter, and salt, stirring gently (the mixture will boil vigorously when the liquid is added). Return the pan to medium heat and stir until the caramel dissolves and the sauce is smooth, about 2 minutes. Let the sauce cool until slightly thickened.

Scoop the ice creams into individual bowls, spoon the sauce over, and top with the toffee pieces.

MAKES 6 SERVINGS

POACHED PEARS WITH CONFETTI FRUIT SALAD AND STRAWBERRY COULIS

Choose whichever pears are at their best—ripe and aromatic—and with a nice shape that will look attractive on the plate.

Combine the water, sugar, lemon juice, cloves, and cinnamon stick in a large saucepan and bring to a boil over medium-high heat, stirring occasionally to help the sugar dissolve. While the water is heating, peel the pears, leaving the stems intact. When the water comes to a boil, add the pears, reduce the heat to medium, cover the pan, and simmer until the pears are tender when pierced with the tip of a knife, about 30 minutes. Lift out the pears with a slotted spoon and set aside to cool, reserving ¼ cup of the poaching liquid.

Purée the strawberries in a food processor or blender until smooth and transfer to a small bowl. Stir in the reserved poaching liquid, cover with plastic, and refrigerate until ready to serve. Toss together the mixed fruit and mint in a medium bowl.

When ready to serve, cut the pears in half horizontally and remove the core. Spoon the strawberry coulis onto individual plates, swirling so it evenly coats the bottom of the plate. Set the pears in the center, fill the pears with the fruit salad, and garnish each plate with a mint leaf.

MAKES 8 SERVINGS

2	quarts water
1¼	cups sugar
3	tablespoons freshly squeezed lemon juice
12	whole cloves
1	piece cinnamon stick (about 3 inches long)
8	ripe but firm pears
2	cups strawberries, stemmed
2	cups ¼-inch diced mixed fruit (such as orange, pineapple, apple, kiwi, papaya, and/or fresh berries)
6	mint leaves, minced, plus 8 whole leaves for garnish

SPICED OATMEAL SHORTCAKES WITH SUMMER FRUIT

Strawberry shortcake is a classic American favorite. This new twist uses nectarines and berries spooned onto shortcakes that have extra texture from oats and added flavor from warm aromatic spices.

Preheat the oven to 425°F. Lightly grease a large baking sheet or line it with parchment paper. Stir together the all-purpose flour, whole-wheat pastry flour, oats, brown sugar, baking powder, salt, cinnamon, allspice, and cardamom in a large bowl. Use a pastry blender or your fingertips to cut the butter into the dry ingredients until the mixture resembles coarse meal. Combine the milk and vanilla in a small bowl and add this to the dry ingredients, stirring with a wooden spoon just until the dough comes together. Do not overmix or the dough will be tough. Cut the dough into 6 even pieces and form them into rounds about 3 inches in diameter and ½ inch thick. Put the biscuits on the baking sheet, about 2 to 3 inches apart, and sprinkle with the granulated sugar. Bake until firm to the touch and golden brown, about 15 to 20 minutes. Transfer the shortcakes to a wire rack to cool.

For the filling, combine the nectarines and berries, brown sugar, lemon juice, and cinnamon in a large bowl and gently toss to mix. Let the mixture sit until juices begin to form, about 30 minutes. Whip the cream, powdered sugar, and vanilla with an electric mixer at medium-high speed until it holds soft peaks; refrigerate until ready to serve.

To serve, halve the shortcakes crosswise with a serrated knife and put the bottom half of each on a dessert plate. Spoon the fruit and collected juices over the shortcakes, top with the Mixed Berry Sauce followed by the whipped cream. Add the top half of each shortcake and serve right away.

MAKES 6 SERVINGS

◆ Opt for a late-harvest gewürztraminer or riesling wine with this dish.

1 1/2	cups all-purpose flour
1/2	cup whole-wheat pastry flour
1/2	cup rolled oats
1/2	cup packed light brown sugar
1	tablespoon baking powder
1/2	teaspoon salt
1/4	teaspoon ground cinnamon
1/4	teaspoon ground allspice
1/4	teaspoon ground cardamom
1/2	cup unsalted butter, cut into small pieces and refrigerated
2/3	cup milk
1/2	teaspoon vanilla extract
2	tablespoons granulated sugar

FILLING

1	pound nectarines, pitted and sliced
1	cup blueberries
1	cup blackberries or raspberries
1/3	cup packed light brown sugar
2	tablespoons freshly squeezed lemon juice
1/2	teaspoon ground cinnamon

Mixed Berry Sauce, recipe on page 232

TOPPING

1	cup whipping cream
2	tablespoons powdered sugar
1/2	teaspoon vanilla extract

MIXED BERRY SAUCE

4 cups mixed fresh berries (blackberries, raspberries, blueberries, and/or loganberries) or 12 ounces frozen berries, thawed

2 tablespoons freshly squeezed lemon juice or water

1/4 cup powdered sugar, or to taste

2 tablespoons crème de cassis or berry liqueur

Berries are the quintessential Northwest treat. This sauce is delightful served atop a small scoop of vanilla ice cream or lemon sorbet.

Combine the berries and lemon juice or water in a medium saucepan over medium heat. Cook, stirring occasionally, until the berries fall apart, about 10 minutes. Pass the mixture through a sieve, pressing with the back of a spoon to extract all the fruit purée while removing the seeds. Stir in enough powdered sugar to sweeten the sauce to taste. Set aside to cool, then stir in the liqueur.

MAKES 2 CUPS

FROZEN CAPPUCCINOS

1 cup strong brewed coffee, at room temperature

1 cup ice cubes

2 tablespoons half-and-half or milk

2 tablespoons sugar

1/4 teaspoon cinnamon

Blend the coffee, ice, half-and-half or milk, and sugar in a blender until smooth and thick. Pour into glasses and sprinkle with the cinnamon.

MAKES 2 SERVINGS

NECTARINE AND BERRY COBBLER

Who doesn't love fruit cobbler, one of the best ways to showcase fresh seasonal fruit? Here it's a blend of nectarines with blueberries and raspberries, though you could alter the filling to suit your taste and what's in season, using peaches, plums, blackberries, and/or other soft fruits instead.

Preheat the oven to 400°F. Lightly butter an attractive 2-quart baking dish.

Toss together the nectarines, blueberries, raspberries, sugar, cornstarch, and almond extract in a large bowl. Transfer the fruit mixture to the baking dish and bake until the filling is hot and begins to bubble, about 25 minutes.

While the fruit is baking, make the topping. Stir together the flour, ¼ cup of the sugar, the baking powder, baking soda, and salt in a large bowl until evenly mixed. Add the butter and rub it in with your fingertips until the mixture resembles coarse meal. Slowly add the buttermilk, stirring constantly, and mix just until the dough comes together.

Take the fruit from the oven, set the dish on a wire rack, and reduce the oven temperature to 375°F. Drop the topping by spoonfuls onto the baked fruit and sprinkle with the remaining 1 tablespoon sugar. Bake the cobbler until the topping is golden brown and a toothpick inserted in the center comes out clean, about 20 minutes. Set the cobbler on a wire rack to cool for 15 minutes. Serve warm with whipped cream or ice cream.

MAKES 6 SERVINGS

You could also bake the cobbler in individual dishes, about 6 ounces each. To make it easier to transfer them in and out of the oven, set the individual dishes on a baking sheet for baking.

1	pound nectarines, pitted, quartered, and cut into ½-inch pieces
1½	cups fresh blueberries
1½	cups fresh raspberries
3/4	cup sugar
2	tablespoons cornstarch
½	teaspoon almond extract
	Whipped cream or vanilla ice cream, for serving

TOPPING

1¼	cups all-purpose flour
¼	cup plus 1 tablespoon sugar, divided
3/4	teaspoon baking powder
3/4	teaspoon baking soda
¼	teaspoon salt
¼	cup unsalted butter, cut into ½-inch pieces and refrigerated
3/4	cup buttermilk

RHUBARB CUSTARD MERINGUE DESSERT

1 1/2   cups sugar

1/2   cup whipping cream

3   eggs, separated

2   tablespoons all-purpose flour

1/2   teaspoon ground cinnamon

1/2   teaspoon vanilla extract

    Pinch salt

2 1/2   cups 1/4-inch diced rhubarb (about 5 stalks)

CRUST

1   cup all-purpose flour

1   tablespoon sugar

1/2   teaspoon salt

1/2   cup unsalted butter, cut into small pieces and refrigerated

MERINGUE

1/3   cup water

1   tablespoon cornstarch

1   egg white

1/2   teaspoon vanilla extract

1/4   teaspoon cream of tartar

1/2   cup sugar

Rhubarb is always a welcome sight in stores, meaning that spring is in the air and winter is waning. Just the right time to think about a showy treat for a Mother's Day dinner or perhaps a graduation party.

Preheat the oven to 350°. Lightly butter a 9-inch square baking pan.

For the crust, combine the flour, sugar, and salt in a food processor and pulse once or twice to blend. Add the cold butter pieces and pulse until they are the size of small peas. Pat the dough into the prepared pan and bake until lightly browned, about 15 minutes.

For the custard filling, whisk together the sugar, cream, egg yolks, flour, cinnamon, vanilla, and salt in a medium bowl. When the crust is ready, take it from the oven and immediately sprinkle the rhubarb evenly over it. Pour the custard filling over the rhubarb and return the pan to the oven. Bake until the custard is set (a knife inserted in the center will come out clean), about 50 to 60 minutes. Start making the meringue 10 minutes before the rhubarb comes out of the oven so that you can spread it on while the rhubarb is still hot.

For the meringue, combine the water and cornstarch in a small saucepan over medium heat and bring to a simmer, whisking constantly. When the mixture comes to a low boil, thickens, and turns translucent, take the pan from the heat and set aside to cool. Beat the 4 egg whites and vanilla with an electric mixer at medium-high speed until frothy. Mix the cream of tartar into the sugar. With the mixer running, add the sugar mixture to the egg whites a spoonful at a time, until all the sugar is incorporated and the whites are glossy and form soft peaks. Add the cooled cornstarch mixture a spoonful at a time and continue to beat until the meringue forms stiff peaks.

Spread the meringue over the hot custard. Be sure the meringue goes all the way to the edges of the pan to completely cover the custard layer. Use the back of a spoon or a rubber scraper to create peaks or swirl designs in the meringue. Return the pan to the oven and bake until the meringue is golden brown, about 15 to 20 minutes.

MAKES 9 SERVINGS

BRIMMING BAKED PEACHES

This is a delightful combination of fresh summertime fruit with the richness of nutty cookies—a delicious way to cap off a casual meal. Amaretti cookies are imported from Italy, often wrapped in colorful paper. Look for them in gourmet shops or well-stocked grocery stores.

Preheat the oven to 325°. Lightly butter a baking dish into which the peach halves will fit snugly.

Scoop some flesh from each peach half, leaving about a ¼-inch shell. Put the flesh in a large bowl and mash it. Stir in the crushed macaroons and amaretti, then stir in the egg followed by the marsala or amaretto.

Set the peach halves in the baking dish and spoon the peach filling into the shells. Bake the stuffed peaches until the filling is firm, about 45 to 50 minutes.

While the peaches are baking, whip the cream to soft peaks. Refrigerate until ready to serve.

Take the peaches from the oven, drizzle the tops with melted butter, and let sit a few minutes before serving. To serve, arrange 2 peach halves on each plate and top with a dollop of whipped cream.

MAKES 6 SERVINGS

◆ The musky fruit flavors in a semi-sparkling muscat complement the peach, while the fizz makes it festive.

6	medium peaches, halved and pitted
1/2	cup crushed plain coconut macaroons (about 4)
1/2	cup crushed amaretti cookies (about 12)
1	egg, lightly beaten
1/2	cup marsala wine or amaretto liqueur
1	cup whipping cream
2	tablespoons unsalted butter, melted

Patriotic Mascarpone Pavlovas

1½ cups small strawberries, stemmed and quartered

3 cups assorted berries (such as raspberries, blueberries, and blackberries)

2 tablespoons orange marmalade

2 tablespoons Whidbey's liqueur, Chambord, or crème de cassis

1 cup mascarpone cheese

⅓ cup well-chilled whipping cream

¼ cup sugar

MERINGUES

4 egg whites, at room temperature for 30 minutes

¼ teaspoon cream of tartar

1 cup sugar

2 teaspoons cornstarch

1 teaspoon vanilla

Mint leaves, for garnish (optional)

These meringues can be made a day ahead and stored between layers of waxed paper in an airtight container. The berry mixture and mascarpone cream can be made up to 2 hours ahead, but the pavlovas should be assembled just before serving. Dry days are best for cooking meringues, as damp days make it harder to fully dry out the meringue to delicious crispness. On a rainy day, you could fill individual tart shells with the berry mixture and top with the mascarpone cream.

Preheat the oven to 200°F. Line 2 large baking sheets with foil or parchment paper.

For the meringues, whip the egg whites and cream of tartar with an electric mixer at medium-high speed to soft peaks. With the mixer running, add 1 cup of the sugar, a tablespoon at a time, and continue beating until stiff and glossy. Add the cornstarch and vanilla and beat 1 minute longer. Spoon the meringue into a pastry bag fitted with a ½-inch plain tip. Pipe a 2½-inch diameter ring or heart shape on a baking sheet lined with foil or parchment paper, and then pipe another on top of the first to form a 2-level rim. Pipe more meringue inside the shape to make a thin, solid base. Repeat, forming 6 meringue shells total. Bake the meringues for 1½ hours (they will not color), then turn off the oven and leave the meringues in the closed oven for 1½ hours longer.

Toss all the berries in a large bowl. Combine the marmalade and liqueur in a small saucepan over medium heat and simmer until the mixture has reduced by about one quarter. Let cool, then pour the mixture over the berries and toss together gently with a rubber spatula to evenly coat the berries.

Just before serving, beat together the mascarpone cheese, cream, and sugar with an electric mixer at medium-high speed until the mixture holds stiff peaks. Spoon the cream into the cooled meringue shells and spread it evenly. Mound the berries decoratively on top, with a drizzle of the berry juices as well. Garnish with the mint leaves and serve.

MAKES 6 SERVINGS

CHAMPAGNE WITH A ROSEMARY BLACKBERRY SWIZZLE

Spear a fresh blackberry on a 2-inch sprig of fresh rosemary, from which you have stripped about 3/4 inch of the leaves from the lower end. Add to a flute of your favorite Champagne or sparkling wine. This combination is just subtle enough to complement the very best Champagne. This is also a great way to dress up a goblet of sparkling water or lemonade.

Our Father
SHERRY MARKOVITZ

T his piece from the Northwest Art Collection of the Junior League of Seattle is particularly intriguing to children because of the image and the use of paints and sequins on the canvas. Our trained docents bring the collection to schools to show how flora and fauna from our area can inspire art in many forms.

CHERRY ALMOND TART

Using prepared puff pastry instead of a homemade crust makes this rich, delicious tart a snap to make.

On a lightly floured surface, roll out the puff pastry sheet to about ⅛ inch thick. Cut an 11-inch circle from the dough and use it to line a 9-inch removable base tart pan. Chill the tart shell in the refrigerator for about 30 minutes.

Grind the toasted almonds to a fine powder in a food processor. Be careful not to overwork the almonds or they may turn to a paste. Add the butter, 5 tablespoons of the sugar, the egg, almond extract, and pulse until evenly blended.

Preheat the oven to 425°F. Remove the crust from the refrigerator and prick the base several times with a fork. Spread the almond mixture over the crust and refrigerate for 15 minutes longer.

Scatter the cherries evenly over the almond layer and bake for 15 minutes. Sprinkle the remaining 1 tablespoon sugar over the tart and continue baking until golden brown, about 5 to 10 minutes. Let the tart cool on a wire rack for at least 10 minutes, then remove the sides from the tart pan and serve warm or at room temperature.

MAKES 8 SERVINGS

1	sheet frozen puff pastry, thawed
3/4	cup toasted blanched almonds
4	tablespoons unsalted butter, at room temperature
6	tablespoons sugar, divided
1	egg
1/2	teaspoon almond extract
1	pound pitted dark sweet cherries, fresh or frozen

CHERRIES

Washington State is the country's premier region for sweet cherries, which are grown primarily in the eastern part of the state. Many different varieties of cherries are available in the Northwest, the most prized among them Bing and Rainier. The Bing cherry is a large, deeply colored, very juicy cherry as much eaten fresh by the handful as cooked in summertime recipes. The Rainier cherry — named for the glorious mountain that dominates the Puget Sound-area skyline — has pale flesh with yellow skin that has a pink blush. A handy kitchen tool for cherry lovers is the pitter, which makes quick and easy work of removing the pits from cherries. Cherries are picked fully ripe, so should be used within a day or two of purchase.

Shortbread Lemon Tart

1 1/2	cups granulated sugar
4	eggs
1/2	cup freshly squeezed lemon juice
1/4	cup all-purpose flour
2	teaspoons grated lemon zest
2	teaspoons grated orange zest
1	teaspoon baking powder
1/2	teaspoon salt

CRUST

1	cup all-purpose flour
1/3	cup powdered sugar
1	teaspoon grated lemon zest
1	teaspoon grated orange zest
1/2	teaspoon salt
1/2	cup unsalted butter, cut into 1-inch pieces and refrigerated
1	egg, separated

ingredient list continued on next page

This refreshing, vibrantly flavored tart could also be served with a drizzle of puréed strawberries, alone or on top of whipped cream and fresh strawberries.

Preheat the oven to 350°F.

For the crust, combine the flour, powdered sugar, lemon and orange zests, and salt in a food processor and pulse once or twice to blend. Add the butter and egg yolk and pulse until the dough begins to form a ball. Form the dough into a flat disc, wrap in plastic, and refrigerate for 30 minutes.

Pat the dough into a 10-inch removable base tart pan. Lightly beat the egg white and brush a thin coat on the crust (do not use all of the egg white). Set the tart pan on a baking sheet and bake just until the crust begins to turn golden brown, about 10 to 12 minutes.

While the crust is baking, whisk together the sugar, eggs, lemon juice, flour, lemon and orange zests, baking powder, and salt until thoroughly blended. When the crust is browned, take it from the oven and pour in the filling. Continue baking until the filling is set and lightly browned on top, about 18 to 20 minutes.

recipe continued on next page

For the topping, stir together the sour cream, sugar, and vanilla in a small bowl. When the lemon filling is set, spread the topping over and continue baking until the topping is set, about 6 to 8 minutes. Let cool completely on a wire rack, then refrigerate at least 4 hours or overnight before serving. To serve, remove the edges of the tart pan and cut the tart into wedges. Garnish each wedge with a small dollop of whipped cream and a strawberry fan.

MAKES 8 SERVINGS

To make strawberry fans for garnish, halve a strawberry with the stem intact. Set the strawberry cut-side down on a chopping board and make thin slits, up to but not through the stem so that the slices remain together. Press gently to fan out.

◆ For afternoon tea, offer Lavender Lemonade.

TOPPING

1 1/2	cups sour cream
1/4	cup granulated sugar
1/2	teaspoon vanilla extract
	Lightly sweetened whipped cream, for serving
8	strawberry fans, for serving

LAVENDER LEMONADE

5	cups water, divided
1	cup sugar
1/4	cup fresh lavender flowers or 1 1/2 tablespoons dried lavender
1	cup freshly squeezed lemon juice
6	lavender sprigs, for garnish

Combine 2 1/2 cups of the water and the sugar in a medium saucepan and bring to a boil over high heat, stirring until the sugar is dissolved. Add the lavender flowers, take the pan from the heat, cover, and steep for 30 to 45 minutes. Strain into a large pitcher, discarding the lavender. Stir in the lemon juice and remaining 2 1/2 cups water. Stir well. Refrigerate until fully chilled, then pour over ice in tall glasses. Garnish with a sprig of fresh lavender.

MAKES 6 SERVINGS

Tarte Tatin with Oatmeal Crust

6 tablespoons unsalted butter

1/3 cup granulated sugar

1/3 cup packed light brown sugar

2 teaspoons grated lemon zest

2 1/2 pounds medium Golden Delicious apples, peeled, halved, cored, each half cut into 3 wedges

PASTRY

1/3 cup rolled oats

2 tablespoons granulated sugar

1 1/4 cups all-purpose flour

1/8 teaspoon salt

1/2 cup unsalted butter, cut into 1/2-inch pieces and refrigerated

About 4 tablespoons ice water

As the tart cools, the crust gets flakier, so let the tart sit for about 30 minutes before serving for best results. While the tart is cooling, prepare Hot Cranberry Apple Cider.

For the pastry, combine the oats and sugar in a food processor and pulse until the oats are finely ground. Add the flour and salt and pulse to mix. Add the butter and pulse until the mixture resembles coarse meal. Add the ice water, a tablespoonful at a time and pulsing between additions, until the mixture begins to lump together. Form the dough into a disc, wrap it in plastic, and refrigerate for at least 1 hour.

Preheat the oven to 425°F. Melt the butter in a heavy medium nonstick ovenproof skillet over medium heat. Gradually stir in the granulated sugar and brown sugar, and continue stirring until the sugars begin to dissolve and the mixture starts to bubble, about 2 minutes. Stir in the lemon zest and take the skillet from the heat. Arrange the apple wedges on their sides in a circle around the edge of the skillet, fitting them tightly. Put several wedges snugly in the center. Cut any remaining apple into 1/2-inch pieces and scatter over the apple wedges, mounding them slightly in the center.

Put the skillet over medium heat and cook until the juices start to bubble, about 3 minutes. Cover the skillet and cook another 5 minutes. Uncover the skillet and continue to cook until the apple juices and sugars make a syrup, but the apples are still firm to the touch, about 10 minutes. Take the skillet from the heat.

Roll out the dough between sheets of floured waxed paper to a 12-inch round. Peel off the top sheet of paper. Use the bottom sheet as an aid to invert the dough onto the warm apples in the skillet, then peel off the paper. Tuck the pastry edges down and inside the skillet around the apples.

recipe continued on next page

Bake until the crust is a deep golden brown, about 40 minutes. Use a small knife to cut around the crust to loosen it. Let the tart stand 1 minute, then set a large platter upside-down on top of the skillet. Use oven mitts to hold the platter and skillet tightly together, and then quickly invert to unmold the tart onto the platter, lifting away the skillet slowly to allow the caramelized juices to drip down. Rearrange any apples that may have dislodged. Let cool to lukewarm, about 30 minutes, then cut into wedges to serve. A dollop of whipped cream will make this dish even richer.

MAKES 8 SERVINGS

HOT CRANBERRY APPLE CIDER

1	cup cranberries, fresh or frozen
1	quart apple cider
	Grated zest and freshly squeezed juice of 1 orange
1	tablespoon packed light brown sugar
1	cinnamon stick
2	whole cloves
	Pinch allspice
1/2	apple, peeled, cored, and diced

Crush the cranberries in a medium saucepan. Add the cider, orange zest and juice, brown sugar, cinnamon, cloves, and allspice. Simmer, covered, over medium heat until hot and aromatic, about 30 minutes. Strain, ladle into mugs or punch cups, and top each with diced apple.

MAKES 4 TO 6 SERVINGS

GINGERBREAD SOUFFLÉS WITH VANILLA SAUCE

1/4	cup unsalted butter
1/4	cup all-purpose flour
1	cup milk
2/3	cup sugar
1/4	cup molasses
2	tablespoons dark rum
2	teaspoons powdered ginger
1	teaspoon vanilla extract
1	teaspoon ground cinnamon
	Pinch salt
5	egg yolks
6	egg whites
1/2	teaspoon cream of tartar

VANILLA SAUCE

2	cups half-and-half
1	vanilla bean, split lengthwise, seeds scraped out
1/3	cup sugar
4	egg yolks
2	tablespoons high quality bourbon, such as Woodford Reserve

The warm and slightly spicy essence of gingerbread makes a great transition to ethereal soufflés in this elegant dessert.

For the sauce, combine the half-and-half, vanilla bean, and vanilla seeds in a medium saucepan and bring to a low boil over medium heat, then take the pan from the heat. In a medium bowl, whisk together the sugar and egg yolks, then gradually whisk in the hot half-and-half. Return the mixture to the saucepan and stir with a wooden spoon over medium-low heat until the custard thickens enough to coat the back of the spoon, about 5 minutes. (Do not boil the sauce or the egg will curdle.) Strain the sauce through a fine sieve into a small bowl and stir in the bourbon. Let cool to room temperature, then cover with plastic wrap and refrigerate until fully chilled, at least 4 hours or overnight.

Preheat the oven to 400°. Butter eight 8-ounce ramekins. Coat the insides evenly with sugar and shake out the excess. Put the dishes on a large baking sheet and set aside.

Melt the butter in a heavy medium saucepan over medium heat. Add the flour and whisk until the mixture is smooth and bubbly, about 2 minutes. Gradually whisk the milk into the flour mixture, whisking constantly until the milk is thickened and the mixture is smooth, about 2 to 3 minutes. Take the pan from the heat and whisk in the sugar, molasses, rum, ginger, vanilla, cinnamon, and salt. Let the mixture cool until warm, about 10 minutes. Whisk in the egg yolks and set aside.

Whip the egg whites with an electric mixer at high speed until frothy. Add the cream of tartar and beat until the whites are stiff, but not dry. Gently fold the egg whites into the yolk mixture in 3 additions. Divide the batter among the prepared dishes and run the tip of a knife around the top of the mixture, about ½ inch in from the edge, to facilitate crowning. Bake the soufflés until puffed and golden, about 15 minutes. Serve right away, making an indentation in the soufflés and drizzling in the sauce.

MAKES 8 SERVINGS

Upside-Down Hazelnut Cake with Brandied Pears

1/3	cup toasted hazelnuts
1 1/2	cups sugar, divided
2 2/3	cups cake flour
1	tablespoon baking powder
1 1/2	teaspoons salt
3/4	cup unsalted butter, at room temperature
1	teaspoon vanilla extract
1/2	teaspoon almond extract
3	eggs
1 1/2	cups whipping cream, at room temperature

BRANDIED PEARS

2	ripe but firm pears
2	tablespoons freshly squeezed lemon juice
6	tablespoons unsalted butter, divided
8	tablespoons packed light brown sugar, divided
6	tablespoons pear or apple brandy, divided
	Pinch salt
2 – 4	tablespoons water, if needed
1/2	cup hazelnuts, toasted, skinned, and coarsely chopped

Anjou pears work especially well in this recipe, but other ripe, firm pears can be used. Make sure the pears are not over-ripe or they will fall apart during cooking. Ripe plums or apples may be substituted for the pears. Because the cake is not too sweet, it can also be served without the whipped cream for a fall brunch. This cake is best served within 2 hours of baking. Serve with a dollop of whipped cream from the Spiced Coffee with Whipped Cream (page 56).

Lightly grease a nonstick 10-cup Bundt pan.

For the brandied pears, peel and core the pears, cut each into about 12 slices and toss with the lemon juice. Melt 2 tablespoons of the butter in a large nonstick skillet over medium heat. Sprinkle 1 tablespoon of the brown sugar over the butter and add half the pear slices. Cook, gently turning the slices once, until the pears soften slightly and release their juices, about 2 to 3 minutes. Take care to not overcook or they'll become mushy and fall apart. Add 3 tablespoons of the brandy, cook another minute, then remove the pears from the pan with a slotted spoon and set aside on a plate. Cook all pears.

When all the pear slices are cooked, stir the remaining 2 tablespoons butter, 6 tablespoons brown sugar, and salt into the juices in the skillet. If needed, add enough water to the liquids in the pan to total about 3/4 cup. Cook, stirring constantly, until the sauce is thick enough to lightly coat the back of the spoon, about 2 to 3 minutes. Immediately pour the sauce into the lightly greased 10-cup Bundt pan. Sprinkle the chopped hazelnuts over the sauce, and arrange the pear slices on top of the nuts. Set aside.

recipe continued on next page

Preheat the oven to 350°F. Combine the hazelnuts and 1 tablespoon of the sugar in a food processor and process until the nuts are finely ground. Take care to not over-process the nuts or they'll turn into paste. In another large bowl, mix the ground hazelnuts, flour, baking powder, and salt. Cream the remaining sugar and the butter with an electric mixer at medium-high speed until light and fluffy. Reduce the speed to medium and add the vanilla and almond extracts. Add the eggs, 1 at a time, beating well after each addition. With a rubber spatula, carefully alternate folding in the dry ingredients in 3 parts, and the cream in 2 parts.

Spoon the batter over the pears, smoothing it carefully so as to not disturb the arrangement of the pears. Bake until a toothpick inserted in the center comes out clean, about 40 to 45 minutes. As soon as the cake is removed from the oven, invert it directly onto a serving plate, leaving the cake pan in place. Let the inverted cake stand for a few minutes on the serving plate. Slowly remove the pan and cut the cakes into wedges to serve warm or at room temperature.

MAKES 12 SERVINGS

◆ Late-harvest semillon will have a toasty richness suited to the nuts and brandied pears.

HAZELNUTS

Oregon's Willamette Valley is home to many thousands of hazelnut trees, part of a legacy of nut-growing that goes back to the mid-nineteenth century when the first hazelnut tree is said to have been planted in the state. Fall is harvest time, but the nuts—in many forms from whole nuts to hazelnut oil to chocolate-coated candies—are available year-round. As with most other nuts, toasting hazelnuts before using significantly develops their flavor. Toasting is also the time to remove the hazelnut skins. When the nuts are nicely browned and aromatic, transfer them to a damp kitchen towel and wrap up to steam until cool, about 15 minutes. Rub the hazelnuts in the towel to remove as much of the skin as possible, though some persistent skin will stick, which is fine.

ORANGE AND LEMON SOUR CREAM CAKE

3 cups all-purpose flour

1 1/2 teaspoons baking powder

1 1/2 teaspoons baking soda

1 1/2 cups unsalted butter,
at room temperature

1 1/2 cups sugar

1 1/2 cups sour cream

6 eggs, separated,
at room temperature

2 tablespoons finely grated
orange zest

2 tablespoons finely grated
lemon zest

Pinch cream of tartar

6 thin slices lemon, for garnish

6 thin slices orange, for garnish

1 cup whipping cream (optional)

ORANGE SYRUP

1 1/2 cups sugar

1/2 cup Grand Marnier or other
orange liqueur

1/2 cup freshly squeezed orange juice

6 tablespoons freshly squeezed
lemon juice

1/2 teaspoon salt

This is a great cake to make for on-the-go events, such as a picnic in the park or tailgate lunch before a big football game. In place of the lemon and orange slices, you could garnish this cake with fresh whole berries and strawberry purée.

Preheat the oven to 325°F. Butter and flour a 10-inch tube pan.

Sift together the flour, baking powder, and baking soda into a medium bowl. Cream together the butter and sugar with an electric mixer at medium speed until light and fluffy. Add the sour cream, egg yolks, and orange and lemon zests, and beat until thoroughly blended, about 5 minutes. Stir in the dry ingredients. Using clean, dry beaters in a clean bowl, beat the egg whites with the cream of tartar until stiff but not dry. Gently fold half the whites into the batter to lighten it, then fold in the remaining whites. Pour the batter into the prepared pan and bake until a tester comes out clean, about 1 hour. Let the cake cool in the pan for about 15 minutes, then invert it onto a wire cooling rack.

For the syrup, combine the sugar, Grand Marnier, orange juice, lemon juice, and salt in a small saucepan and cook over medium-low heat, occasionally swirling the pan gently to help the sugar dissolve. Increase the heat to medium-high and boil until the syrup thickens slightly, about 8 minutes. Let cool until warm.

Use a bamboo skewer or toothpick to pierce the top of the cake many times, the more the better. Slowly pour the syrup over the cake, allowing it to soak in before adding more. Garnish with the lemon and orange slices and serve with the whipped cream, if you like.

MAKES 12 TO 14 SERVINGS

When whipping eggs for cakes such as this, an ice-cold egg fresh from the refrigerator won't beat up as lightly as one that's closer to room temperature.

◆ To dress up this simple dessert, add a dollop of unsweetened whipping cream and drizzle it with a late-harvest riesling. Offer glasses of the wine to sip alongside.

CHOCOLATE LAVA CAKES

The molten chocolate centers in these cakes make them extra special. Use high quality chocolate in this recipe—it will make a real difference. Serve the warm cakes with a scoop of ice cream or a dollop of whipped cream, if you like.

Preheat the oven to 325°F. Butter and flour six 6-ounce ramekins or custard cups.

Combine 5 ounces of the chocolate and the butter in a medium heatproof bowl set over a saucepan of barely simmering water. Stir occasionally, until just melted and smooth, then set aside.

In the bowl of an electric mixer, whisk together the whole eggs, egg yolks, and sugar on medium-high speed until the mixture is thick and pale, about 5 minutes. Add the flour, espresso powder, vanilla, and salt, and continue beating until just combined. Slowly add the melted chocolate mixture to the egg mixture and continue beating at medium speed until glossy, about 5 minutes. Pour half the batter into the prepared dishes. Top each with the remaining chopped chocolate in the center of each dish, then add the remaining batter. Set the dishes on a baking sheet for easy handling and bake the cakes until the sides and tops are set but the center is still a bit runny, about 15 minutes.

For the sauce, melt the chocolate and butter in a small saucepan over low heat, whisking often until smooth. Add the water, corn syrup, and vanilla, and whisk until smooth and warmed. Take the pan from the heat and set aside.

When the cakes are done, let them sit on a wire rack for about 5 minutes. Run a small knife around each cake to loosen it and immediately turn the cake out on to a dessert plate by setting a plate upside-down on top of the dish and inverting them together, then lifting off the dish. To serve, spoon the sauce around the cakes, and garnish with a sprinkling of powdered sugar or an espresso bean.

MAKES 6 SERVINGS

7	ounces bittersweet or semisweet chocolate, coarsely chopped, divided
10	tablespoons unsalted butter, cut into pieces
3	whole eggs
3	egg yolks
1/4	cup plus 2 tablespoons sugar
5	tablespoons all-purpose flour
2	tablespoons espresso powder
1	teaspoon vanilla extract
1/2	teaspoon salt
	Powdered sugar or chocolate-covered espresso beans, for garnish

CHOCOLATE SAUCE

4 1/2	ounces bittersweet or semisweet chocolate, coarsely chopped
2	tablespoons unsalted butter, cut into pieces
1/3	cup hot water
1/4	cup light corn syrup
1/2	teaspoon vanilla extract

CHOCOLATE DUET CHEESECAKE

This spectacular cake will be only as good as the quality of chocolate that you use, so choose the best! The cheesecake can be made up to 2 days before serving, but cover the pan after it has initially chilled for a few hours. It will be easier to cut the cake if it is removed from the refrigerator about an hour before serving.

Preheat the oven to 325°F. Butter a 9-inch springform pan.

For the crust, pulse the cookies in a food processor to make coarse crumbs. Add the melted butter, salt, and cinnamon, and pulse a few times until evenly blended. Press the crumb mixture firmly onto the bottom and 1 inch up the side of the springform pan. Bake the crust for 8 minutes, then set aside on a wire rack to cool.

Melt the white chocolate and the bittersweet chocolate separately, in small heatproof bowls set over saucepans of barely simmering water. Stir them occasionally, until just melted and smooth, then set the bowls aside. Beat the cream cheese and sugar with an electric mixer at medium speed until smooth and fluffy, about 3 minutes. Add the flour, then beat in the eggs, 1 at a time, scraping the sides of the bowl between additions. Add the whipping cream and vanilla and mix to blend. Transfer 2¼ cups of the batter to a medium bowl and stir in the melted white chocolate. Stir the melted bittersweet chocolate into the remaining batter in the mixing bowl. Pour the bittersweet chocolate batter into the prepared crust and smooth the top. Bake until the chocolate filling is softly set in the center and beginning to puff at the edges, about 50 minutes. Take the pan from the oven and let cool on a wire rack for 5 minutes to firm slightly, leaving the oven on.

Starting at the edge of the pan, spoon the white chocolate batter in concentric circles onto the dark chocolate layer, then smooth the top. Bake until the white chocolate filling is set in the center, about 35 minutes. Let the cake cool on a wire rack for 10 minutes before making the topping, leaving the oven on.

recipe continued on next page

8	ounces bittersweet chocolate, finely chopped
6	ounces white chocolate, finely chopped
4	packages (8 ounces each) cream cheese, at room temperature
1 1/3	cups sugar
2	tablespoons all-purpose flour
4	eggs
2	tablespoons whipping cream
1	tablespoon vanilla extract

CRUST

1	package (9 ounces) chocolate wafer cookies, coarsely broken
6	tablespoons unsalted butter, melted
1/8	teaspoon salt
1/8	teaspoon ground cinnamon

ingredient list continued on next page

TOPPING

1 1/2   cups sour cream

1/3   cup sugar

1   teaspoon vanilla extract

    White and bittersweet chocolate curls, for garnish (optional)

    Fresh raspberries or other fresh berries, for garnish (optional)

For the topping, stir together the sour cream, sugar, and vanilla until smooth. If the cheesecake has puffed up too high for the topping to fit, press it down gently with a spatula. Pour the topping over the cheesecake and gently smooth it with a spatula. Bake until the topping is lightly set, about 10 minutes. Let the cake cool to room temperature, then refrigerate, uncovered, for at least 4 hours before serving, or the cake may fall apart when cut.

Slide a small knife around the outer edge of the cheesecake to loosen it from the pan, then release and remove the sides. Garnish the cake with chocolate curls or berries if desired.

MAKES 8 TO 12 SERVINGS

♦ Offer a sparkling wine; its refreshing bubbles will allow you to enjoy every bite.

HOW TO MAKE CHOCOLATE CURLS

It's easy to make chocolate curls for garnishing the top of the cake — or as a fancy finish to a layer cake, chocolate mousse, or any number of desserts. Firmly hold a piece of chocolate (preferably at least 1/2 inch wide) in your hand and use a vegetable peeler to strip away curls from the side of the chocolate. Work over a piece of foil or waxed paper, lifting it to scatter the chocolate directly onto the cake. You won't have to handle the delicate curls (which might melt in your hands).

CHOCOLATE TIRAMISÙ MOUSSE

This divine chocolate treat is great for a dinner party, as it can be made up to a day in advance.

In a shallow dish, combine the coffee, granulated sugar, and rum; set aside, stirring occasionally to ensure the sugar dissolves. In a medium bowl, combine the cocoa powder with ¼ cup of the cream and stir to mix, then stir in the mascarpone cheese until smooth and evenly blended.

Whip the remaining 1 cup of the cream with an electric mixer at medium-high speed until soft peaks form. Add the powdered sugar and vanilla and continue to whip until stiff peaks form. Fold the whipped cream into the mascarpone mixture, then fold in half of the grated chocolate.

Dip 1 side of half the ladyfingers in the coffee mixture. Line the bottom of a 9- by 13-inch pan (or a 10-inch springform pan or trifle dish) with the ladyfingers, espresso side up. Cover them with half of the mascarpone filling. Dip 1 side of the remaining ladyfingers in the coffee mixture. Lay them, espresso side down, over the filling. Spread the remaining mascarpone mixture over the ladyfingers and cover the dish with plastic wrap. Refrigerate for at least 3 hours or overnight.

Just before serving, sprinkle the remaining grated chocolate over the tiramisù. Dust with powdered sugar, if desired, and cut into squares to serve.

MAKES 12 TO 16 SERVINGS

1	cup double-strength coffee or 1½ tablespoons instant espresso powder dissolved in 1 cup water
¼	cup granulated sugar
¼	cup rum, light or dark
⅓	cup unsweetened cocoa powder
1¼	cups whipping cream, divided
2	cups mascarpone cheese
¼	cup powdered sugar, more for optional garnish
2	teaspoons vanilla extract
4	ounces semisweet chocolate, grated, divided
24	ladyfingers, hard or soft type

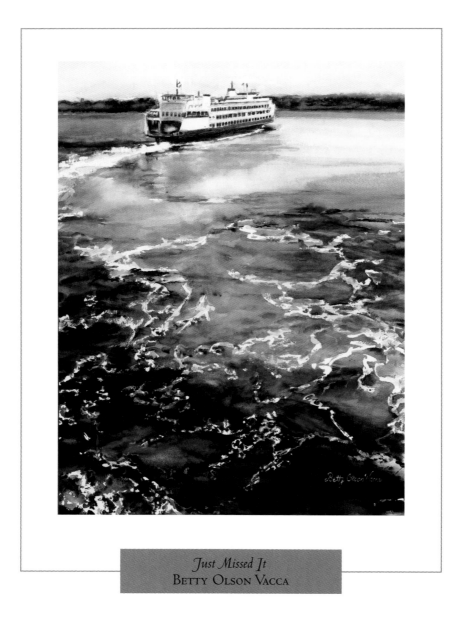

Just Missed It
BETTY OLSON VACCA

The ferry boat is a much-loved symbol of life in the Pacific Northwest, traversing the typically calm waters of Puget Sound all year long, from places like Vashon Island to Seattle or further north to the San Juan Islands and Victoria, British Columbia. Tourists and residents alike delight in the relaxing atmosphere aboard, and sometimes lucky riders spot a pod of Orcas swimming nearby.

Cookbook Committees

PRODUCTION REVIEW COMMITTEE
2003–2004

- Elizabeth Arganian *Chair*
- Stephanie Reeves *Vice-Chair*
- Beth Douglass *Editor-in-Chief*
- Barbara McClure *Design Editor*
  Mary Chapman Mascarella
      Text Editor
  Joanne Petitto *Marketing*
  Lolo Levy *Business Development*
- Helen DiMeco *Secretary*
- Margery Hokonson
      Sustainer Co-Chair
  Susan Minahan *Sustainer Co-Chair*
- Ann Kirtman *Sustainer Advisor*

SUSTAINER ADVISORS
1999–2004

- Margery Hokonson *Chair*
- Kristin Adams
- Bernice Bellamy
- Bonnie Brown
  Colleen Clancy-Eastman
- Dana Cocales
- Jacky Grotle
- Kellanne Henry
- Mary Herche
- Ann Kirtman
  Sally Lindberg Goetsch
  Sue Minahan
- Susie Ostrander
  Cindy Eder Porter
- Gail Richards
- Barbara Ries
- Karen Roed
  Tricia Tiano

CHAPTER COORDINATORS
2000–2004

- Beth Douglass *Recipe Editor 1999–2003*
- Jacky Grotle *Recipe Editor 1999–2003*
- Leslie Adams *Poultry*
- Helen DiMeco *Pasta*
- Jacky Grotle *Brunch*
- Ann Kirtman *Appetizers*
- Danielle Majestic *Meats*
- Jennifer Martinkus *Salads*
- Barbara McClure *Side Dishes*
- Susan Pugel *Desserts*
- Stephanie Reeves *Soups*
- Kathleen Skinner *Seafood*

RECIPE TESTING COORDINATORS
2000–2001

Monica Barber *Appetizers*
Elaine Say *Brunch*
Ellen Stearns *Appetizers*
Deborah Stubbs *Poultry*

FUNDRAISING COORDINATORS

- Dana Cocales
      In-League 1999–2003
- Kellanne Henry
      Corporate 2000–2002
- Kerry Kozlowski
      Corporate 2002–2003

MARKETING COORDINATORS

- Leslie Feller *1999–2002*
- Susie Ostrander *1999–2002*
  Joanne Petitto *2003–2004*
- Stephanie Reeves *2002–2003*

COMMITTEE CHAIRS
1998–2004

- Elizabeth Arganian *2003–2004*
- Kristin Adams *2000–2003*
- Julie Dreyfoos *1999–2001*
  Stacy Peterson *1999–2000*
- Margery Hokonson *1998–1999*

ADDITIONAL COMMITTEE MEMBERS
1999–2004

Christine Kay Acarregui
Diana Ackerley
Lisa Allworth
Mihoko Baker
Kris Betts
Kate Keckler Dandel
Kathy Eddings
Hilary Hansen
- Kathleen Jeffcoat
Karen Kennedy
Kristine Klappenbach
Mary Francis Klug
Marie Maxwell
Lynn Mizulo
- Jeanette Petersen
Debra Pinckney
- Heather Rees
Annmari Ryan
- Elise Spencer
Jimi Lou Steambarge
Kathy Thurston
- Briana Turner-King
Ruthanne Weaver
Kathy Weber
Annette Williamson

- Two or more years of contribution

SPONSORS & CONTRIBUTORS

$10,000	$1,000 — $2,499	$500 — $999	$250 — $499	$100 — $299
Nordstrom	Kristin Adams	Maxine Barnard	Barbara Jo Allen	Ellen Allen
	Elizabeth and David	Marilene Bysshe	Patty Barrier	Susan Amato
	Arganian	Leslie and David Feller	Lauren Bennett	Bonnie Jean Anderson
$5,000	Maureen Benoliel	Judith Holder	Susan Black	Stephanie Anderson
	Deborah S. Cleveland	Claudia Marks Johnson	Cheryl Claeys	Patricia Bartok
Brown-Forman	Cathryn Fortune	Ann Berlinger Kirtman	Colleen Clancy-Eastman	Sally Skinner Behnke
JoAnne and	Cindy Freimuth	Bonnie Larson	Dana Cocales	Bernice Bellamy
Clayton Jones	Jane Hawkanson	Lolo and Rick Levy	Corinne Cowan	Sue Blethen
Microsoft	Kellanne Henry	Geraldine Lucks	Karen Evenden	Bunko Babes of Issaquah
Lesa A. Sroufe	Mary R. Herche	Maria Mackey	Beverly B. Fuhs	Jane Cable
Evelyn Zabo and	Margery and Neil	Meredith McClurg	Dot Fuller	Chris Carpenter
Rick Schroder	Hokonson	Diane R. McDonald	Megan Goodrick	Tracy Hallock Crail
Marcia Zech	Beverly J. Jefferson	Carole Ann and Larry	Cathi Hatch	Dee Dickinson
	Lisa Kittilsby	Milton	Mrs. A. J. Hedgcock III	Sharon Bender Dillon
	Kerry Kozlowski	Susan Minahan	Joan Hibbs	Beth Gaskill Douglass
$2,500	Marilyn Leck	Dana Pigott	Kathleen Hoff	Suzanne Dragon
	Sue Mecklenburg	Stephanie and Randy	Marion Hopkins	Kathi Effenberger
Joanne Petitto	Jeanette and Kurt	Reeves	Leena Piik Jacobs	Kellie K. Eickerman
Susan H. Swindells	Petersen	Peggy Walton	Lisa Lindstrom	Megan Elliott
Korynne Halvorson	RBC Dain Rauscher	Deborah Woodhouse	Martha Longbrake	Mary Fite-Black
Wright	Gail Richards	Ann P. Wyckoff	Marie Maxwell	Sally Foster
	Patricia E. Roberts		Tina Negri	Elizabeth Fox
	Karen Roed		Susan Olson	Nancy Franz
			Janet O'Neil	Betty Freeman
			Stacy Peterson	Maureen Gavin
			Heather Rees	Carmen Gayton
			Linda Reichenbach	Linda K. Goodrick
			Sheri Salo	Susan Goplen
			Stephanie Selin	Carolyn Gray
			Jaimie and Matt Shea	Neva Green
			Beverly Van Hartesvelt	Margaret Habegger
			Stephanie VonGortler	Janet Huguenin
			Ruthanne Ketcham	Suzanne Lile Hunter
			Weaver	Marli Iverson
				Carol Jaffe

SPECIAL THANKS

The Junior League of Seattle gratefully thanks its members, special friends and community businesses for their generous support and contributions. We would also like to convey our appreciation to the many artists who willingly shared their unique images of Northwest life and landscape. Our deepest gratitude goes to all those listed on the following pages, and to anyone we may have failed to mention. As this project owes its success to the talent and support of so many, we invite you to share in our pride as we join together to make a difference in the lives of children and families.

Under $100

Kathleen Sue Jeffcoat
Clair Jenkins
Sandra O. Kachlein
Laura Landau
Paula Lefavor
Anne Malmo
Andrea T. Mann
Jacqueline Mansfield
Beverly Martin
Kathleen Maryatt
Marty Matthews
Sally McCray
Ann McCurdy
Howardine McInnis
Macy Moring
Kimberly Morris
Mary Murphy
Rhonda Neben
Nancy Piantanida
Sherry Portuese
Lisa Raab
Leslie Reynolds
Nancy Senseney
Carissa Smith-Hunt
Roberta Stern
Linda Stull
Catherine Taflin
Sally Thomson
Tricia Tiano
Mary M. Turner
Jill Turville
Marilyn Ward
Leigh Watson
Kate Webster
Karen Wickstrand
Sandra Zinsmeyer

Julie Adams
Leslie Adams
Leslie Allen
Lisa Allworth
Eileen Baird Askew
Elizabeth D. Bailey
Trudy Baldwin
Valerie Barrett
Kris Betts
Alisa Betz
Lisa Bockenstedt
Margaret Breen
Bonnie Brown
Mary W. Cahill
Katherine Calhoun
Lynda N. Caporale
McLean Carroll
Amy Chavez
Adrienne Hobert Clark
Linda Colwell
Lisa Connor
Katherine and Jeff
    Cordick
Mary Rae Cowles
Sally Davidson
Joan Davis
Julia Davis
Monica Deck
Melissa Demouche
Alandra Dilley
Helen DiMeco
Raquel Dobbins
Julie Doces
Connie Edwards
Carol Primrose Enden
Cynthia Pierce Epsen
Jeanette Ferguson
Diane Fiduccia
Claire and Zane Fitterer
Bridget Franklin
Amy Frederick
Jennifer Georges

Susan Georgulas
Heather Goldsmith
Kristen Gormley
Sandy Green
Jacky Grotle
Anna Guerra
Kristi Hartman
Arden Hofler
Sara Comings Hoppin
Katherine C. Howard
Charlotte Hutton
Darcey James
Aimee Jamison
Jayme Johnson
Julianne Johnson
Molly Johnson
Caroline Johnston
Stephanie Keeton-Honan
Jessica Kircher
Kacey Kroeger
Allison Lee
Michele Levinger
Windsor Lewis
Miaenn Lillie-Olander
Ann-Marie Linde
Jennifer and Jim Lord
Jennifer Colwell Loy
Sheila Magnano
Danielle and Mike
    Majestic
Lisa Mar
Mary Chapman
    Mascarella
Barbara McClure
Denise McCullough
Eleanor Merz
Christine Miller
Linda Miller
Dawn Mills
Lynn Mizulo
Joanne Krause Montague
Caroline Burke Moore

Terry Timm Moos
Sally R. Morbeck
Erin Moyer
Barbi Monroe Nelp
Mary Nelson
Kimberly Nielson
Susie Ostrander
Laurie Parrott
Susan Peters
Cindy Eder Porter
Susan Pugel
Kate and Jeff Rader
Lorene Richards
Katie Roed
Jean Rolfe
Anne Rosauer
Nancy Schmoll
Sherry Schroeder
Kimberly Lum
    Schwarzhoff
Brianne Shally
Holly Shrikhande
Gwen Smith
Elise Spencer
Nancy Steel
Katherine Maury Stein
Connie Strope
Deborah Stubbs
Morgan Thomas and
    Steven Schwartz
Elizabeth Thorson
Kathy Thurston
Briana Turner-King
Candice Wheeler
Henrietta Whitehall
Diane R. Whitfield
Donnelly Wilburn
Annette Williamson
Deborah Wilson
Debbie Winn
Cindy Zech

In-Kind Donations

Brown-Forman
BV Winery
Choc Elan, LLC
Converters Express
Digital Image
Ernst & Young, LLC
Event Success
Heart of Washington
Kim Kimmy Enterprises
Made in Washington
Mary Cunningham
    Graphic Design
Matt Mizulo LLC
Palisade Restaurant
Paste-Well Corp
Redhook Ale Brewery
Schnitzer Northwest, LLC
Seastar Restaurant
Starbucks Corporation
Sun Luck Brands
Tully's Coffee
Uwajimaya
Wilson Sonsini
    Goodrich & Rosati,
    Professional
    Corporation

Photography Props

Allusia
Capers
Made in Washington
Martha E. Harris
    Flowers and Gifts
    of Madison Park
Sur La Table
Table Top Shop
Tiffany & Co.
Uwajimaya
Watson Kennedy
    Fine Home

CONTRIBUTORS OF RECIPES, TESTING, TIME & TALENT

Christine Kay Acarregui
Diana Ackerley
Sarah Ackley
Julie Adams
Kristin Adams
Leslie Adams
Marge Adams
Gordon Adkins
Janet Adkins
Clacy Albert
Ellen Allen
Lisa Allworth
Annette Alt
Susan Amato
Jean Amick
Debbie Andersen
Libba Anderson
Mary Anderson
Pamela Anderson
Roger Anderson
Stephanie Anderson
Tricia Anderson
Elizabeth Arganian
Paige Armentrout
Erika Arndt
Eileen Askew
Alison Athay
Elizabeth Bailey
Cindy Baker
Mihoko Baker
Crissi Baldwin
Diane Baldwin
Mitch Barber
Monica Barber
Constance Barnes
Janice Barnes
Valerie Barrett
Patti Barrier
Deborah Batjer
Kathryn Bauman
Tim Bauman
Candy Baunsgard
Curt Baunsgard
Kay Baxter
Jeanne Bayley
Sheryl Beirne
Bernice Bellamy
Lauren Bennett
Hilary Benson

Julie Berard
Laurie Besteman
Kris Betts
Marisa Bingham
Susan Black
Tony Black
William Blackwell
Mary Ann Blake
Helen Blakemore
Rose Bohner
Brittiony Borges
Kim Boynton
Jill Brahms Keto
Mary Brandin
Carrie Brice
Lorie Brighton
Kathryn Roed Bronstein
Carolyn Brookhart
Bonnie Brown
Jennifer Brown
Melanie Bruch
Illis Burke
Belinda Buscher
Kristen Bush
Sue Butts
Marilene Bysshe
Jane Cable
Joe Cantu
Pat Cantu
Karen Carlton
Shelley Carson
Callie Castillo
Katie Chace
Wendy Chaffee
Evelyn Chapman
Melody Charuhas
Amy Chavez
Terri Chedzik
Ami Chung
Colleen Clancy-Eastman
Mary Clanton
Shelby Clayton
Kristen Clifford-Holm
Pamela Cobb
Doris Cobleigh
Dana Cocales
Elizabeth Cole
Nina Nguyen Collier
Joan Cook

Betsy Copeland
Leslie Cordell
Katherine Cordick
Pauline Cotton
Mary Coughlin
Corinne Cowan
Tracy Crail
Georgia Crockett
Kimberly Crouch
Barbee Crutcher
Sally Culverwall
Priestley Cummings
Melanie Currier
Laura Custer
Sue Cutting
Michelle Czech
Jackie Daehler
Ngoc Dai
Nikki Dalgarn
Bobbie Damon
Dottie Daves
Agnes Davis
Jennifer Davis
Joan Davis
Julia Davis
Jennifer Davis
Kimberly Dawgs
Rebecca Dawson
Monica Deck
Ellie Deets
Charity Dempsey
Deborah deSauvignon
Catherine Dietrich
Joan Dillon
Helen DiMeco
Karen Dion
Julie Doces
Fiona Dodd
Margaret Doeve
Ann Douglass
Beth Douglass ◆
David Douglass
Suzanne Dragon
Patty Dreyer
Julie Dreyfoos
Julie Drzewiecki
Nancy Dupre
Cami Eals
Kathy Eddings

Connie Edwards
Julita Eleveld
Kate Elftmann
Megan Elliott
Mary Emerton
Carol Enden
Shirley Espy
Leslie Feller
Jeanette Ferguson
Diane Fiduccia
Arnie Fleck
Emily Flodstrom
Heather Flodstrom
Laurie Flynn
Janet Folley
Theresa Ford
Barbara Forrest
Laura Fowler
Scott Fraser
Amy Frederick
Cindy Freimuth
Julie Fry
Beverly Fuhs
Dot Fuller
Kim Gabica
Stephanie Gales
Laura Garcia
Becky Gaskill
Gerry Gaskill
Sandra Gaskill
Donna Gelinas
Susan Georgulas
Heather Goldsmith
Megan Goodrick
Lara Gorman
Tessa Gorman
Karen Gouras
Andrea Gregg
Ontie Griebel
Sue Grinstein
Jacky Grotle
Judy Grotle
Ken Grotle
Marc Grotle
Tyan Grout
Anna Guerra
Michelle Halstead ◆
Beth Hamlin
Nicole Hammes

Hilary Hansen
Marcia Harrington
Heather Harrison
Sally Harter
Cathi Hatch
Jane Hawkanson
Brooke Hawley
Nancy Hawley
Sharon Heine
Jill Hendel
Kellanne Henry
Rene Henry
Mary Herche
Gregory A. Hicks
Klara Hicks
D'Linda Highum
Evelyn Hill
Susan Hilliard
Kathleen Hoff
Janis Hoffman
Joan Hoierman
Margery Hokonson
Judy Holder ◆
Kathy Holert
Betsy Holland
Diana Holland
Cathy Holton
Connie Holton
Marcia Horwitz ◆
Deborah Hsing
Susan Hubbard
Elizabeth Hudd
Tiffany Huey
Heather Jackson
Janice Jeffcoat
Kathleen Jeffcoat
Peter Jeffcoat
Beverly Jefferson
Mrs. Orvin Jenkins
Debbie Jennings
Christine Johnson
Gwen Johnson
Linda Johnson
Caroline Johnston
Jenny Johnstone
Christiana Jones
JoAnne Jones
Seon Kang
Sally Katovsich

Kate Keckler Dandel
Karen Kennedy
Meri Kerekanich
Kim Kimmy
Ann Kirtman   ◆
Louis Kirtman
Kristine Klappenbach
Mary Francis Klug
Diane Knoll
Kerry Kozlowski
Emily Kruger
Laura Landau
Bonnie Larson
Rebecca Lawrence
Marilyn Leck
Alison Lee
Lolo Levy
Carol Leyton
Merrilee Libby
Sally Lindberg Goetsch
Ingegerd Linden
Sally Lindquist
Jane Lindsay-Scott   ◆
Lisa Lindstrom
Maureen Linekin
Vicki Lockard
Carol Loforte
Martha Longbrake
Jill Loveland
Jennifer Lowry
Caroline Loy
John Lynch
Maria Mackey
JC Madison
Linda Madison
Molly Madson
Danielle Majestic
Mike Majestic
Shelley Malcolm
Lawrence Maltz
Tina Maltz
Andrea Mann
Jackie Mansfield
Ken Marks
Jennifer Martinkus
Pam Martinkus
Mary Mascarella
Marie Maxwell
Barbara McClure   ◆
Jeff McClure
Marianne McCrary
Sally McCray
Denise McCullough
Kathy McCullum
Molly McDaniel
Nancy McFadden
Lisa Mead

Susan Mecklenburg
Kristi Mehal
Dina Meier
Lucille Merget
Teresa Messina
Linda Michael
Mimi Miller
Carole Ann Milton
Larry Milton
Susan Minahan
Kimberly Miner
Heidi Mitchell
Lynn Mizulo
Kim Moore
Christine Moorman
Ginny Morris
Jean Morris
Marla Moss   ◆
Dorothy Naeymi
Rhonda Neben
Tina Negri
Lynn Neil
Jane Nellams
Barbi Nelp
Mary Nelp
Karen Nelson
Suzanne Nelson
Cathy Newman
Pam Newman
Susan Newton
Lynn Nichols
Kimberly Nielsen
Anne Nisbet
India Nishi
Gunnar Nordstrom
Shirl Oelschlager
Debbie O'Flynn
Nancy Olsen
Susan Olson
Margaret Opalka
Melanie Ortega
Pamela Ortega
Susie Ostrander
Pennie Palmer
Anne Passantino
Jane Patterson
Sheila Peddy
Peggy Peery
Marie-Claire Peron
Jeanette Petersen
Kurt Petersen
Lois Peterson
Stacy Peterson
Joanne Petitto
Mary Clare Phelps
Indy Phiffer
Wade Phiffer

Angela Pickens
Debra Pinckney
Charles Pinkert
Adele Piro
Cathy Pleasant
Susan Plunkett
Susan Pollock
Sarah Pommer
Wayne Pommer
Sara Johns Ponte
Cindy Eder Porter
Nancy Porter
Sherry Portuese
Elliott Post
Greg Post
Nancy Post
Kristian Prill
Sue Pruner
Jane Pugel
Jim Pugel
Susan Pugel
Toni Pugel
Barbara Quinn
Nancy Quinn
Kate Rader
Kathy Randall
Kathy Ray
Judith Redshaw
Heather Rees
Laurel Rees
Stephanie Reeves   ◆
Kasey Rehme
Jacki Reichanadter
Judy Redshaw
Gail Richards
Lorene Richards
Nancy Richardson
Toni Richmond
Barbara Ries
Tracy Rippy
Pat Roberts
Kim Robinson
Teresa Robinson
Rebecca Rodda
Karen Roed   ◆
Carol Rogers
Kathy Romstad
Trish Ropell
Anne Rosauer
Edye Ross
Julitta Ross
Debra Rowden
Karen Ruby
Boyd Ruckhaber
Carrie Ruckhaber
Annmari Ryan
Heidi J. Sadler

Sheri Salo
Allison Sander
Curt Sanford
Suz Sanford
Tina Sankwich
Cameron Satoris
Penny Satoris
Elaine Say
Janet Schmid
Rachel Schmidt
Ann Schneider
Dorothy Schoenleber
Kirsten Schoenleber
Margaret Schoenleber
Lisa Scott
Seattle Police
    SWAT Team
Kristin Secreto
Stephanie Selin
Ann Sestero
Darcy Shaver
Lesley Shay
Jaimie Shea
Denny Shepherd
Kathleen Skinner
Jean Smith
Susan Smith
Patti Solaski
Cheryl Soskin
J. Scott Soutter
Elise Spencer
Jonathan Spencer
Katie Staffield
Jimi Lou Steambarge
Ellen Stearns
Katherine Stein
Deborah Stubbs
Linda Stull
Darrel Stutesman
Joanna Stutesman
Marie Sullivan
Patrice Sullivan
Stacy Sullivan
Elizabeth Sundem
Pat Sundgren
Derenda Sweeny
Peggy Swistak
Mia Syre
Cathy Taflin
Lynda Tarvin
Gayle Taylor
Judy Taylor
Morgan Thomas
Kathy Thurston
Tricia Tiano
Laura Tolen
Janet True

Heidi Tucker
Briana Turner-King
Nancy Urner
Sharon Urry
Beth Van Blaricom
Alice Van Nada
Tara Vanniman
Kathryn Volk
Eden Waggoner
Tamra Wahl
Norma Wainright
Shannon Wainright
Tamra Wake
Nancy Walker
Robin Walker
Jean Wall
Angie Walls
Peggy Walton
Valerie Waltz
Leigh Watson
Katie Watts
Rebecca Weaver
Ruthanne Weaver
Kathy Weber
Jarvis Weld
Regan Wesley-Kirschner
Erin Westphal
Candice Wheeler
Robin White Grad
Barbara Whitt
Karen Wickstrand
Dana Wikan
Larry Wikan
Annette Williamson
Debbie Wilson
Debbie Winn
Courtney Witter
Debby Woodhouse
Stuart Woodhouse
Katie Worth
Korynne Wright
Ann Young
Jeff Yusen
Natalie Yusen
Evelyn Zabo
Terri Zambrovitz
Todd Zambrovitz
Liz Zeitlin
Sandra Zinsmeyer

◆ Tasting Party Hostess

Biographies of Professional Artists & Contributors

HEIDI-MARIE BLACKWELL *Artist*

Heidi-Marie is a Northwest native and studied painting and graphic design at the University of Washington. She has also studied in France, traveled throughout Europe, and worked in Los Angeles. She is the owner of Blackwell Studios in Seattle and primarily works in painting now. Heidi-Marie was the featured artist in *Simply Classic*, and a more extensive biography is available there.

ANGIE NORWOOD BROWNE *Photographer*

From her Southern roots to her Pacific Northwest studio, Angie has been creating award-winning food photography for over twelve years. Her distinctive work has appeared in cookbooks, magazines, and advertising campaigns around the world. Clients agree that her attention to detail creates photographs that reveal texture, depth, and grace.

ROSS BUCKLAND *Artist*

A lifetime aviation enthusiast, Ross Buckland has always used this as a subject for his drawings and paintings. He began studying art in high school and continued on his own with inspiration from artists such as Sargent, Wootton, Ferris, and Remington. He has won several awards and held many shows.

JOE MAX EMMINGER *Artist*

Joe Max was born and raised in Seattle, where he still lives. He is a self-taught painter and enjoys spending time on his art everyday. He describes his work as expressing what he sees and feels and lives, so the subjects of each piece evolve as he paints them.

KRISTY GJESME *Artist*

Kristy studied at California State University Long Beach and Moore College of Art in Art Education, Painting and Art Therapy. She is a Certified Expressive Arts Therapist and teaches art and watercolor in Washington State. Her work is exhibited and sold in La Conner, Whidbey Island, and the San Juan Islands, where she resides.

WILLIAM HEWSON *Artist*

William has lived in the Pacific Northwest for almost twenty years. He previously studied in Paris, Stockholm, and with Charles Reid; now he is a well-known teacher throughout the Puget Sound. William is inspired by the local watery landscapes and infuses his love of post-impressionism into his paintings.

MARSHALL LYSANDER JOHNSON *Artist*

Marshall was born and raised in Washington. He primarily paints with oil on canvas, using a palette knife and brush work. His distinctive style is reflected in vibrant colors, which convey the energy of the Northwest. His works have also been made into prints and limited lithographs.

TED KUTSCHER *Artist*

Ted's passion for painting began as a child, watching his mother paint. He creates oil paintings as a hobby, aside from his career in financial planning on Vashon Island, Washington. He describes painting as magical — a way to be captivated by the interaction of light, color, form, and structure.

SHERRY MARKOVITZ *Artist*

Sherry grew up in the Midwest and studied art from age ten at the Art Institute of Chicago, then came to Seattle and studied at the University of Washington. She is influenced by many global traditions, often using animals and ornament to create quiet and soothing works of art.

STEPHEN MATTHIAS *Artist*

With influences from his studies in Rhode Island, Virginia, Washington, D.C., and France, Stephen taught art at the University of Washington in Seattle, and now paints on Bainbridge Island. His works have appeared in the combat archives from the Vietnam War located in Washington, D.C., and numerous other prestigious galleries around the nation.

PIERCE MILHOLLAND *Cover Artist*

Focusing on visual treasures familiar to the Pacific Northwest, the painting style of Pierce is reminiscent of the Post-Impressionists. He uses warm imagery and striking color, coupled with a unique balance of tone and light, to transform what may be commonplace into something quite special.

Cynthia Nims *Food Writer*

Born and raised in the Northwest, Cynthia Nims has also studied cooking in France, earning a *Grand Diplôme d'Etudes Culinaires* from La Varenne, where she worked on numerous cookbooks with the owner, Anne Willan. Previously editor of *Simply Seafood* magazine, Cynthia is now the food editor of *Seattle Magazine*, local editor of the *Zagat* restaurant guide, and a cookbook author.

Anne Nisbet *Wine Writer*

Anne Nisbet has been writing about wine for *Seattle* magazine since 2000. Her stories about wine and the Northwest wine scene have also appeared in Alaska Airlines' magazine, *Northwest Palate, The Oregonian*, and the *American Institute of Wine and Food*. She is the author of *The Gourmet's Guide to Northwest Bed & Breakfast Inns*. In addition to writing, Anne orchestrates culinary logistics for three of the Northwest's most prestigious wine and food events, the International Pinot Noir Celebration, the Auction of Washington Wines, and Taste Washington. She lives in Magnolia with her husband, their two dogs, and an ever-growing collection of cookbooks and wine.

Ann Rutter *Artist*

Ann grew up in Colorado and later studied in Spain and Germany before settling in Seattle. She discovered painting as an adult, and now her works appear in corporate and private collections in the US and abroad. Ann is a member of the NW Watercolor Society and other arts groups.

Barbara VanDyke Shuman *Artist*

As a third-generation Northwesterner, Barbara studied art with Seattle University and the University of Washington. She then taught art and English as a second language, both locally and in Turkey and China. Barbara devoted herself to being an artist full-time in 1996, and her art has appeared in many gallery exhibits.

Nancy McDonnell Spaulding *Artist*

Born in Colorado, Nancy has lived in Vermont, Spain, Arizona, New York and then settled in the San Juan Islands in Washington State. She has chaired many art juries and shows, including the Best of the Northwest show in Seattle. Her artwork has ranged from serigraphs to pastels.

Pat Tolle *Artist*

The highly colorful oil paintings by Pat Tolle typically depict aerial landscapes and scenes from the Pacific Rim. Her pieces have been shown in many galleries, and she also won a Washington State Arts Commission award from the City of Bothell for the University of Washington Bothell/Cascadia Community College campus.

Betty Olson Vacca *Artist*

This Seattle native is both an artist and teacher of painting. Her works concentrate on the Pacific Northwest and her family through a personal journey of learning, feelings, and the joy of seeing. She has won many awards, has had many shows, and appears in numerous private and public art collections.

Patty Wittmann *Food Stylist*

Patty Wittmann began her culinary career as a restaurant chef and now enjoys styling food for advertising, packaging, magazines, and cookbooks. She also attended art school and finds this especially valuable in the creative process of developing cookbooks. Her work appears in *Ray's Boathouse, The Perfect Match*, and *Nordstrom Family and Friends*. Wittmann juggles her work as a food stylist with a passion for writing and illustrating children's books. Her latest picture book is *Don't Wake Up The Bear*.

Xiaogang Zhu *Artist*

Born in China, he was an art professor and textile designer before coming to study and teach in Vermont in 1989. He now lives in Washington and paints in oils and gouache. His art has appeared in several museum exhibits and books on painting, in addition to being in art gallery shows.

RESOURCE GUIDE

For the Home

ALLUSIA
6421 Phinney Avenue N
Seattle, WA 98103
206-789-8300

*Unique home décor and
furnishings, table top, and giveables*

CAPERS
4521 California Avenue SW
Seattle, WA 98116
206-932-0371

*Gifts, home furnishings, and
accessories*

MADE·IN·WASHINGTON.com
1711 W Nickerson
Seattle, WA 98119
800-645-3474
www.madeinwashington.com

*Stores feature smoked salmon,
gourmet foods, cedar planks, gift
baskets, glass art, pottery, music,
books, apparel and more.*

*·Use the donation code JLGIVE
during checkout when asked for
"promotion code," and JLS
community projects will benefit.*

**MARTHA E. HARRIS
FLOWERS AND GIFTS OF
MADISON PARK**
4218 E Madison
Seattle, WA 98112
206-568-0347

*Gifts, home accessories, linens,
fresh florals, and more*

NORDSTROM
1617 Sixth Avenue
Seattle, WA 98101
888-282-6060
www.nordstrom.com

*This national retailer is widely
known for providing superior
service and high quality, distinctive
merchandise. When you are ready
to shop, so are we.*

SUR LA TABLE
1765 Sixth Avenue S
Seattle, WA 98134
800-243-0852
www.surlatable.com

Gourmet cooking supplies

TABLE TOP SHOP
1105 Bellevue Way NE
Bellevue, WA 98004
425-454-7322

Fine linens and tableware

TIFFANY & CO.
600 Pine Street
Seattle, WA 98101
206-264-1400
www.tiffany.com

Fine tableware, gifts, and jewelry

**WATSON KENNEDY
FINE HOME**
1022 First Avenue
Seattle, WA 98104
206-652-8350
www.watsonkennedy.com

*Distinctive objects for gracious
living and gift giving*

Food and Spirits

**BEAULIEU VINEYARD
(BV WINES)**
1960 St. Helena Highway
Rutherford, CA 94573
800-373-5896
www.bvwines.com

*Winemakers and distributors
of fine wines*

BROWN-FORMAN
850 Dixie Highway
Louisville, KY 40210
www.brown-forman.com

*Producer and marketer of fine
consumer products which include
Jack Daniel's, Southern Comfort,
Finlandia Vodka, Fetzer California
Wines, and Bolla Italian Wine*

**CHEF JOHN HOWIE'S
CEDAR PLANKS**
www.plankcooking.com

*Baking and barbeque planks,
spice rubs, cookbooks, and fresh
seafood packs*

CHOC ELAN, LLC
4580 Klahanie Drive SE,
PBN 236
Issaquah, WA 98029
425-890-4440
www.chocelan.com

*Truly enthusiastic about chocolate,
Choc Elan is the Northwest's
premium chocolaterie.*

HEART OF WASHINGTON
105 S. 18th Street, Suite 205
Yakima, WA 98901-2149
866-376-6469
www.heartofwashington.com

*Find information about our state's
agricultural products, festivals,
recipes and more.*

METROPOLITAN MARKET
4025 Delridge Way SW
Suite 210
Seattle, WA 98106
206-923-0740
www.metropolitan-market.com

*A shopping experience that exceeds
customer expectations through
attentive and friendly service, and
a wide variety of excellent products*

PALISADE RESTAURANT
Elliott Bay Marina
2601 West Marina Place
Seattle, WA 98199
206-285-1000
www.r-u-i.com

*A Seattle signature - for elegant
waterfront dining, private parties
and events*

REDHOOK ALE BREWERY
14300 NE 145th Street
Woodinville, WA 98072
425-483-3232
www.redhook.com

Brewers of craft beers

RESTAURANTS UNLIMITED, INC.
1818 N. Northlake Way
Seattle, WA 98103-9097
206-634-3082
www.restaurantsunlimited.com

*A national restaurant group
specializing in fine food in a casual
atmosphere*

SEABEAR
605 30th Street
PO Box 591
Anacortes, WA 98221
800-645-FISH
www.seabear.com

*Offering the best Northwest
salmon since 1957 —
wild salmon fillets, traditional
Northwest smoked salmon,
chowders, and more direct from
the Pacific Northwest*

**SEASTAR RESTAURANT
AND RAW BAR**
205 108th Avenue NE
Bellevue, WA 98004
425-456-0010
www.seastarrestaurant.com

*Serving fresh Pacific Northwest
foods influenced by world cuisine*

STARBUCKS CORPORATION
PO Box 3717
Seattle, WA 98124
800-782-7282
www.starbucks.com

*Purveyor of fine coffee, coffee-
related products, and gifts*

Sun Luck Brands
600 Fifth Avenue S
Seattle, WA 98104
www.sunluckbrands.com

*A full line of Asian foods
tailored to customers interested
in cooking authentic Asian
meals at home*

Tully's Coffee
3100 Airport Way South
Seattle, WA 98134
206-233-2070
www.tullys.com

Gourmet coffee and gifts

Uwajimaya
600 Fifth Avenue S
Seattle, WA 98104
800-889-1928
www.uwajimaya.com

*Retail stores and mail order
providing a wide variety of Asian
seafood, meat, produce, groceries,
and giftware*

Art Galleries

Blackwell Studios
by appointment only
2935 Mayfair Avenue N
Seattle, WA 98109
206-281-8694
www.blackwellstudios.com

Blackwell

Fountainhead Gallery
625 West McGraw Street
Seattle, WA 98119
206-285-4467
www.fountainheadgallery.com

Hewson, Matthias

Greg Kucera Gallery
212 Third Avenue S
Seattle, WA 98104
206-624-0770
www.gregkucera.com

Markovitz

Grover Thurston Gallery
309 Occidental Avenue S
Seattle, WA 98104
206-223-0816
www.groverthurston.com

Emminger

Gunnar Nordstrom Gallery
127 Lake Street South
Kirkland, WA 98033
425-827-2822
www.gunnarnordstrom.com

Tolle

Howard Mandville
120 Park Lane Suite D
Kirkland, WA 98033
800-544-4712
www.howardmandville.com

Zhu

Island Studios
270 Spring Street
Friday Harbor, WA 98250
360-378-6550
www.islandstudios.com

Gjesme, Spaulding

Kindred Circle Art Gallery
409 Main Street
Edmonds, WA 98020
425-776-3778
www.kindredcircle.com

Olson Vacca

Kirsten Gallery
5320 Roosevelt Way NE
Seattle, WA 98105
206-522-2011
www.kirstengallery.com

Buckland, Johnson, Rutter

Painted Ladies Art Studio
485 Front Street, No. F2
Issaquah, WA 98027
206-769-9008
www.bvdart.com

VanDyke Shuman

Patricia Rovzar Gallery
118 Central Way
Kirkland, WA 98033
800-889-4278
www.rovzargallery.com

Milholland

Silverwood Gallery
23927 Vashon Highway SW
Vashon Island, WA 98070
206-463-1722
www.silverwoodgallery.com

Kutscher

Services

Davis Wright Tremaine, LLP
2600 Century Square,
1501 4th Avenue
Seattle, WA 98101
206-622-3150
www.dwt.com

*A national law firm representing
businesses based throughout the
United States and around the world*

Digital Image
316 Occidental Avenue South,
Suite 101
Seattle, WA 98104
206-667-9757

Digital prepress services

Ernst & Young, LLC
999 3rd Avenue
Seattle, WA 98104
206-621-1800
www.ey.com

*Global leader in professional
services, including tax, audit, risk
management, and corporate finance*

Event Success
16300 126th Avenue NE
Woodinville, WA 98072
206-849-9770
www.nweventsuccess.com

*Event planning/consulting
for weddings, corporate, and
special occasions*

Mary Cunningham Graphic Design
1108 19th Avenue E
Seattle, WA 98112
206-229-1949

Print graphic design and illustration

Nicole Bigler Epicurian Bay
P.O. Box 200654
Denver, CO 80220
720-232-8477
www.cookbookmarketing.com

*Sales representation and marketing
consulting - specializing in
cookbooks and other culinary titles*

Schnitzer Northwest, LLC
225 108th Avenue NE, Suite 400
Bellevue, WA 98004
425-452-3700
www.schnitzernorthwest.com

*Real estate investment,
development, and asset management*

Tamara Wilson Public Relations
The Tower Building
1809 Seventh Avenue
Suite 1403
Seattle, WA 98101
206-838-8977
www.tamarawilson.com

*TWPR offers seamless events,
including product launches,
restaurant openings, and store
openings*

WSGR

**Wilson, Sonsini, Goodrich & Rosati
Professional Corporation
Attorneys at Law**
5300 Carillon Point
Kirkland, WA 98033
425-576-5800
www.wsgr.com

*A leading law firm representing
technology companies at all stages
of their growth*

Index

◆ *Photograph*

THE JUNIOR LEAGUE OF SEATTLE
COMMUNITY PROJECTS & PARTNERSHIPS
Celebrating Community Service Since 1924

Access Seattle –
 Easter Seals Society of Washington

Art Education and Culture Cube –
 Bellevue Art Museum

Art Studio – Seattle Art Museum

Arts Alive!

Baby Food Pantry –
 Northwest Harvest Food Bank

Back To Work Scholarships

Braille Library for the Blind

Broadview Emergency Shelter

CASA (Court Appointed Special
 Advocates) – Family Court
 Guardian Ad Litem Program

Child Health Immunization and
 Nutrition Program

Children's Protective Services

Community Volunteer Career
 Development Youth Model

Council for Prevention of
 Child Abuse and Neglect
 Public Awareness Campaign

Displaced Homemaker Center –
 Bellevue Community College

Done in a Day Projects

Eastside Community Mental Health
 Center's Children of Divorce Project

Eastside Domestic Violence Program

English as a Second Language –
 Volunteer Service Program

Family Counseling Service

Guidebook for Handicapped and Aging

Healthy Child Information Fairs

Healthy Futures Art Project

Historic Site Guide

Homemaker Service

Kids on the Block

Lifebooks Project

Magnuson Park Playground

Mentoring Moms Project –
 Arbor House Young Parent

Northwest Art Collection

Northwest Indian TV Programs

Northwest Mediation Service

Puget Soundings Magazine

Radio and Television Series
 for Children

Rebuilding Together (formerly
 Christmas in April, Seattle)

Scholarships

Scoliosis Screening Project

Senior Rights Assistance Program

Specific Language Disability Project

Storysharing Project

Transitional Housing Program of
 Friends of Youth

Victim/Witness Advocacy
 Referral Project

Wise Penny Next-to-New Shop

Woman to Woman Alcohol Education
 and Prevention

Youth Suicide Prevention Project

This list is a sampling of the kinds of projects that benefit from the proceeds of our cookbooks.

To order another copy of *Celebrate the Rain* or our other award-winning cookbook, SIMPLY CLASSIC, please contact:

THE JUNIOR LEAGUE OF SEATTLE, INC.
4119 East Madison Street
Seattle, Washington 98112
PHONE 206-324-3638
FAX 206-324-0811
ORDER ONLINE www.jrleagueseattle.org